Birth of the European Individual

This book examines the birth of the European individual as a juridical problem, focusing on legal cases from the European Court of Justice as an electrifying laboratory for the study of law and society. Foucault's story of the modern subject constitutes the book's main theoretical inspiration, as it considers the encounter between legal and other practices within a more general field of juridical power: a network of active relations between different social spheres.

Through the analysis of cases of delinquent individuals – each expelled from one of the Member States – the raw material for constructing the idea of the European individual is uncovered. The European individual, it is argued, emerged out of the intersection of regimes of law, security and economy, practices of knowledge-power and juridical practice.

Birth of the European Individual: Law, Security, Economy will be of interest to those studying the individual in law, as well as anyone considering the relationships between power and the individual.

Samuli Hurri is based at the University of Helsinki, Finland.

Birth of the European Individual

Law, Security, Economy

Samuli Hurri

Routledge
Taylor & Francis Group

LONDON AND NEW YORK

First published 2014 by Routledge

2 Park Square, Milton Park, Abingdon, Oxfordshire OX14 4RN
711 Third Avenue, New York, NY 10017

Routledge is an imprint of the Taylor & Francis Group, an informa business

First issued in paperback 2018

British Library Cataloguing in Publication Data
A catalogue record for this book is available from the British Library.
    Hurri, Samuli, author.
    Birth of the European individual : law, security, economy/Samuli Hurri.
    pages cm
    1. Personality (Law) – Europe. 2. Persons (Law) – Europe.
    3. Sociological jurisprudence. I. Title.
    KJC1012.H87 2014
    342.2408--dc23
    2013043934

Library of Congress Cataloging-in-Publication Data
A catalog record has been requested for this book.

ISBN: 978-0-415-72173-8 (hbk)
ISBN: 978-1-138-37753-0 (pbk)

Typeset in Baskerville by
Florence Production Ltd, Stoodleigh, Devon, UK

Contents

Acknowledgements

I am grateful to Kaarlo Tuori, Emilios Christodoulidis, Sakari Hänninen, Panu Minkkinen, Kevät Nousiainen, Sabine Frerichs and Lars D. Eriksson for their reading of the manuscript at different stages. I am also grateful to Scott Veitch, Kimmo Nuotio, Ari Hirvonen, Susanna Lindroos-Hovinheimo and Toomas Kotkas, who have read individual chapters.

At the Faculty of Law of the University of Helsinki, I had the good fortune to work for a long time with Academy Professor Kaarlo Tuori, who supported me in countless ways. I am a member of The Centre of Excellence in Foundations of European Law and Polity, as well as the research project The Many Constitutions of Europe, both led by Kaarlo Tuori and funded by the Academy of Finland. I am also a member of the research project European Bonds: the Moral Economy of Debt led by Sabine Frerichs and funded by the Academy of Finland.

Colin Perrin, Rebekah Jenkins, Nicola Prior and Laura Brookes at Routledge have done a big job to make this book come true, my sincere thanks to them.

Chapter 2 of this work partially reproduces my 2009 article 'A Legal Space for the Representation of Danger' in *No Foundations* 6: 39–68. What I say about *epieikeia* in Chapter 9 and Chapter 10 builds on my 2013 article 'Justice *kata nomos* and justice as *epieikeia* (legality and equity)' in L. Huppes-Cluysenaer and N. Coelho (eds) *Aristotle and the Philosophy of Law: Theory, Practice and Justice* (Dordrecht: Springer).

Material from Michel Foucault's *Abnormal* has been reproduced here with the kind permission of Verso.

Chapter 1

Introduction

Case 41/74

In May 1973, Ms Yvonne van Duyn, a Dutch national, flew to the UK to take up a job with the Church of Scientology at its college in East Grinstead, which is one hour to the south by train from London. At Gatwick airport she was interviewed by an immigration officer. The officer refused her leave to enter, because it turned out that she had worked in a Scientology establishment in Amsterdam for six months, that she had taken a course in the subject of Scientology, that she was a practising Scientologist and that she was intending to work at the Scientology establishment in the United Kingdom.

Case 67/74

Mr Carmelo Angelo Bonsignore, an Italian national, had been living and working as a chemical worker in Cologne, Germany, since 1968, that is, since he was 18. In May 1971, during a family gathering at his sister's home, he wanted to show the party there his newly purchased gun, a 6.35 calibre automatic Beretta pistol. Accidentally, the gun fired and the bullet killed his younger brother. The criminal court at Cologne found him guilty but did not impose punishment because of mitigating circumstances. The *Oberstadsdirektor* of Cologne decided to deport Mr Bonsignore from the territory of the Federal Republic of Germany and ordered immediate execution of this measure.

Case 36/75

Mr Roland Rutili, an Italian national, had lived in France all his life. His home was in Audun-le-Tiche, a town in Meurthe-et-Moselle, one of the three Lorraine departments bordering on Luxemburg in northern France. He was married to a Frenchwoman, had three children with her and a steady job. As a trade union activist, he had participated in the political actions of 1967–1968. On the grounds of that participation, Mr Rutili's presence in the departments of Lorraine was considered by the French Minister of the Interior to be likely to disturb *ordre public*, and he decided to prohibit Mr Rutili from residing there.

Case 48/75

In the 1960s, Mr Jean Noël Royer, a French national, had been prosecuted in France for armed robberies and convicted of procuring. From November 1971 to January 1972, he had been residing in Grâce-Hollogne, Belgium. He had not complied with the immigration formalities in the way required by the Belgian system. To 'suppress gangsterism' the Belgian *Police Judiciaire* ordered Mr Royer to leave the country and not to come back. Some time later, Mr Royer disobeyed that order by entering Belgium once again. He was arrested and eventually sent to prison. He was soon released, and again expelled from the country, this time by ministerial decree. Later, an appellate tribunal in Liège sentenced Mr Royer for his illegal residence to one month's suspended imprisonment and fined him 3000 Belgian francs.

Case 30/77

Mr Pierre Bouchereau, a French national, lived and worked in the UK. In January 1976, Mr Bouchereau was convicted by a criminal court in London of possession of small quantities of amphetamine and cannabis. Six months later, in June 1976, he again pleaded guilty to unlawful possession of drugs. This time it was 28 tablets of LSD and three packets of amphetamine salt. According to the British system, the criminal court had the power to recommend the deportation of Mr Bouchereau to the immigration authorities. Upon deciding the case of Mr Bouchereau, the Marlborough Street Magistrates' Court was minded by the Home Office to make that recommendation.

Case 115/81

In June 1980, Ms Rezguia Adoui, a French national, applied for a permit to reside in Belgium from the Liège immigration authorities. The permit was refused by a decision of the Minister of Justice and she was ordered to leave Belgium within 15 days. The ground was that she was working 'in a bar which was suspect from the point of view of morals and in which waitresses displayed themselves in the window and were able to be alone with their clients'.

Case 116/81

Ms Dominique Cornuaille, a French national, had resided in Belgium since June 1978. She had then applied for a residence permit, but the *Office des Étrangers* had received information from the police describing her as a waitress of questionable moral character who displayed herself in scant dress to clients. The Consultative Committee, a body giving recommendations in immigration matters in Belgium, issued an opinion that she should be expelled from Belgium. The defence argued that the 'Belgian authorities make no secret of the fact that they are systematically expelling all French waitresses, perhaps because they may be "the logistic support" for the French underworld'.

Laboratory for human-making

The above cases were preliminary rulings of the ECJ on requests by national courts concerning 'special measures' taken – or to be taken – by EC Member States against EC nationals. The special measures were individual decisions by immigration authorities prohibiting entry, ordering deportation or restricting a permit to reside in one way or another. In other words, they were measures that restricted Community law freedom of movement. EC law required (as today's EU law still requires) that Member State authorities justify these decisions on the grounds of *ordre public* or public security. Moreover, it required that the grounds in question must be based on the personal conduct of the individual in question. This rather microscopic structure of two notions – *ordre public* and personal conduct – inserted in the sundry mass of European law constitutes something that can be called a laboratory for human-making.

For the present research, the files of the above cases also constitute a laboratory of legal theory. The point at which everything starts is contact between two sets of legal structure: immigration law and the law regarding nationals. The reaction between these two legal structures generates the birth of a new and extraordinary legal creature, *the European individual*. Concomitantly, it reveals certain structures of legal practice that can be considered as generally prevailing in the legal field. Moreover, with proper semiotics, the laboratory further reveals certain non-juridical forces, rationalities and powers that the files themselves say very little about.

The vision of the way in which legal practice interlaces and counteracts these forces and powers is what the birth of the European individual puts forward as an object of research. Ultimately, the European individual is created in this interlacing and counteraction, in the power relations between the field of legal practice and other practices and fields.

For some, the idea of a laboratory may appear to be nothing but a nifty gadget with which it is convenient to describe work done as a contribution to Science with a capital 'S'. Use of the word 'laboratory' suggests that a controllable (verifiable/falsifiable) way exists of producing experimental knowledge that would uncover the laws of reality beyond the humdrum flow of phenomena. This position would be blind positivism. It is unreflective of the researcher's own embedded involvement in the production of social structures in his observations. It is also unreflective of the nature of social life generated by commitments, beliefs and illusions of active human beings. Symbolism, the practice of representing things through language, has the effect that the character of social objects and social actions is not factual. 'Things' are filtered through systematic use of symbols and sets of symbols, which create symbolic orders. Symbolic orders are society, the symbolic universe, and cannot be experimented with externally, because one cannot step out of symbolic orders.

I agree with the above in that there are no virginally empty laboratory test tubes; they are all charged at once with the symbolic universes of meaning that both the actors and their onlookers carry. The process of conceptualisation that eventually squeezed out the text that follows was not controllable as work in laboratories perhaps should be. Moreover, in its final stage of consolidation, this process has been dominated by one eminent figure, Michel Foucault, and his rather specific analysis of forces and powers (by which he attempted to get symbolism out of his system). The point about the laboratory is neither to do away with the influences of the thought of others on the 'laboratorian', nor with the special effectivity of symbolic universes of meaning. The point about the laboratory is to express what this work has attempted to facilitate by its close readings of individual cases: a microscopic vision of precisely those universes, as well as their power. Moreover, the point about the laboratory is that, within its confines, one may embark on a specific enterprise, that of outlining *a theory of legal practice*. This notion has two meanings.

The first sense relates to what can be called legal praxeology. There the objective is to expound on a set of general structures belonging to the legal field as a field of practice. In other words, the goal is to lay down a theory of the ways in which the law is practised. The second sense is perhaps the more intricate one. Outlining a theory of practice means not only a theoretical rendering of practice, but a study of the ways in which practice renders visible the theories prevailing in its field.

'Theory of practice' indicates not theoretical reflections of actors, but theories carried by practitioners in their activities. As a matter of course, the same concrete persons conduct both reflection and action. The distinction is analytical. For theorists, theories are schemata of intelligibility and understanding, whereas for those who practise theories are schemes of action. In an outline of theory of legal practice, the material consists not of accounts that actors might occasionally give of their practice, their reflective discourse, but of their much more convoluted – but nonetheless strategically streamlined – discursive action. For a project that aims at reconstruction of a theory of practice in these senses, a microscopic view is indispensable.

While the view is microscopic, the overall prospect is nothing less than to explore what humans are made of, what are the powers that make them so and what are their possibilities to resist. These prospects may sound not only pretentious, but also misguided to some. They would perhaps rather look upon the law as a system belonging to those macrocosmic spheres where it would be totally archaic to put individual human beings at their centre. It is the old Ptolemaic fallacy, this time going down to the modern philosophical tradition still trapped by the idea of the subject.

In truth, human beings play non-significant roles. They are accidental side effects of the steady roll and drift of objective social structure. Subjects are a mere substratum for the symbolic orders that reign over them, soldiers who cannot know where the troops are heading or why they are heading there. Certain types of theorising are more adequate for modern law and society, say others, than theorising that revolves around the subject. Systems theory, for example, would consider social systems such as law as operating quite independently from what it would call 'personality systems', by that meaning humans.

For this writer, all these types of criticism are self-imposed. I look upon social systems, apparatuses and regimes as if they were structures for the structuring of individuals; structures that undertake to transform humans into the subjects of these systems, apparatuses and regimes. The legal order is one of these structuring structures, as are the economic order and the security order. So, too, are all the political entities housing these structures: the European Union and the Member States. All of these need subjects, a need they would satisfy by exercising symbolic power over human individuals. This exercise is an activity of recruitment, persuading or forcing individuals to enlist as subjects of the regime. In turn, individuals may resist by fomenting one regime against the other. A proud and sturdy barbarian battle carried out alone against all domination is not a conceivable or realisable strategy.

From another critical point of view, the cases cited could be considered as mere epiphenomena incurred by the broader historical-political process of post-war European integration. In the big picture, would not a focus on such small events present only a number of minor cracks and virtually insignificant dysfunctions? Are they not details that can attract only the purest of academic interests?

Integration is a massive political task taken up by a formidable band of politicians and all kinds of social engineers. Their objective has been to raise an organisation, to develop a technology of governing, for the materialisation of an important commission: the making of a political society, a strong power, out of Europe. Perhaps the cases studied here are not of planetary significance to this undertaking. The point about focusing on these individual cases has been, as Foucault said, 'to look at power from the other side' (Foucault 2003b: 168). That is, from the side of those who are subjected to it.

The formation of Europe as a process of social integration, within and laterally to the old political societies, of course started to accelerate long before the post-war founding of the European Communities. Perhaps the time at which the railways came was significant to the mingling of Europeans:

Europe was immediately sensitive to the changes in behaviour that the railroads entailed. What was going to happen, for example, if it was possible to get married between Bordeaux and Nantes? Something that was not possible before. What was going to happen when people in Germany and France might get to know one another? Would war still be possible once there were railroads? In France, a theory developed that the railroads would increase familiarity among people, and that the new forms of human univer- sality made possible would render war impossible. But what the people did not foresee – although the German military command was fully aware of it, since they were much cleverer than their French counterpart – was that, on the contrary, the railroads rendered the war far easier to wage.

(Foucault 2000g: 353)

My laboratory, which is about social and symbolic structures, can be compared with the physical and technical structure of railways in two ways. First, like railways, establishment of freedom of movement of workers brings with it prospects of peaceful coexistence, but also disappointments, unhappiness and fears of losing something prestigious in local communities.

In connection with the other fundamental freedoms (notably that concerning capital), it has become evident that the legal liberation of movement has not only opened an avenue for acclimatisation and future harmony between nations, but also an avenue that has 'rendered the war far easier to wage' in the form of economic conquests and manoeuvres. All in all, opening up societies to foreign elements, including human elements, is the one sense in which railways and my laboratory can be likened. This opening has generated the cases under study.

The second sense in which the problematic of my laboratory can be compared with the problematic of the railway is more important. The cases cited attest to instances where, in the language of the quote, 'new forms of human universality' have failed to deliver. What we now know by the name of European citizenship is precisely this kind of new form of human universality, prospected by the elites for the purposes of arousing Europhoria long before Maastricht, the Jupiterian apex of constitutionalism. The birth of the European individual, as a human form with its rather limited own specificity, took place when universal human forms failed to deliver.

Let me now explain the dimensions within which this work moves. There are three dimensions, and each of them can be taken as an independent set of problems. The first of these dimensions is the way in which the *European individual* is born – as a new, special and problematic human form – in the legal practice of the ECJ in the 1970s. The second dimension consists of the structures of the practice of law, what will be called its *omnihistorical elements*. These will be laid down through a close reading of the cases that gave birth to the European individual.

The third dimension is what will be called a *semiotic of subtexts*. This is developed with the help of Foucault's analytical models. This should make perceptible the non-juridical mechanisms of power at work in the cases. (Subtextual indicates things that are not made as explicit discourse in the texts.) In the background of this last dimension is Foucault's overall project of writing a genealogy of the modern subject. This is a historical ontology for what human individuals have come to be, expounding on the ways in which individuals carry the political history of struggles and domination in their present human constitution.

These three dimensions are independent sets of problems, but at the same time they put up a network of dimensions that is absolutely necessary for the conception of each dimension as a set of problems. Through reading of Foucault's genealogy of the modern subject, one gets to know what the subtextual mechanisms of power are. Through reading of the subtextual mechanism of power one gets to know the power relations in which the elements of legal practice take place. Through reading of the elements of legal practice, one gets to know how the European individual was born as a legal problem. Therefore, despite the independent value of each set of problems, the dimensions are interconnected.

The European individual is born as a problem

Let us say that the provisional and transient goal of integration has been that European individuals should be treated, not as foreignerss, but as equals with the nationals of the Member State. Yet the very equalisation of these two categories of persons (Europeans and nationals of a Member State) implies nonetheless that a difference exists. Equalisation mechanisms are not needed if there is no difference. This rather elementary insight directs the focus away from equaliser-mechanisms and towards mechanisms of difference-making. The European individual, the subject of this book, is born in one of these mechanisms of difference-making. The task is to distinguish between the Member State national, the European and the foreigner.

The mechanism for difference-making at the heart of this work consists of the provision for derogation from the right to free movement. This mechanism has two parts. The first part of the mechanism is that derogations are possible if the *ordre public* of a Member State would otherwise come under threat.[1] The second part of the mechanism is that these threats must be the result of the personal conduct of the individual in question.[2]

Together, derogation requires *threats posed to the* ordre public *of the society by the personal conduct of the individual*. This mechanism arranges the discursive space of legal norms in which the practice of law – by its insertions, substantiations, compositions and modifications of the ingredients of that space – gives birth, materiality and form to the European individual. I will return to the details of legal norms later in the next chapter. Let me at this moment indicate two points about the European individual.

The first point comes out of the fact that the mechanism of difference-making is not created in a vacuum. When inserted into the Member State legal systems, it brings two types of law into contact with each other. The first type is immigration law, which facilitates the exercise of power by the authorities responsible for controlling non-national immigrants. The second type is, roughly speaking, what remains: the law regarding nationals. The latter appears not to be a type of law, but to refer to the law in general. In its turn, immigration law is truly a law that has its own specificity. The point about this rather awkward distinguishing of 'the law regarding nationals' as a special kind of law is to pin down the liminal space into which the cases insert the European individual.

The concrete meaning of this becomes apparent in what is the very basic practice of immigration administration: granting residence permits to immigrants. The normal practice is that, upon entering the country, a foreigner applies for a residence permit and then, after the relevant authority has made its affirmative decision, the residence of the person in question is legal. What happens between filing the application and the decision is a diagnosis of the person: would he or she be dangerous or not? By contrast, the law regarding nationals, as we see it, can be defined by its lack of this kind of element of proactive diagnostics. In criminal law, for example, decisions about punishment are made only after the fact of an offence is proven.

The conclusion is that nationals are presumed to be safe, ie secure, whereas non-national immigrants are presumed to be dangerous. Both presumptions may turn out to be mistaken in individual cases. The presumption of security, as for nationals and the presumption of dangerousness, as for immigrants, nonetheless remain at a general level. The control-powers that the law regarding nationals instals are *reactive*. In immigration law, the authorities must examine each individual case specifically, the result of which alone can create a basis for confidence. The control powers that immigration law instals are *proactive*.

The analytical clarity that this brings forth with respect to our mechanism of difference-making is this: European individuals entering a country also enter an unclear symbolic boundary space, where the practice of law faces a problem. Are European individuals to be considered *de jure* secure, like nationals, or could there be a *de facto* diagnosis of the dangerousness of each individual as in the case of immigrants? To put it simply, the problem is whether one can and should trust Europeans. The problem of the European individual is born in a space stretched between two types of exercise of power that function differently. In turn, these functions construct the individual differently: dangerous individual, safe/secure individual. The European individual becomes a hybrid between these two constructions.

The second point to be made with respect to the mechanism for difference-making by *ordre public* and personal conduct concerns the specificity of the types of *knowledge* that are involved in the mechanism. First, the personal conduct requirement opens up the way for a very special kind of discourse to enter into the cases. The discourse put forward in the field of legal practice is unusual in that the subject of this discourse is not the subject of externally realised acts, omissions and undertakings, as is usual in law.

In order to find out about the dangerousness of the individual, one must get down to the task of examining the interior spheres of the individual, their propensities and tendencies. Past action of the individual is not relevant in the normal legal way, but only as material to be decoded for the purposes of prognostication about that individual's future action. The security-diagnosis made of an individual cannot ultimately stay on the level of past offences and misconduct, because it aims at finding out about future threats. It must produce knowledge of the individual in their individuality, which is fundamentally different from normal legal practice that proceeds on the basis of pre-set taxonomies.

The other type of knowledge involved in the mechanism of distinction-making is no less curious from the point of view of legal practice. In the context of the cases, the meaning of the notion of *ordre public* relates to its usage in the security administration of the state. This is the branch to which immigration control institutions traditionally belong. Whereas the personal conduct requirement opens up a way to the secrecies of the inner reality of the individual human being, the *ordre public* requirement opens up a way to the secrecies of the inner reality of the state. State knowledge of threats to *ordre public*, managed by immigration control institutions as part of the security service, belong to the sphere of the so-called *arcana imperii*.

This fact has made immigration administration a very special branch in that it is almost impenetrable to the practice of law. When the security services have assessed an immigrant as dangerous, and on the basis of this assessment the immigration authorities refuse a residence permit, legal review of the substantive grounds of refusal is often blocked by invoking the security interests of the Member State.

The European individual is born in a space that breaks away from Member State shields of secrecy; all the cases make perceptible attempts by certain parties to place the notion of *ordre public* on a new basis, as well as attempts by other parties to continue on the traditional basis of immigration law. The security administration and its secret interests are nonetheless ever-present. The cases constantly bring to the surface knowledge of the type that pertains to the *arcana imperii*, which is fundamentally different from publicly promulgated information (legislation) that usually forms the basis of legal practice.

So two types of knowledge are involved: the knowledge of the individual and the knowledge of the state. The former kind of knowledge is about the threats that an individual can pose to society. The latter kind of knowledge is about the things that can put society in danger. This way, the cases move in the sphere of fears and secrecies, which infiltrate into the practice of law through the mechanism of difference-making between nationals, European individuals and strangers. The point of contact between the practice of law and these knowledge sets is where the European individual is born.

Structures of legal practice

Important though the role of the knowledge of the individual and the knowledge of the state may be, on the one hand, and the input of the apparatuses that work on the basis of these types of knowledge, on the other hand, the European individual is not developed by them. The scene for this drama lies in the field of law. The actors, whoever they are in the different cases and whatever they represent, must practise law. This raises the question of the specificity of the practice of law.

In the cases under study, one has a privileged vision opened to the workings of the structures of legal practice. It is privileged because the mechanism of difference-making enables observation of the differences between the legal field and other fields, the fields of security and economy in the first place. In the cases studied, the structures of legal practice are the law's ways of dealing with those other fields. These dealings make visible power relations that are not relations between individuals, but relations between regimes and apparatuses. Power relations will be revisited shortly; let us first introduce the structures of legal practice.

The first problem is the nature of these structures. In this work, they have been made visible through a microscopic study of only certain individual cases. What guarantees that these structures are generalisable? I have made them visible only through the practice of the ECJ. What guarantees that they are not only structures pertaining to that specific institution? The context of the cases is a very special branch of EC law and an even more special branch of Member State laws. What guarantees that they are nothing but structures belonging precisely and particularly to these branches? I should like to put forward three good reasons in this respect.

The first good reason is a simple one, and it concerns EC law. The way I have embarked on the study of these cases has been constantly to be on my guard not to get mixed up with doctrinal EC law. I have intentionally struggled against the horizon of normative meaning provided by EC law scholarship. That horizon is not completely out of sight of this book, but sufficiently so. This is of course a risky undertaking, and it certainly makes the work appear an awkward one to all readers versed in those doctrines and conducting their daily work within them. Yet it is the first and absolutely necessary precondition for any attempt to undertake research on the general structures of legal practice that one does not let the cases pass through the filters of EC law doctrines. The conviction is that it is not those doctrines that have generated the European individual, but the general structures of legal practice at work in the cases.

The second good reason concerns adapting one's gaze, so to speak. What I have been in search of is those structures that make the law move. The presumption is that the existence of these structures (that can make the law move and change) is a condition for the existence of legal practice, because all practice is about movement. Movements of legal practice are in the nature of tactical manoeuvres filtered through strategies, and the structures that have been sought are those that allow the strategic and tactical game of law to carry on. While the undertaking is theoretical, its schemata of intelligibility coincide with schemes of action deployed in practice.

Taken separately, the structures indicated below may appear as nothing but the most established elements of traditional jurisprudence. And, indeed, so they are. Yet it is precisely the strategic conjoining and arranging of these traditional elements in their mutual relations, the *use* made of them in the manoeuvres of different litigants that provides a vision of these structures as motors of movement. In short, the most stable elements in traditional legal theory turn out to be destabilising elements in the field of practice. A theory of practice requires that the possibilities for conjoining these elements tactically and strategically are made perceptible. And this requires a microscopic view.

The third good reason concerns the perspective adopted. This is, once again, to look at power from the other side, from the side of those who are subjected to its exercise. This perspective has some rather special consequences, and it must be distinguished from any perspective that concentrates, for example, on the legal status of an individual and his or her rights and duties in different situations. This would only be another perspective where the individual, the legal subject, is an object. To look at power from the other side means that *one really looks at power*, not at the individual. When one looks at power, one looks at the mechanisms that, in their turn, look at the individual as an object subjected to these mechanisms. The idea in this work is to look back upon those mechanisms. The individual is the perspective, while the exercise of power and the structure of power is the object. This choice of perspective is necessary for the purposes of making the structures of legal practice visible.

However, all these methodological choices are only good reasons, of course, not absolute guarantees. Working with a microscope makes certain things visible, whereas working with a telescope makes other things visible. I have chosen the microscope. Let me present briefly what the microscope will point out, in the work that follows, as the basic elements employed in legal practice.

Fundamental categories: rights and decisions

The dilemma underlying the juridico-political understanding of power is this: individual rights pre-exist establishment of a sovereign power, but acts of sovereignty likewise pre-exist rights. The dilemma is not resolved by suggesting that what really pre-exists is simply a prior state of law. Rights and decisions are not only structured by the law but belong to the basic structures of the law. This is why the one is always formative of the other and the dilemma of pre-existence cannot be solved. In the work that follows, the rights-decisions mechanism appears as one of the legal schemes of action and will be rendered as a device for analysing the concrete practice of law. However, as categories per se, rights and decisions are indispensable elements of legal practice.

The practice of law cannot do away with decisions because its *modus operandi*, the way it works, is that the law is pre-established in the form of a decision. Legal practice looks back to prior authorisation of the exercise of power and to the spheres of freedom that remain. Yet there would be no practice of law if all conflicts had their solutions in pre-set legislation. That is why the *opus operatum*, the work wrought, of the practice of law is that new decisions are inserted into the law all the time. This dialectic between the *modus operandi* and the *opus operatum* is constitutive to the practice of law. The practice of law cannot do away with individual rights either, because the material existence of the law depends on that element. If there were no subjects making legal claims, there would be no legal practice. The language for making legal claims is through rights, a device made use of by individuals. Their assertion of rights materialises the law, feeds action into the practices and rituals of law, and thus upholds the whole apparatus.

Ultimate principles of justification: the rule of law and general good

What the legal field requires from anyone entering the law is to be capable of providing a specific type of discourse, making constructions of justifications. The ultimate principles of justification in the field of law are the rule of law and the general good. Since Plato and Aristotle, these principles have formed the criteria by which just and corrupt forms of government are to be distinguished. Legal philosophy today situates these principles within the framework of the democratic constitutional state, which is a legal framework for political decision-making. The rule of law makes it possible to deliberate on general good according to manners cultivated for that purpose and to pronounce the results of these deliberations in the form of general law.

The substance of the principles is more or less the same in the context of legal practice, but there they function rather differently. The rendering that these principles of justification receive in the theory of legal practice is that they constitute the genuinely legal form of battle. 'Battle-form' gives shape to confrontational situations. Confrontational situations are the struggles by which human individuals lead their lives, but also the struggles occurring at the objective level of social regimes and systems. Not only individuals, but also regimes and systems attempt to exert power over others. Hence, in the background of confrontational situations between individuals stands the relations of power (struggles and disputes) at the level of social structures.

At first, the ultimate principles of justification underlie the tactics used by individuals in their struggles on the legal battlefield. At the same time, however, the legal battlefield on the whole confronts other fields by imposing the requirements of the rule of law and general good on the contestants. Normative scrutiny of the necessities and exigencies of security and economy, for example, requires that these necessities are presented in the normative form of general good. This makes them commensurable and allows an assessment of the choices made between them.

Basic concepts of justice: legality and equity

One is used to thinking that justice belongs to the sphere of extra-positive moral standards, by which the system of positive law may be criticised, evaluated and corrected. Alternatively, one may think that justice is maintained by the legal system itself as its omnipresent *telos* or formative idea inscribed into its social functioning.

Let me indicate two classic examples representing the latter view. Gustaf Radbruch considered justice as a value inherent in the law, not external to it, albeit that a constant tension exists between justice and the two other values, legal certainty and expediency (Radbruch 1950: 107ff). For Rudolf von Jhering, in turn, the whole life of the law is a struggle against wrong. Whether they like it or not, individuals who struggle for their subjective rights also struggle against injustice at the objective level (Jhering 1879). These abstract theoretical statements call for specification: what kind of justice operates in the legal field of action?

Rendering justice in the context of practice makes use of the two genuinely legal concepts of justice: legality and equity. It is in the nature of generally applicable laws that they must be detached from any singular factual circumstances and from any singular confrontational situation. The work of legal practice is to bring together what has occurred, on the one hand, and general laws, on the other hand. The interplay between legality and equity is inserted into this space of practice between general laws and factual circumstances. Justifying derogation from rigid legality, an argument from equity invokes the uniqueness of the circumstances of the case.

As an open-ended form of justice, the function of equity is to correct the unavoidable imperfection of the legislator. Yet the object of criticism is not the existing legal norms themselves, but the factual presuppositions in the background of laws. When special circumstances occur that do not fit in the range of presupposed ordinary paths of life, one becomes aware of the silent normative force of those paths. Once they have entered normative debate, they may be defended as views of what is 'natural'. But before its silence is thus broken, we can call this force *normalisation*. The struggle for justice in the sense of equity is not directed against legality, but against normalisation. In other words, it is a struggle for the right to be different.

I would like to designate the above structures as *omnihistorical* to the practice of law. The meaning of this term is not to say that they are transcendental or universal. The meaning is precisely the contrary: they are the mechanisms that make the practice of law a historical thing insofar as historical stands for change. Structures are constant only in the sense that they make change constant. This is due to the fact that they are plans that the actors practising the law deploy in different tactical combinations and through different strategic filters. My analysis of the cases consists of microscopic analysis of these combinations and filters. They are made perceptible in the submissions of the different litigants, as well as in the submissions of the Advocates General and the final judgments of the judges.

The predicate omnihistorical means, therefore, that these categories, principles and concepts are present in every confrontational situation that takes place on the legal battlefield. They are the armour available everywhere in the field as deployable, practicable structures. Finally, the import of the predicate omni-historical is not that these structures should have been the same from time immemorial. The import is that, at the present time, at every present time, these structures constitute the historicity of the practice of law. They make the law a moving thing. They constitute the law as a set of elements that can be, and need to be, practised.

The question posed earlier was whether something guarantees that these structures apply generally and not only to the individual cases studied. The best reason to support that is yet to be stated. Omnihistorical elements are structures by which the law guarantees its own specificity. The omnihistorical structures of legal practice enable this practice to transfix into its own operations what comes out of other systems, regimes and apparatuses. They are also the elements that conjoin the legal mechanisms of power to the mechanisms of other types of power. In other words, omnihistorical structures insert the legal field into the general field of power, where they facilitate the exercise of juridical power. At this point, let us turn to Foucault.

Foucault: semiotic of subtexts

Foucault provides a *semiotic* for comprehending the trifling and fractional signs passing by relatively quickly in the text of the cases. In a meticulous close-reading of the cases, however, the pull of these hardly perceptible signs grows with every reading. These signs start to work as references to the *subtexts* of the cases.

The nature of the subtexts is not only literary. They should open a view to the reality in which legal practice is contained, to the way in which it enters the power relations between different systems, regimes and apparatuses of the exercise of power. The practice of law is an exercise of juridical power over individuals but, at the same time, it is an exercise of power in relation to the other members of the general field of power. One should note, moreover, that the general field of power is not simply something derived from Foucault and then read into the cases. The subtextual power structures are built into the mechanism of distinction-making (personal conduct, *ordre public*) at the heart of the work. As one recalls, this mechanism took the form of two types of knowledges: knowledge that concerns the dangerousness of the individual, on the one hand, and knowledge that circulates in the safety/security apparatuses of the state, on the other hand; in other words, the knowledge of the individual and the knowledge of the state. The exercise of power that the cases deal with passes through the production of these types of knowledge.

As in the distinction-making mechanism, so too in Foucault's research the mechanisms of power passing through these two kinds of knowledge are central. Broadly speaking, they are knowledge deployed in the government of living human beings. Strictly speaking, they are knowledge of the individual and knowledge of the state. However, two specifications must be indicated straight away. First, the knowledge of the individual is not only the *knowledge about* individuals that circulates in the apparatuses and practices of controlling and governing them. It is very much also the individual's *own knowledge* of himself, where the role of the external power mechanisms is to instal procedures of knowledge-production that individuals are expected to make use of on their own.

Secondly, the state is not an essential political entity constituted juridically in public law. Foucault's state is dispersed throughout society; it works in the different apparatuses and mechanisms of power that all create power by making it pass through their procedures of knowledge production. At the same time, these apparatuses and mechanisms are run alongside the juridically conceived state, and connect to juridical power in different ways.

Foucault's mechanisms of power connect to legal practice and its structures, but not in such a way that they would always work together. On the contrary, they most often work against each other. The types of knowledge that Foucault propounds are all *anti-juridical*. This is why the subtextual mechanisms of power remain subtextual in the cases.

Ultimately, this is because the structures of legal practice are not structures meant for government of living humans and living populations as Foucault's 'knowledges' are, but for government of the legal subject, *homo juridicus*, and for government of the juridically conceived state. This friction effects the negative concealment of the subtexts of the cases, but the same friction is also the positive generator of the materials under study. This is, once again, because the point of contact is inscribed in the mechanisms of distinction-making (personal conduct, *ordre public*) at their very heart.

How, then, is one to get down to the subtextual analysis? The Foucauldian semiotic should provide the key and chart that opens a view to the multiplicity of rationalities at work in modern society. These rationalities contribute to the overall rationalisation of individual, social and political life, but at the same time rationalisation tears apart this life, because the rationalities by which each member of the general field of power works are not only different, but *antagonistic*.

On the one hand, antagonism exists between all the rationalities going on and generating the struggles and disputes that vitalise history. Constant movement, transformation and reorganisation of power structures is happening. On the other hand, the central antagonism is the antagonism between the rationalities of knowledge and juridical rationality. Sometimes these rationalities 'join hands, but only after such a mess, such a shambles!' (Foucault 1986b: 209).

There are six types of anti-juridical knowledge involved in this work, all of which come out from close readings of Foucault. The anti-juridical nature of each knowledge is the guiding principle in each exposition, giving a certain common structure to the book as a whole. Accordingly, the book is organised into three 'triptychs', each consisting of two anti-juridical types of knowledge that flank a central juridical case analysis on both sides. Case analyses undertake to present structures of legal practice as elements by which juridical power should be able to confront its adversaries in the general field of power. The following very brief introduction of the triptychs lays down a rudimentary synopsis of the main part of the book.

First, economic knowledge, juridical power and psychological knwledge. The problem of the first triptych is depicted as one concerning *human forms*. One of these forms, *homo œconomicus*, will be discussed first in an account of Foucault's rendering of classic economic liberalism in his lectures. As a kind of background figure or counterpart for *homo œconomicus*, Foucault also elaborates on the legal form of humanity, *homo juridicus*. The elements formative of this latter figure, legal rights and legal powers to decide on rights, will be the subject recast in the next chapter discussing the case of *Royer*. The third chapter completes the triptych by introducing another pair of human forms: the *delinquent* of criminal psychology and the *law-breaker* as a person who commits crimes. This pair will be illuminated by Foucault's analysis of a number of expert psychiatric opinions presented before legal courts in criminal cases.

Secondly, historical knowledge, juridical power and reason of state. The second triptych addresses the exercise of power especially from the point of view of the possibilities that an individual may have for developing resistance in the legal field, by way of practising law. Foucault's reconstruction of *war* as a principle of intelligibility for power and society will be discussed first. This, according to Foucault, is something advanced by historical knowledge. The second element, the centrepiece, is analysis of the *Bouchereau* case, which undertakes a scrutiny of legal practice from the point of view of tactics, strategies and conquests, as if in a war. In the third part, Foucault's explorations of the Renaissance political knowledge known by the name of *reason of state* will be discussed.

The third and last triptych addresses directly the types of knowledge sets involved in the cases: knowledge of society and knowledge of the individual. The first part will be a reconstruction of Foucault's knowledge-power, which is about the different ways in which knowledge circulates in the exercise of power. The second part consists of an analysis of the case of *Adoui and Cornuaille*, where knowledge is inserted into the legal mechanism of legality and equity. The last part consists of a reconstruction of what Foucault called his project of the history of the desiring man, that is, his genealogy of the procedures for extracting knowledge of the individual from the individual's own introspective discourse.

I am not going to move immediately into the framework I have presented above. The edifice entailed by this framework was constructed only after a long and arduous journey and the next chapter will show that the problems all first emerged from analyses of concrete legal practices, namely the cases. Using Foucault's words, this has required 'an operation that makes visible to itself the totality of the field of experience at each of its stages, and dissipates all its opaque structures' (Foucault 1989: 114). In our case, opaque structures perhaps do not dissipate entirely, but the operation at least makes the problems visible.

Notes

1 Article 48 of TEC provided that freedom of movement entails a set of rights 'subject to limitations justified on grounds of *ordre public*, public security or public health'.
2 Council Directive 64/221/EEC of 25 February 1964 art 3.1 states that: 'Measures taken on grounds of *ordre public* or of public security shall be based exclusively on the personal conduct of the individual concerned'.

Chapter 2

Problematisations

A monologising dynamic is walled into the normative structure of legal discourse. The 'legal condition', so to speak, is that everyone participating in practice must struggle to demonstrate that their interpretation is the only one that accords with the existing law. The fortifications of monologue have developed in a counter-factual manner. Legal practice, the basic business of which involves conflict, is constantly faced with the polyphony of social life. This continuous encounter with the fact of diversity has created an especially strong monologising dynamic in the structures of legal practice.

However, in the meantime, it has also afforded legal practice a peculiar awareness of the fundamental heterogeneity of social life. The strategic centrality of the oneness of existing law – the 'idea of law as a complete, consistent, closed and decidable whole' (Bengoetxea 1994: 65) – nevertheless subjugates the awareness of disagreements that lie on the basis of legal practice.

Pierre Bourdieu noted that what could be called the 'juridical sense' or 'juridical faculty' is precisely this 'universalising attitude'. Neutralisation and universalisation seem to be for Bourdieu the cornerstones of the juridical habitus (the embodied action-disposition consisting of schemes that generate perception and judgment). These two, according to Bourdieu, constitute the real 'entry ticket into the juridical field'. The universalising attitude shows itself in the language of lawyers, Bourdieu thinks, when they speak of their interpretations of norms in the 'indicative mood'; that is, as if they were facts. However, an appearance of coherence, autonomy and neutrality created by legal professionals for themselves is not 'a simple ideological mask' but 'the expression of the whole operation of the juridical field and, in particular, of the work of rationalization to which the system of juridical norms is continually subordinated' (Bourdieu 1987: 820).

This chapter presents analyses of the first three cases of the European Court of Justice (ECJ)[1] in my materials: *van Duyn, Bonsignore* and *Rutili*. For these three cases, I put forward a style of research that attempts to preserve the polyphonic nature of legal case materials. This choice of method has served the work in later chapters by delineating the right problems – by raising them from the field of legal practice. To make problems perceptible, this chapter will first have to open and to vivify the different perspectives voiced in the proceedings and recorded in the case files.

These perspectives usually trail off in the interpretive schemes of those who work with cases under the spell of the monologising dynamic.

Next, one will have to engage in a dialogue with these perspectives, as if they were one's real interlocutors. One must try not to commit the authorial unifying monism natural to any contemplation. One should try to disintegrate, dissolve one's own contemplative unity and let it be scattered in the ocean of legal practice as it is put forward in the action of the different players. Of course, one has to balance this endeavour, because nonetheless the task remains of providing the 'voice-over', the background discourse that fills in gaps and ties things together in the story.

However, it should not be a story that ends in unity of minds. In particular, it should attempt to avoid lifting the Court's rulings, and thereby the judges' perspective, above the perspectives of other participants. Focus is just as much on reports of proceedings, recording the submissions of the litigants, as on the opinions of the Advocate General and final judgments. One should also attempt to avoid, in the privileged position of an author, reconstructing any right answers to legal questions with which practitioners work. Before the analyses, let us briefly explain the legal norms that are under discussion.

Personal conduct, *ordre public*

Article 48 of the Treaty establishing the European Economic Community (TEC)[2] compromised something that used to belong to the sovereignty of Member States. Namely, Article 48 TEC removed the Member States' power to determine and to decide freely who is allowed to enter and remain in their territories. Article 48 established 'freedom of movement for workers', entailing a list of concrete rights conferred on the nationals of EU Member States. These rights include the right to move freely and to remain in Member States while employed or looking for employment and under certain conditions even the right to remain in a Member State after the end of employment. Migrant workers should be treated on an equal footing with nationals of the host Member State. This is considered an expression of the more general principle of non-discrimination in the EC, laid down in Article 7 TEC.[3]

Rights entailed by freedom of movement were subject to 'limitations justified on grounds of *ordre public*, public security or public health' (Article 48(3)).[4] Member States may derogate from free movement rights and non-discrimination and take measures against migrant workers if they can justify these by *ordre public*. This means that society is in danger and must be protected. *Ordre public* relates to the practice of the security apparatuses of Member States, one of which is their immigration administration.

It should be noted at this point that this work transgresses the scientific rules of citation in that the English rendering of *ordre public*, 'public policy', is translated systematically back to *ordre public* even within quotes. The problems with the English notion of public policy were explicitly recognised in the case materials, notably in the opinion of the Advocate General in the case of *Bouchereau* (at 2024–25).

However, the derogation clause did not mean that Member States are again free from the constraints of EC law and back to their full sovereignty if *ordre public* is endangered. Action justified by the derogation clause is legally controlled. Member States are not exempt from the law on the whole; rather, a space exists for manoeuvre within legal limits. One of these limits appears in Article 3(1) of Directive 64/221/EEC:[5] 'Measures taken on grounds of *ordre public* or of public security shall be based exclusively on the personal conduct of the individual concerned'. The personal conduct requirement means, essentially, that immigration authorities seeking to banish an EC national must be able to provide evidence that attests to the likelihood that precisely this particular individual constitutes a danger to society.

Lastly, procedural requirements purport to guarantee adequate remedies for EC nationals. Articles 5–9 of Directive 64/221[6] establish the procedural system to which Europeans are entitled if threatened by exclusion. Article 6 is crucial: 'The person concerned shall be informed of the grounds of *ordre public*, public security, or public health upon which the decision taken in his case is based, unless this is contrary to the interests of the security of the State involved'. Let us call this the right to information.

Let me recapitulate and summarise what we have here so far:

- first, the right to move freely among and to remain in Member States
- secondly, a derogation justified by *ordre public*
- thirdly, the personal conduct requirement that limits derogation and
- fourthly, the right to information on the reasons/grounds for exclusion.

This reductive exposition of the particular requirements imposed on Member States and their security authorities is sufficient for our purposes. It forms what in the previous chapter was called the mechanism of difference-making. The heart of that mechanism consists of the *ordre public* requirement, on the one hand, and of the personal conduct requirement, on the other hand.

Van Duyn

The ECJ gave its preliminary ruling in *van Duyn* on 4 December 1974. The case involved Scientology: does a person's association with Scientology form 'grounds of *ordre public*' on which exclusion is justified? The case of *van Duyn* forms a groundwork for later cases. In *van Duyn*, the two basic notions – personal conduct and *ordre public* – develop into a rough conceptual framework within which later practice may hold (even if loosely) to the idea of the socially dangerous individual.

The following exposition will be divided into two main parts, the first of which concerns *ordre public* and the second personal conduct. After describing the facts, I will move to the views of each participant in the proceedings: Ms van Duyn herself, the UK Government, the Commission, the Advocate General and the judges of the ECJ, as a collective.

The report on the facts and procedure in *van Duyn* begins by reproducing the statement on Scientology made by the UK Minister for Health in the House of Commons in 1968:

> Scientology is a pseudo-philosophical cult . . . The Government are satisfied having reviewed all the available evidence that Scientology is socially harmful. It alienates members of families from each other and attributes squalid and disgraceful motives to all who oppose it; its authoritarian principles and practice are a potential menace to the personality and well-being of those who submit to them. There is evidence that children are now being indoctrinated. (at 1339)

According to the minister, the trouble with Scientology was that there 'is no power under existing law to prohibit the practice of Scientology' (at 1339). Nonetheless, he said, the government was convinced that Scientology is 'so objectionable' that it is 'right to take all steps within [the government's] power to curb its growth' (at 1339). Therefore, it had decided that '[w]ork permits and employment vouchers will not be issued to foreign nationals . . . for work at a Scientology establishment' to prevent foreigners coming to the UK 'to study Scientology and to work at the so-called College in East Grinstead' (at 1340). East Grinstead was where Scientologists had their headquarters.

Five years later, in May 1973, Ms Yvonne van Duyn from the Netherlands sought entry to the UK at Gatwick airport. The immigration officials determined that she was the kind of foreigner that the minister had referred to. She was on her way to the college in East Grinstead to begin working there as a secretary for the Scientologists. The immigration officers at the airport followed the directions of the UK Government, barred her from entering the UK and sent her back home.

In the meantime, however, the UK had joined the EEC, which, as the treaty said, was founded on non-discrimination of individuals on grounds of nationality and on the free movement of workers. The question that arose was whether the treatment of Ms van Duyn constituted discrimination on the part of the UK, if the UK does not intervene in the practice of Scientology by UK citizens, but nonetheless endeavours to curb the growth of Scientology by acting against foreigners practising Scientology.

Ms van Duyn initiated proceedings in the English High Court of Justice. The High Court was to determine whether discrimination had occurred that constitutes a breach of Community law, or whether the policy and the action implementing it were within the limits of permitted derogation. The High Court decided to refer the case to the ECJ and requested it to clarify the meaning of Community law on this point.

The situation according to UK law was clear. Legally, any foreigner could be refused entry if the refusal is 'conducive to the public good'. The Secretary of State could give personal directions on this, but in any case immigration officers had wide independent discretion: an officer may exclude anyone if it 'seems right' to do so 'for example, in the light of the passenger's character, conduct or associations' (at 1340).

Under UK law, 'conducive to the public good' described what Community law has as the *ordre public* condition. In effect, the powers of the immigration authority remained practically intact in UK law on immigration, except for providing these powers formal legality.

The position of the UK Government in the *van Duyn* proceedings was that Community law changes nothing about the UK definition of *ordre public*. The meaning of the *ordre public* requirement (that restrictions to free movement must be 'on grounds of *ordre public*') would be essentially the same as the requirement in UK law that restrictions should be 'conducive to the public good'. Along these lines, the UK Government representative referred to Scientology as something 'sufficiently undesirable', something 'a Government may consider contrary to the public good' (at 1345).

The Commission disagreed with the UK Government. It submitted that *ordre public* is a concept of Community law. It 'must first be interpreted in the context of Community law, and national criteria are only relevant to its application'. Freedom of movement, in the Commission's view, can only be maintained 'on the basis of uniform application in all Member States'. The UK Government's interpretation, according to which the Community concept of *ordre public* means the same as the UK concept of 'public good', was an incorrect way to deal with Community law. The idea is not that patterns of national law are imposed on Community law, but vice versa (at 1344).

The Advocate General disagreed with the Commission. It remarked that Member States have undeniably retained their powers 'to ensure [. . .] the safeguarding of their *ordre public* and, in particular, of public security within their territory'. The Advocate General's opinion is that a Community concept of *public security* does not exist (it is not possible to 'deduce' that concept, he said) despite the fact that the concept appears in the texts of the treaty and of the directive (at 1356).

Community public security does not exist, but what about Community *ordre public*? Insofar as 'a "Community *ordre public*" exists', the Advocate General thought that 'it can only be an economic *ordre public*'. It should relate to market, trade, customs or competition. As to *ordre public* in the area of public security, the Community does not act in that area at all. 'Member States have the sole power', the Advocate General submitted, 'to take measures for the safeguarding of public security'. Moreover, Member States have the sole power 'to decide the circumstances under which that security may be endangered'. Unlike the Commission, the Advocate General found that the 'concept remains, at least for the present, national, and this conforms with reality inasmuch as the requirements of public security vary, in time and in space, from one State to another' (at 1357).

The judges of the court found themselves with the task of striking a delicate balance. On the one hand, they should guarantee that *ordre public* derogations do not vitiate freedom of movement altogether. Individuals do have enforceable rights that the courts must protect. On the other hand, these rights are 'subject to limitations' and the Member States may derogate if a case of *ordre public* exists. But what circumstances fall within this concept?

The judges conceded that 'the particular circumstances justifying recourse to the concept of *ordre public* may vary from one country to another and from one period to another, and it is therefore necessary in this matter to allow the competent national authorities an area of discretion'. Nonetheless, the judges insisted that the concept 'must be interpreted strictly, so that its scope cannot be determined unilaterally by each Member State'. In the future, the Community institutions, including the Court itself, will have to control application of the *ordre public* limitation. Moreover, the judges ruled that if Member State authorities have 'clearly defined their standpoint as regards the activities of a particular organization and where, considering it to be socially harmful, they have taken administrative measures to counteract these activities', they may 'rely on the concept of *ordre public*' (at 1350).

Let us sum up the discussion thus far. The UK Government claimed that the *ordre public* requirement is essentially the same as the requirement that one should consider what is conducive to the public good. The Commission contradicted this by insisting that *ordre public* is a Community concept, which must have the same uniform application in all Member States. Against that, the Advocate General maintained that *ordre public* is a national concept, which has virtually nothing to do with the Community. The judges declined to define *ordre public* substantively as a Community concept, but nevertheless ruled that it should be interpreted strictly in the Community context. Member States do not have the sole power to qualify anything as *ordre public*, but substantively the concept remained *non liquet* for the time being.

Let us now turn to the discussion of 'personal conduct' in *van Duyn*. How would the topic of dangerousness emerge in the frames of that concept? In *van Duyn*, the question was recast in the form: does association with Scientology form a part of the individual's 'personal conduct'? Remember that the directive required that exclusion 'be based exclusively on the personal conduct of the individual concerned' (Article 3(1) Directive 64/221/EEC).

According to the report on the facts, an immigration officer at the airport had interviewed Ms van Duyn, on the basis of which the immigration officer regarded Ms van Duyn's presence in the UK as 'undesirable' and decided she should be sent back to the Netherlands. The facts that emerged in the interview were as follows: Ms van Duyn 'had worked in a Scientology establishment in Amsterdam for six months; she had taken a course in the subject of Scientology; she was a practising Scientologist; and she was intending to work at a Scientology establishment in the United Kingdom' (at 1340).

In its request for a preliminary ruling, the UK court wanted to know whether a Member State is 'entitled to take into account as matters of personal conduct' one's connections with Scientology. More precisely, these connections meant Ms van Duyn's *association*, on the one hand, with Scientology, which is an organisation considered contrary to the public good, but not unlawful and, on the other hand, her intention to take up *employment* in that organisation.

Ms van Duyn stated that her past activity had been blameless. She emphasised that both the activities of the Church of Scientology itself and of the people working for it are perfectly legal in the UK. 'Merely belonging to a lawful organization, without necessarily taking part in its activities cannot', according to Ms van Duyn, 'amount to "conduct"', because 'conduct implies activity' (at 1343).

The UK Government disagreed. It submitted that association with an organisation is relevant if the organisation in question is 'sufficiently undesirable' and if the association of the person in question is 'sufficiently close' to that organisation. 'Whether, in any given case, such exclusion is justified will depend on the view the Member State takes of the organization'. This view by no means needs to be expressed by making the organisation illegal in the country; 'as is common knowledge', said the UK Government, 'the United Kingdom practises a considerable degree of tolerance in relation to organisations'. Employment as such 'is a very material aspect of the individual's personal conduct' (at 1345).

The Commission disagreed with the UK Government. The Commission did not deny that association with an organisation generally relates to the personal conduct of an individual. However, the point of personal conduct *qua* associations is that these must make the personal conduct unacceptable. The Commission insisted that the unacceptability of the association is the decisive factor. For example, 'a membership of a militant organization proscribed in the host Member State' would be a relevant element in assessing someone's personal conduct. But if the association is acceptable to UK nationals, as in this case, it cannot be unacceptable to others, said the Commission (at 1344).

The Advocate General disagreed with the Commission. For the Advocate General, 'there is no doubt' that the facts of the case 'fall within the concept of "personal conduct"'. Association 'with the Church of Scientology is an element of a person's conduct'. Personal conduct as associations raised for him no problems concerning agency. The idea of the personal conduct requirement is merely that the grounds of each exclusion decision are examined individually, which enables the courts to review these grounds (at 1358).

The judges went further than the Advocate General. They produced a concise but full statement on personal conduct in relation to associations. The following can, of course, be contested from all sides, but it is a clear position:

> Although a person's *past association* cannot [,] in general, justify a decision refusing him the right to move freely within the Community, it is nevertheless the case that *present association*, which reflects *participation* in the activities of a body or of the organization as well as *identification* with its aims and its

designs, may be considered a *voluntary act* of the person concerned and, consequently, as part of his personal conduct within the meaning of the provision cited. (at 1349, emphasis added)

Association, insofar as it involves participation and identification, is voluntary action. There is a syllogism: voluntary action is personal conduct, association is voluntary action; ergo, association is personal conduct. After this agency-theoretical feat, the judges concluded that Member States need not make the activities of an organisation unlawful to take into account someone's membership in it. Rather, it is enough that a Member State has clearly defined its standpoint and taken administrative measures to counteract the activities of that organisation (at 1350).

To conclude the analysis of *van Duyn*, let us ask what exactly it was about Ms van Duyn's personal conduct that constituted a danger to society? For the UK Minister for Health, Scientology is dangerous because it brainwashes people: 'its authoritarian principles and practice are a potential menace to the personality and well-being of those who submit to it' (at 1339). Scientology is dangerous in this way, but was not Ms van Duyn herself then a victim of Scientological brainwashing, rather than a perpetrator? Was she not someone whose capacity for autonomous judgment is muted because of brainwashing? Her behaviour was not personal conduct, but personal enactment of Hubbard's *dianetics* – 'the modern science of mental health'.[7] The UK Minster of Health perhaps meant that it was precisely the fact of her mind's mutilation by this 'science' that made Ms van Duyn dangerous.

What are the effects of such mutilation? Are they not that one can no longer 'act voluntarily'? At the bottom of the problem of one's associations is the question of whether – after a certain kind of identification and participation – one remains a free person. Is this incapacity the reason why Ms van Duyn was dangerous? The brainwashing argument of the Minister for Health in any event seems to ruin the judges' argument based on the philosophy of agency.

In a similar vein, the logic of the security system ruins the logic of the law. The practice of law, however, is not in any way ruined by that. As with any practice, it is of course 'logical' only to the extent that being logical is practical.[8] The practice of law works *together with* some practices, such as the practice of the Minister for Health who, in this case, cares for people's mental health. The practice of law works *against* other practices such as Scientology, which also seem to affect the minds of individuals in some curious way. In both relations, the practice of law would impose its own categories on the categories of other practices.

Bonsignore

Bonsignore was a case from Cologne, Germany, on which the ECJ ruled on 26 February 1975, less than three months after deciding *van Duyn*. In *Bonsignore*, the question confronted was the relation between exclusions in immigration law and convictions in penal law. In this connection, Article 3(2) of Directive 64/221[9] provides that 'previous criminal convictions shall not in themselves constitute grounds' of *ordre public*. This does not mean that such convictions are insignificant; it means merely that they do not constitute sufficient ground, because they do not necessarily say enough about the present dangerousness of a person. What can be held 'personal conduct' if not past deeds? Perhaps future deeds?

In the following, each participant's views are again presented one after another. The participants in *Bonsignore* were the *Oberstadtdirektor* (Chief Administrative Officer) of the City of Cologne, the Representative of the Public Interest, the Italian Government, the Commission, the Advocate General and the judges.

As in the *van Duyn* case, the analysis has two parts: one part that deals with *ordre public* and another part that deals with personal conduct. In *Bonsignore,* however, the issue is not so much clarification of what these notions in a legislative text refer to in the external reality of the lives of individuals and societies. In *Bonsignore,* the practice of law confronts the reality of the police and security services, the reality of the immigration authorities. This creates, in *Bonsignore,* the need to draw boundaries between the system that upholds that reality and the legal system.

Carmelo Angelo Bonsignore, a 20-year-old immigrant from Sicily, had accidentally shot and killed his younger brother, using a gun for which he had no permit. The Criminal Court of Cologne (*Amtsgericht*) found him guilty of causing death by negligence, but imposed no punishment because of mitigating circumstances. For his offence against the Firearms Law, he was fined. The *Oberstadtdirektor* deemed Mr Bonsignore a threat to the *ordre public* and decided to deport him. Mr Bonsignore appealed this decision in the Administrative Court of Cologne.

The Administrative Court recognised that, according to Article 3(1) of Directive 64/221/EEC, deportations must 'be based exclusively on the personal conduct of the individual concerned'. This it took to mean that deportation is lawful only if 'there was a risk of repetition'. With regard to Mr Bonsignore no such risk was present, so the court held that 'the deportation order must be clearly "vitiated by error"'. Despite that, the *Regierungspräsident* (Chief District Administrative Officer), who was the next to deliberate on the matter, declared that the risk did exist and confirmed the deportation decision. Mr Bonsignore then returned to the Administrative Court to have the decision finally annulled (at 310).

The Administrative Court decided to request a preliminary ruling from the ECJ on two counts. First, is it possible to exclude someone 'for the purposes of deterring other foreign nationals' (criminal law 'general prevention')? That question concerns the notion of *ordre public*. Secondly, need there be 'clear indications' that a convicted person 'will commit further offences or will in some other way disregard public security or *ordre public*' (criminal law 'special prevention')? That question, in turn, concerns the notion of personal conduct (at 300).

In *Bonsignore,* a discourse on danger was heard from all parties, but especially in the submissions of the national security authorities. This is how the

Oberstadtdirektor saw the duties of the authorities handling *ordre public (öffentliche Ordnung)*:

> The task facing the administrators of the police and security services is not only to put an end to existing disturbances, but also and primarily to provide a preventive defence against dangers threatening public security and *ordre public*; such a 'danger' may consist in the possibility of harm which the competent authorities, on the basis of their experience, consider likely to occur. (at 300)

The *Oberstadtdirektor* first drew upon German legislation concerning immigration that regarded offences against firearms regulations 'as of particular danger to the peaceful, secure coexistence of Germans and foreigners' (at 300–301). The German Federal authorities had instructed the local immigration authorities to apply national immigration law so that certain offences, such as illegal possession and trafficking of guns and narcotics 'must, in principle, result in the deportation of aliens who are responsible for them' (at 312). According to the *Oberstadtdirektor*, foreigners who commit these offences 'constitute a particularly serious threat to the peaceful coexistence of a large population which is concentrated – in the large towns – in a restricted area' (at 301).

The *Oberstadtdirektor* explained, however, that people such as Mr Bonsignore must be expelled primarily because the acts for which they are convicted 'are of particular danger to the population', while the 'desirable consequence that news of such a measure [ie of the deportation of a foreigner] spreads and has an unquestionable deterrent effect' is only a subsidiary ground for taking this measure (at 301).

The Representative of the Public Interest, intervener in the action before the Administrative Court, held that the concept of *ordre public* is 'developed in legal systems based on Roman law' and embodies 'all provisions drawn up in the general interest'. The crucial part of that general interest is 'an interest in maintaining the respect of foreign workers for the German system of law and order' (at 301).

Foreigners, especially, need to be integrated 'into the existing order', that is, 'into the way of life of the Federal Republic' (at 302). This involves 'instilling an awareness of the importance of public security and order, in particular in large industrial centres', said the Representative of the Public Interest (at 301). In cases such as Mr Bonsignore's, deportation 'is necessary as a collective deterrence', and collective deterrence in general is an important means 'in the context of the maintenance of order' (at 302).

Moreover, deportations of foreigners, including deportations of Europeans 'are objectively justified [. . .] when they are capable of fulfilling their purpose of acting as a deterrent'. This fact of purposiveness is what also makes deportations 'lawful according to the directive, as being measures taken on grounds of *ordre public*' (at 302). In other words, in the context of *ordre public*, ends and expediency justify the means. The end is not exactly deterrence, but integration by deterrence.

In their defence before the Cologne Administrative Court, the national authorities had also drawn on the fact that 'offences by aliens involving the use of arms had risen to a substantial degree'. Therefore, in their view, 'a further increase in these crimes of violence must be *countered* by the immediate expulsion of aliens who [commit these crimes and] had come to the notice of the authorities' (at 310).

The Italian Government, an intervener in the proceedings, disagreed. It said that the meaning of the personal conduct requirement is precisely that such things as general prevention are not permitted as grounds for exclusion. That is, deportations of individual foreigners may not be used as a means to deter or integrate other foreigners. In addition, Italy was of the opinion that exclusions of Europeans in order to deter other foreigners in the country would be 'both contrary to principles of justice and equity and incompatible with the very foundations of the Community legal system'. This 'might lead to a real discrimination based on nationality' (at 303).

The Commission supported Italy's views. The Commission held that the personal conduct requirement in Article 3(1) of the directive means that each case must be examined individually. This 'is also valid as regards the objective sought by such measures'. Moreover, the objectives must relate to the individual, not groups of individuals. Therefore, 'the desire to deter other foreigners [. . .] must be [. . .] irrelevant' (at 303). 'This interpretation', said the Commission, 'corresponds to the spirit and objective of the directive' (at 304).

Neither the Commission nor the Italian Government engaged in the discourse on danger started by the Cologne authorities. The basic parameters within which the Commission and the Italian Government moved were not those of the security system, but rather the principles of justice and equity, the foundations of a legal system, discrimination, the spirit and objectives of the law. These matters, however, were not at all the concern of the immigration authorities. Their presumption was, perhaps, that these other parameters just do not count because one simply *derogates* from what they constitute, that is, from the system of law. Would such exit from the law then be an entrance to a free space of juridical indiscernibility? Or is it rather an entrance to another kind of law?

Unlike the Commission and the Italian Government, the Advocate General did engage in the discourse on danger. He recognised the 'fact that in the industrialized countries which provide employment for large numbers of foreign workers, statistics [. . .] show that certain forms of criminal behaviour are peculiar to the immigrant population' (at 312). This is explained by what 'sociologists would term [. . .] a feeling of alienation', that is, a failure to adapt due to a variety of structural causes that amplify the 'feeling that in practice they remain outside society in the host country' (at 312).

Consequently, the Advocate General foresaw a possibility that the system for derogation from freedom of movement could have been created differently from what it actually was, and more in the way of the German *Ausländergesetz*. One could imagine a list of offences likely to be 'contagious', that is, a list of the types of misbehaviour that threaten to spread throughout the population (as infectious diseases travel from one body to another). Were the Community authorities to promulgate in public such 'offences which are considered to involve [. . .] a risk of "contagion"', it would secure uniform application of derogations from freedom of movement in Member States. This sounded good to the Advocate General, but it 'is not the system employed by the Council directive' (at 313).

Instead, the system requires that each person's conduct be assessed individually 'to remove any possibility of [. . .] taking security measures of a collective nature in respect of' Community nationals. Moreover, the Advocate General considered it 'necessary to go still further [. . .] by acknowledging that the concept of personal conduct and the desire to act for reasons of a general preventive nature are *incompatible* and *irreconcilable*' (at 315, emphasis added).

This suggests that incompatibility and irreconcilability indeed also lie between the two systems, the legal system and the police and security services system. However, the Advocate General was prepared to imagine the kind of legal arrangement that is based on promulgation by Community authorities of a defined variety of misbehaviour, and which establishes the sanction of exclusion on that misbehaviour in a formalistic manner. Notably, this solution, warmly recommended by the Advocate General for the future, would accord with the positivist logic of the legal norm: tort, imputation and sanction.

The Advocate General was convinced that the Community legislator should move in this direction. Then 'the grounds of deportation would have to be based on Community criteria which would be uniformly applicable' (at 316). This would to the Advocate General's mind represent a considerable step in the progress of integration:

> At least we will then have abandoned once and for all the old concept of deportation, which is a security measure available at the discretion of the administrative authorities and which gives them the power to expel 'undesirable' immigrants from their territory, and was in practice, until quite recently, not subject to an effective review by the courts. (at 316)

As for the idea that deportations of individual foreigners would deter – and thereby integrate – other foreigners, the Advocate General was sceptical. He reckoned that exclusions possess a feature that 'satisfies the feeling of hostility, sometimes verging on xenophobia, [. . .] in the indigenous population', rather than any sincere efforts at governing life in society towards peaceful coexistence (at 315).

The judges provided little discussion of the concept of *ordre public* in this case. In their ruling, the judges merely stated that derogation from freedom of movement 'cannot be justified on grounds extraneous to the individual case'. This is the effective meaning of the personal conduct requirement. Therefore, Community law 'prevents the deportation [. . .] if such deportation is ordered for the purpose of deterring other aliens' (at 307).

To sum up so far, one could say it is somewhat confusing that the legal mechanism of TEC Article 48 and Directive 64/221, based on a combination of *ordre public* and personal conduct, seems to undermine what one is used to having as the basis of all law: the formalistic logic of imputation on the basis of the principle of legality. In criminal law, this is expressed by the principle of *nulla poena sine lege*.

Instead of that logic, however, the *ordre public* derogation based on personal conduct seems to establish a logic of singularity: things are to be decided on a case-by-case basis and not according to publicly promulgated rules of law. More puzzles ensue as it also seems that the representatives of the police and the security services, who should follow another kind of logic than that of the legal system, really do emphasise the importance of pre-established categories of offences that would automatically bring about the administrative consequence of deportation.

Let us now focus more closely on the problem of 'personal conduct' in *Bonsignore*. This focus will further illustrate the difference between the ideal-typical systems of law and security service, as well as the real confusion between them in practice. To begin with, the Advocate General provided a brief, although still relatively detailed, description of the concrete event that triggered the entire process:

> Mr Carmelo Bonsignore, an Italian national born in Sicily in 1950, arrived in Germany in October 1968. He was employed at the Ford works in Cologne as a chemical worker. In May 1971 he unlawfully purchased from an unknown person a 6.35 calibre automatic Beretta pistol and cartridges. He did not possess a firearms permit.
>
> Several days later, on 30 May, during a family meal at his sister's home he produced the pistol which he had just obtained, wishing to show how it was fired. He removed the magazine and found that a cartridge remained in the breech. He attempted to remove it but was unsuccessful. Being unfamiliar with the handling of firearms he unintentionally pulled the trigger and his young brother, Angelo, who had recently arrived in Germany, was fatally injured in the head by the bullet. (at 309)

As mentioned above, the Cologne Criminal Court (*Amtsgericht*) had held that Mr Bonsignore was guilty of causing death by negligence, but did not impose punishment on that count owing to mitigating circumstances. These mitigating factors were that Mr Bonsignore was 'young and inexperienced' and 'very deeply affected by the death of his brother'. He had 'in no way attempted to deny his liability' and promised 'never again to touch a gun' (at 309–10). Therefore, the *Amtsgericht* found 'that no purpose would be served' by punishing Mr Bonsignore 'in view of the circumstances, notably the mental suffering caused to [him] as a result of the consequences of his carelessness' (at 305). As also mentioned earlier, Mr Bonsignore was sentenced to a fine for illegal possession of a firearm.

It appears that the *Amtsgericht* (the Criminal Court) had in fact arrived at a completely different estimation of Mr Bonsignore's character and conduct from that of the *Oberstadtdirektor*, who found that Mr Bonsignore 'is not prepared to obey the German system of law and order' (at 310). Generally speaking, for the *Oberstadt-*

direktor, the personal conduct requirement posed no problems in cases such as *Bonsignore*: 'a foreigner convicted of an offence always supplies the reason for his deportation by his own personal conduct' (at 299). The Representative of the Public Interest supported this by stating that: 'Mr Bonsignore invited deportation by infringing upon German firearms legislation, that is, through his personal conduct' (at 301).

Offences that relate to firearms are not ordinary offences; they are particularly dangerous offences. Therefore, according to the immigration authorities: 'the unlawful acquisition and possession of firearms is a threat to public security and public order [*öffentlich Ordnung*] and, for this reason, justifies a deportation order' (at 301). In other words, carrying a gun illegally is an offence, 'the very nature' of which 'conceals a potential danger for *ordre public*' (at 312).

This attitude towards guns appears plausible, but the fact remains that the German court had sentenced Mr Bonsignore to nothing more than a fine for this particularly dangerous offence, which was probably in line with the manner in which German citizens themselves were treated for this particular offence. Therefore, the problem boils down to the different status of German nationals and foreigners or, in the EC context, to discrimination against the latter. This is perhaps envisaged by the statement of the German authorities according to which: 'it is intolerable that foreigners enjoying the hospitality of this country should be allowed [. . .] to become a constant danger to the (national) population' (at 310).

The perspective provided by the immigration authorities on 'freedom' in this connection is interesting. They said that: 'the Community is obliged to acknowledge [the right to freedom of movement] only if it does not adversely affect *ordre public*; the consequences of "*undue*" *freedom* of movement are contrary to the purpose sought' by the Community legislator. The 'achievement of *peaceful freedom* of movement', which corresponds to aims to integrate foreigners into German society, requires that deportations be ordered for the purposes of collective deterrence of foreigners (at 302, emphases added).

The Italian Government disagreed again. In its turn, it recalled first of all that previous criminal convictions as such are expressly prohibited as grounds for deportation in Article 3(2) of Directive 64/221. In the view of the Italian Government, the personal conduct requirement of Article 3(1) means that: 'a close and special *correlation* must exist between the expected threat to *ordre public* and the conduct of' the foreigner to be deported. To make it even clearer, the Italian Government restated that: 'the directive requires the existence of a *chain of causation* between the conduct of workers and the feared threat to *ordre public*' (at 303, emphases added.)

The Commission supported the views of Italy. It also recalled Article 3(2), and offered on its behalf that deportation of a convicted person can be ordered 'only when, after a thorough consideration of all the facts of the case, it may be feared that the foreigner in question will again offend against *ordre public* and public security' (at 304). The Commission thereby interpreted the expression 'personal conduct' so that it requires an analysis of future recidivism.

Both the Italian Government's causality argument and the Commission's recidivism argument bring to mind the classic question: can one's past conduct be so thoroughly examined that it can be known what the person will do in the future? Moreover, what are the consequences of this with respect to the voluntary-action philosophy endorsed by the judges in *van Duyn*?

The Advocate General was conscious of the controversies over the possibility of causal determination on the basis of which the probability of future recidivism might be assessed. Despite these controversies – and recalling the express prohibition in Article 3(2) of Directive 64/221 of grounding deportation solely on a previous criminal conviction – he stated that the personal conduct requirement clearly does demand an estimation of *the person* on the basis of their conduct: 'The concept of personal conduct must be examined not only in light of the offences committed, but also in view of the "potential criminality" of the offender, to use the language of the criminologists' (at 316).

The Advocate General held that there must be 'cogent evidence on which to base [the] opinion that there is a serious risk that the individual concerned will commit further offences or, more generally, represent, through his conduct, both past and foreseeable, a danger to the host State' (at 316). So a clear demand exists for the authorities to probe the inner spheres of the mind of the individual, to be able to estimate that individual's future conduct.

Even the most violent crimes, such as murder, if committed in 'a particular psychological context', are not sufficient evidence of the perpetrator's future conduct, said the Advocate General (at 311–12). For example, if a wife kills her husband after having for many years been battered, abused and mentally tortured by him, it is not at all likely that she would commit more murders.

All in all, the import of what has been covered thus far is that imposing punishments on the basis of offences determined in penal law is completely different from deliberating on the necessity of deporting these offenders. Two systems are in operation: the reactive system of criminal adjudication, and the proactive system of immigration administration. One is based on an individual's past action, the other on their future action. Classic criminal law has regarded the actual deed, or at least an attempt, as a *sine qua non* for punishment. Governing security, in turn, has already failed in those cases where actual deeds have realised threats. There is a difference in rationalities: one is reactive, the other proactive.

The bewildering element in *Bonsignore*, however, is that in fact it was the *criminal court* that had made use of the future-argument in its decision not to impose punishment; the crucial thing about the mitigating factors was that these factors provided a vision of the *future* decency of Mr Bonsignore's conduct. Thereafter, and in contrast, the *immigration authorities*, in their decision to deport Mr Bonsignore, acted on the basis of the 'sole fact' (at 302) of his *past* conduct, regardless of the likelihood of his becoming a recidivist. An exchange of rationalities seems to have occurred between these two powers.

However, this exchange occurred only at the level of the mechanism deployed, while the *leitmotiv* of each (justice on the one hand, security on the other hand) of course remained what it was. Obviously, none of our criminal laws would ever allow convictions based on 'potential criminality' without the existence of an actual offence. The improbability or probability of recidivism can be considered only in connection with deliberation on the severity of punishment.

However, one more aspect should be added to the evidence of the vagueness of the distinction between the legal system and the security and police service system. This is, namely, the way in which the immigration authorities lumped together the *ordre public* maintenance technique of *deterrence* and the criminal law logic of *imputation*. Traditionally, the notion of 'general prevention' purports to justify coercive criminal law, and it reflects an idea behind any normative order that works by means of sanctions. Interestingly, the immigration authorities felt that public sanctions that follow publicly defined torts are a better way to influence a population, rather than by really trying to discover criminality in people's minds.

The immigration authorities did not seem to care so much about their own, future-oriented, ideal-typical logic, but invoked the logic of law and, as a specific technique, made it serve the maintenance of social order. Nonetheless, their concept of law was clearly different from the concept of law rooted in the professional *habitus* of every modern lawyer for whom there is something strange in the notions of 'peaceful freedom' and 'undue freedom'. Justifying measures by way of their expediency as a means to an end – in any event where the end is deterrence – sounds even stranger. However, is deterence not also the conventional objective of general prevention?

The Advocate General also contributed to the action-theoretical discussion on freedom and agency. Let us sum up the earlier contributions before moving on to that. Perhaps a certain correspondence existed between, on the one hand, the immigration authorities' discussion of the detrimental consequences of 'undue freedom' together with their emphasis on the importance of 'peaceful freedom' and, on the other hand, the philosophy of voluntary action endorsed by the judges in *van Duyn*.

Similarly, a certain connection existed in the Italian Government's insistence on 'correspondence' and 'chain of causation' between the individual's conduct (the cause) and the social danger (the effect), on the one hand, and the Commission's assumption according to which one's past personal conduct opens the way for predictions of one's future personal conduct.

The Advocate General's perspective is a fresh one, however, and does not seem to connect to any of the others' notions. He grasped the idea of freedom and rights from the perspective of 'the system established' (at 314). That system was the Common Market:

> [. . .] individual rights [. . .] are essential to the realization of the Common Market which, far from being limited to unhindered trade of goods, necessarily involves individual mobility and guaranteed access to the territory of each Member State for the purpose of employment there. (at 314)

In this view, 'rights are fundamental to the system' (at 314). However, this is not to be understood in the way that rights were there first, and then a system was built on them. Instead, the system explains the meaning and purpose of the rights, which is to enhance 'individual mobility'. Individual mobility and circulation of the workforce carries on the life – the bloodstream – of the Common Market. Rights are not fundamental in the sense that they were intrinsically valuable, founding the system as an essential commitment. Rights are the fundamental means to an even more fundamental end.

This grasp of the matter is something quite different from the (romantic or rational) idea of constitutional and human rights that recognises the intrinsic and invaluable autonomy (= reason + freedom) in every individual human being. From the perspective of the 'system established', rights and freedom – as well as, of course, 'workers' themselves – exist to keep the engines of the Common Market roaring.

Finally, we can turn to the views of the judges on the notion of personal conduct. They were terse but precise in their contribution. In their judgment, the Court stated (at 307) that: 'the concept of "personal conduct" expresses the requirement that a deportation order may only be made for breaches of the peace [ie of *ordre public*] and public security which might be committed by the individual affected'.[10] The Court thereby established a rule according to which *future* conduct – 'breaches that might be committed' – is indeed significant and decisive.

It is time for some intermediary conclusions. It is apparent that in some way a tendency exists to view immigrants as objects (objects whose moves should be predictable), but in another way as subjects (as recalcitrant and unpredictable, which is why they are dangerous in the first place). On this plane, in a certain sense, there is something humane in the immigration authorities' perspective: they at least honour immigrants as subjects enough in that the authorities feel they must try to *deter* them and *counter* their violence, rather than to sophisticate them with the inner conduct-determining mechanisms of their immigrant personalities. There is the importance of *instilling awareness*, but the context of maintenance of order really seems to presume and believe in genuine resistance on the part of the subjects.

By far the least humane of the perspectives is that of the 'system established' (ie. the Common Market), represented by the Advocate General. In this system, the migrant worker is not even a distinguishable object really, but a fluid, a mere refill in the tanks of the supranational economy. In any event, these human forms seem to militate against each other, and especially against the voluntary action philosophy of the judges in *van Duyn*.

Rutili

The next case is that of Mr Roland Rutili, ruled on by the ECJ on 28 October 1975, involving the events of May 1968 in France. As is well known, political and industrial protest actions all around the country created considerable public disorder, which evidently was precisely what the participants hoped for.

The existing French social order was, at least on the level of public discourse and cultural hegemony, shaken for a couple of weeks in a manner that was half carnival, half subversive.

The *Rutili* case considerably changes the direction of the story. Undoubtedly the change that occurred in *Rutili* was not as a result of the length of time that had elapsed, because only eight months separated *Bonsignore* and *Rutili*. In *Rutili*, the participants were faced with a complex problem that, among other things, showed an affinity between political rights and procedural rights. Both types of rights assume that an individual is a speaking subject. In *Bonsignore*, the reality faced by the participants was the reality of the security system, which engendered the problem of an individual as a predictable object that can be dangerous. In *Rutili*, the participants encountered political reality and a political subject. This subject is no less dangerous.

In the first place, the problem of *Rutili* concerned the meaning of one single word: 'justified'. This is certainly the key term in all practice of law. The French court asked the following question: 'what is the precise meaning to be attributed to the word "justified"' in TEC 48(3)? (at 1222), on the understanding that this Article provides that freedom of movement entails rights but that these are subject to limitations *justified* on grounds of *ordre public*.

The participants in *Rutili* were Mr Roland Rutili, the French Government, the Italian Government, the Commission, the Advocate General and the judges. The perspectives of the participants will again be presented one by one, but without attempting to organise the exposition into sections about *ordre public* and personal conduct. These words do appear in the *Rutili* files, but the participants did not really discuss the concepts. Before moving to the discussion, let us briefly recount the facts.

Mr Rutili was an Italian national who had lived and worked in France all his life. He had a French wife and they had three children. Mr Rutili had participated in the political and industrial actions of the summer of 1968. Some weeks afterwards, the authorities decided to deport Mr Rutili from France, although they soon revoked their decision, replacing it with another one which ordered Mr Rutili to stay in Puy-de-Dôme, one of the three *Départements* surrounding Paris. After two years of bureaucratic processing, Mr Rutili eventually received a residence permit preventing him from entering the district of Lorraine, where he had previously lived and worked and where his family continued to reside (at 1221).

According to the French administration (at 1238) the alleged facts behind the decisions against Mr Rutili were the following:

- Mr Rutili participated in the election campaign for the 1967 Parliamentary elections
- he took part in subversive activity which occurred during the events of May 1968
- he played an active part in political action during the 14 July demonstrations at Audun-le-Tiche in 1968.

It is important to note that Mr Rutili himself was not informed of these reasons before the appeal proceedings that he initiated in an administrative court in Paris to annul the decision that set limitations on his residence in France. In other words, he learned of the contents of the accusations levelled against him only at this final stage, after he had for several years sought redress from the administration.

In the proceedings before the administrative court, Mr Rutili invoked the rights enshrined in EC law that should have guaranteed his freedom of movement anywhere in France. At this point the Parisian court decided to request a preliminary ruling from the ECJ, explaining 'the precise meaning to be attributed to the word "justified"' in TEC 48(3), which, as already noted, provides that rights of freedom of movement are subject to limitations justified on grounds of *ordre public* and public security.

Mr Rutili's position was that the limitation of his right of residence was 'wholly without justification', both from the perspective of French law and from that of Community law. It constituted 'an infringement of the fundamental right of freedom of movement and of the principle of non-discrimination'. Curiously enough, this is all that Mr Rutili had to say, or at least all that was recorded in the case file (at 1227).[11]

The French Government disagreed. Apparently the opinion of France was that the *Rutili* case presented nothing new to existing Community case law (*van Duyn* and *Bonsignore*). The French Government confined itself to reiterating some of the contents of the previous judgments. Accordingly, the word 'justified' means that restrictions on freedom of movement must be based on *ordre public* which, crucially, is a concept that applies to different circumstances. These circumstances may vary from time to time and from country to country. The ECJ had recognised that national authorities have an area of discretion in determining what constitutes such circumstances. The personal conduct requirement was certainly fulfilled in *Rutili*, so no doubts or problems could arise from that issue (at 1224).

The Italian Government, an intervener in the proceedings, disagreed with the French Government. It stated that 'the term "justified" in the first place means that there must be an exhaustive explanation of reasons' for the decisions, which is something that 'seems manifestly not to have been done' in Mr Rutili's case. The Italian Government raised the issue of the procedural right to information in Article 6 of Directive 64/221:

> The person concerned shall be informed of the grounds of *ordre public*, public security, or public health upon which the decision taken in his case is based, unless this is contrary to the interests of the security of the State involved. (at 1224)

Needless to say, this is a prerequisite for realisation of the rights of appeal. In Italy's view, a decision cannot possibly be regarded as properly 'justified' if this elementary procedural right is not guaranteed. The first thing that 'justified' means at the very least is that the person is informed of the grounds.

The Commission supported the views of Italy. The Commission held the word 'justified' to mean that the decision 'must be reasoned'. However, the objective fact that such reasoning occurred is insufficient by itself; such reasoning must be explained to the person in question 'to enable him to make use of the legal remedies'. Guaranteeing the individual's right to obtain information about his case is essential in 'justifying' a decision. In addition, the Commission opined that the grounds of *ordre public* can 'be resorted to only in particularly serious cases', since this constitutes an exception to free movement of persons, which is 'one of the underlying principles of the Community'. In other words, *ordre public* exceptions must be interpreted restrictively (at 1225).

In its estimation of Mr Rutili's personal conduct, as described by the French authorities, the Commission was of the opinion that it 'can scarcely be considered to affect adversely the *ordre public*'. In fact, the Commission regarded Mr Rutili's conduct as nothing but a 'legitimate exercise of a freedom enjoyed by the public'. This freedom is established in the form of 'fundamental human rights' and recognised by all Member States. Legally determined limitations on 'public freedoms' (that is, political rights) enable simultaneous exercise of these and other rights, as well as protection of society. The limitations are laid down in national laws and in international conventions. Limitations must, in other words, be necessary in a democratic society. There can be no others, and this would 'form a basic criterion for determining at what point an activity may be regarded as constituting "a danger to society"' (at 1225).

The interesting point here – and which should be pointed out straight away – is that 'necessary in a democratic society' seems to refer in intricate ways to the events under discussion (May 1968) that indeed had momentarily shattered the *ordre public* in France. Political rights are certainly necessary in a democratic society, but maybe that society is at once something that necessarily constitutes a danger to society. Clearly, there are two different societies, the society of order and the democratic society, that are dangerous to each other.

The Commission also discussed the concept of 'political neutrality' that describes the special limitations of political rights applicable to foreigners. The idea of this old-time principle of immigration law is simply that foreigners are not entitled to participate in the political life of a country. The principle is enshrined, for example, in Article 16 of the European Convention on Human Rights, which provides that nothing in the Articles on political rights in the Convention 'shall be regarded as preventing the High Contracting Parties from imposing restrictions on the political activity of aliens'. In the Commission's view, the concept of political neutrality must 'be handled with care in the context of a Community which is trying to integrate the migrant worker more and more closely into the host country and which likes to emphasize its political aims' (at 1226).

Advocate General Mayras (the same person who had handled the two previous cases, *van Duyn* and *Bonsignore*) stated that *Rutili* provided the Court with 'an opportunity to define more clearly the outlines of the concept of *ordre public*' (at 1237). He would now consider that the concept was essentially about 'reconciling two different requirements':

- that of the Community which consists in achieving freedom of movement for workers and
- that of Member States, which is concerned with the maintenance of *ordre public* within their territory (at 1242)

The Advocate General nonetheless held to his earlier view that *ordre public* is 'a relative matter' for which 'it is impossible to provide an exclusively Community definition'. Therefore, instead of attempting such a definition, the Advocate General found it 'more realistic' to discuss 'precisely what limits the Treaty and the directives [. . .] have set on the powers of the national authorities' (at 1242).

As for these limits, for the Advocate General the procedural ones appear to be the most crucial in *Rutili*. The right to information is 'an important provision which indirectly but clearly limits the powers of the national authorities in that it compels them to inform the person concerned of the grounds of *ordre public* upon which the decision is based'. The right to information requires that decisions limiting freedom of movement 'must contain a precise statement of the grounds relied upon by the Administration'. The facts 'must be clearly specified' and the 'person concerned [must] be informed of these facts'. The person in question must be informed of the facts 'before the decision is put into effect, in other words, at the latest when it is communicated to him' (at 1242).

The judges began by stating what seems to be obvious: 'only limitations which fulfil the requirements of law, including those contained in Community law, are permissible' (at 1231). The analytic meaning of this basically boils down to a tautology: the law requires that legal requirements are fulfilled. However, all three cases studied in this chapter show that in reality this formulation states more than the merely obvious. In fact, it is a sign of a considerable achievement: the immigration authorities cannot step outside the legal area. In other words, the derogation clause provides them no return to their normal business, that is, to their wide discretionary powers to act essentially in any way they find conducive to the public good.

The judges then reiterated what they had already said in their previous ruling in *van Duyn*, namely that Member States are free to determine *ordre public* in the light of their national needs, but in the Community context the concept must be interpreted strictly and its determination is subject to control by Community institutions. To this they added, however, that restrictions on the individual's rights cannot be imposed unless the individual's '[. . .] presence or conduct constitutes a genuine and sufficiently serious threat to *ordre public*' (at 1231).

The judges closed their discussion on this point by alluding to the European Convention on Human Rights and to its derogation principle of 'necessary in a democratic society'. According to the Court, Community law rules concerning derogations 'are a specific manifestation' of this more general principle of human rights law (at 1232).

Finally, it is important also for the judges that individuals should have adequate legal remedies available to them in each Member State. The right to information is central: the Member State must provide the person in question with 'a precise and comprehensive statement of the grounds for the decision, to enable him to take effective steps to prepare his defence' (at 1233).

Let us conclude by looking into the case of *Rutili* more closely from France's perspective. Insofar as Mr Rutili took part in the events of May 1968 in the typical way, in fact he was the only one of the three persons studied in this chapter who openly sought to create disorder. Presumably, it was his voluntary action and intention to offend the French *ordre public*. However, this action was regarded by learned lawyers as nothing more than the legitimate exercise of his political rights.

This brings us to the heart of the problem. One of the things of which Mr Rutili was accused was his participation in the 14 July demonstrations. This 'fact' is immediately caught in the complex web of historical signification. The date 14 July is the French national holiday that commemorates and celebrates the bombardment of the Bastille fortress in Paris in 1789.

The events of May 1968 certainly cannot be regarded as comparable with the French Revolution but, in view of the *Rutili* case, it is clear that a crucial connection exists. In many ways the republican democracy in which we live and upon which today's legal system relies was founded in 1789 by upsetting and overturning the *ordre public* of the *ancien régime*. This explains why the facts of the case were legally defined as 'the legitimate exercise of political rights', rather than offences against *ordre public*. However, exercise of political rights is an offence against *ordre public*. Thus, a hidden allusion to the foundation of law, to law-making violence, forms the subtext of *Rutili*.

Political rights share an affinity with procedural rights applicable in courts of law, in that both recognise the status of the individual as a speaking subject. In my view, *Rutili* eloquently presents these two side by side in one text. However, something remains to be said with respect to the procedural right to information, something that is perhaps even more fundamental than its connection to the political spirit of revolution. Once again, the right to information requires that allegedly dangerous individuals be informed of the grounds for their exclusion. So information that is either provided to them or denied to them is information about themselves as individuals. This refers not so much to the political constitution of society but to the social constitution of society.

What constitutes a social condition, on the micro level, is not the mere conversation that people have with each other on subjects great and small, which at certain moments of historical significance may result in cities being burnt to cinders. Rather, the ground social condition is the condition in which I as an ego am aware of the fact that others observe and think about me. They make representations about me, and I eagerly want to know about these representations. If they conceal them from me, I am excluded; if they reveal them to me, I am included.

Human forms, power, knowledge

Like Rabelais's Gargantua, the European individual was born in 11 months. It could be said that the systems and regimes were already there in wait for that special and problematic form of individuality, but were still gestating. As will be seen in the following parts of the book, the arguments are not over. Struggles over domination of the European individual have only just started, and the clash will only get more intense. This clash will be the subject, the European individual, of the chapters that follow. What remains for this chapter is to highlight and make explicit what has so far remained implicit, namely problems that have become acute and that will form the primal subject matter of the research in the following chapters. One must get down to the work of deciphering the symbolism, the work of finding out the reality behind the discourses that revolve around the European individual.

The problems are grouped under three headings: the problem of *human forms*, the problem of *power*, and the problem of *knowledge*. The difficulty with problems is that in the reality of practice they are constantly interlaced one with another. All the problems are under all of the headings, where they constitute the polymorphic problematic of the European individual. Let us try, however, to make a coherent problematisation out of the whole.

Human forms

What forms of humanity are imposed on the European individual? In *van Duyn*, the all-pervasive analytical division between humans as *objects* (eg of diagnosis, prediction) and humans as *subjects* (eg of rights, responsibility, action) became almost unnaturally palpable. The object-form went all the way to the individual's mind. The life of the mind, the spiritual life that is generally considered to be the untouchable source of free subjectivity, was indeed the mutilated object – the kernel of the case – in *van Duyn*. The sacred interiority of human beings that should make them so invaluable, make them stand out from the rest as the image of God, is put forward in this case as a fragile, malleable, vulnerable mind. Mind may be the substratum for indoctrination by Scientology, but it is also the primary object for the sanitary policies of the UK Minister for Health. As was put forward in the clash between Scientology and the minister, the human mind is a brain that can be washed and rewashed – cured, too, and protected – but in the first place, by deployment of the right kind of technology, a soul that can be possessed like a chattel.

The reaction of the judges was the philosophy of voluntary action. The judges imposed the absolute imperative of free consciousness on this absolutely mutilated mind. An endless juridical *petitio* seems to underlie the judges' syllogism: Ms van Duyn's action was voluntary, because her action was voluntary. Action was voluntary not because of this or that, but because voluntariness is an axiom. This is indispensable, because it is a form of humanity. It is not the truth of the human being but the truth of the juridico-moral symbolism and its *regimen animarum* – the principle of its rule over souls.

If one looks at the words indicated by the judges – participation, association, identification – do they really tell of the mind's carrier as the man-monad? Or do they rather tell about the travel of an individual in and through symbolic universes, one's absorption into these universes that travel in and through the individual? One of these universes is the juridical order that conjures up the free person out of a living individual and puts that individual into the moral subject-form.

So these are the analytical basic forms: object, subject. Next let us see what appear to be the different ways of conjoining and arranging these forms. What are the elements inserted into them, and what filters are used for their modification?

The first problem will have to be the human form that the Economic Community put forward as 'the system established'. If there is a Community *ordre public*, that must be an economic *ordre public*. What kind of human form is set up for the European individual by the economic order? The Advocate General stated that the purpose of the economic order is to enhance individual mobility. The problem is then to ask: what is individual in mobility?

The English text of Article 48 said that there is free movement of workers, but maybe the French text is more accurate to the economic order: '*La libre circulation*'. Circulation is traffic, rotation, sliding of materials and fluids from one place to another. To make the workforce circulate freely, it is necessary in certain places to open the dams but in other places to provide sandbags. The economic order secures free movement of the workforce because it must be able to flow where demand has increased, and move away from places where the supply has grown too great.

However, the Advocate General also stated that rights are fundamental to the system. The European individual, established by the system, was expected to be carried along by the currents of the labour market, but now it is afforded rights. The economic order would perhaps have meant that this means that the individual has the right to circulate. But then along came the Italian Government and invoked a different idea, namely the principles of justice and equity. What have these to do with free circulation and economic order? Perhaps nothing, but when free circulation is institutionalised in laws, we have another kind of order trying to bury itself in the 'very foundations' of the Community. This is the legal order now, and it has a different idea about the European individual.

Our second problem is to ask: what is this different idea? Rights are there, but there is also the chain of causation between the conduct of workers and the apprehended threat to *ordre public*. The chain of causation means that the European individual is someone who acts and whose action has consequences in reality. The European individual becomes the cause of effects. The legal order imposes this form of humanity upon the European individual, who is now responsible because of being the cause of effects. At this point, we have Carmelo, a concrete European individual entering the stage, who unintentionally pulled the trigger. It was the bullet that killed Angelo, the Advocate General noted, not his brother Carmelo. Carmelo was devastated, but would he still be dangerous? With that, again a new form of humanity appears: the dangerous individual.

A new system enters the stage of the problem of the European individual. Now the individual must be seen not only in light of offences committed but also in view of potential criminality. This problem is someone whose 'awareness of the system of law and order' has been badly impaired. This European individual is a risk; there is a risk of reoffending. The question is whether that individual will commit another offence. How can it be known what the European individual does or what he does not do? The individual was supposed to be the cause of effects and therefore responsible and free.

Insofar as the individual's action is voluntary, he is free, and therefore nobody can answer the question whether he will reoffend. The question cannot even be asked. True, one cannot do so in the case of the juridical human form but something has crept into this form, namely 'a particular psychological context' in the words of the Advocate General. The result of this creeping context is that the juridical form moves off the stage and is replaced by the psychological human form. The European individual is no longer the cause of effects, but the effect of causes. If one knows the causes, one knows what the individual will do. Psychological knowledge deals with precisely those causes, and this reverse kind of causality is our third problem concerning the European individual.

In this book the problematic of these human forms will be examined in Part I.

Power

The Minister for Health had no power under existing law to prohibit the practice of Scientology. The Government of the United Kingdom only had power under the law, the legal system, which made the exercise of this power rather special. The specialness is that it was – it had to be – legitimate. The existing law afforded it legitimacy. The minister's power was great because it was legitimate, but it was also confined. Both aspects ensued from the legal system.

However, completely different powers were also involved. In the same country, in this case the UK, was the power of the immigration officer at Gatwick airport. This person's power was also great: the immigration officer could refuse the entry of anyone into the UK insofar as it seemed right to do so; for example, in the light of the passenger's character, conduct or associations. The power of the immigration officer was also legitimate. According to the law, the immigration officer's decisions would have to be conducive to the public good. Thus this power was also legal.

On the face of it, the asymmetry between the power of the minister and the power of the officer seems enormous. However, what emerges as an elementary power problem is that both of these two powers were legitimate by law, but only one of them seems to have been curbed by law. The sovereign power was curbed, but the power of the security system working at the lower level was not. Therefore we face the problem of the over-world of power, and the underworld of power.

The security services would go down to the underworld, whereas the political government works on the upper floors. Where would legal practice operate? Like the problem of human forms, the power problem too breaks up into three problems.

In *Bonsignore*, we learned that the task facing the administrators of the police and security services is primarily to provide a preventive defence against dangers threatening public security. At first it seems that the practice of law, whose nature is reactive rather than preventive, would really not have much to do with this task. However, this is an incorrect impression: the legal system has connections with the work of the security service in the underworld. They have a common interest: an interest in maintaining respect for the system of law and order. What would happen to legal practice if this system was no longer respected? The security system seems to be serving some great favours to the legal system when it integrates the European individual into the 'existing order'. The security system takes care of the 'peaceful coexistence of a large population' and ensures that this population assimilates into the way of life of the republic. This is the first element of the problem of power: how far does the law belong to the regime of order?

Despite the basic harmony and common interests between the two systems, a difference of opinion occurred in *Bonsignore*. In the underworld, crimes of violence must be countered and therefore the *Oberstadtdirektor* decided to expel a hazardous gunman from the country. The Administrative Court, however, considered that this decision must be clearly vitiated by error because preventive defences were not justified in this case. In fact, the security regime had intruded on the legal regime's ground; it had punished a person rather than defended the state.

Punitive power belongs to courts of law, and the *Amtsgericht* had already exercised this power. The representatives of security could not fathom this: a foreigner convicted of an offence always supplies a reason for the foreigner's deportation owing to the foreigner's own personal conduct. The sole fact that an offence has been committed is sufficient; the gunman had invited deportation by infringing upon German firearms legislation. However, the Court replied that this person no longer seemed dangerous and it served no purpose to expel him. Here we arrive at the second problem of power: the justification of power.

In the case of *Rutili* the French court had asked: what does 'justified' mean? At first it seems strange that a court of law should ask this question. Is this not basic vocabulary for any court? Justified means that action is authorised by law or that some good purpose is served by it. However, the reasoning of the security system turned out to be rather curious from the legal point of view of justification. According to this reasoning, security measures are objectively justified when they are capable of fulfilling their purpose. What purpose? The purpose of collective deterrence, an efficient way to integrate the European individual into the existing order. Spreading news of expulsions is also helpful, because of its unquestionable deterrent effect upon the population. With these rather disorienting notions emerges the third problem of power: what is the nature of the rationality that prevails 'in the context of the maintenance of order'?

In this book, these three problems of power constitute the subject matter of Part II.

Knowledge

'Scientology'– what a parody of knowledge! How did this pseudo-philosophical claptrap ever come to be given such an inept name: the *logos* of science? However, there is nothing funny at all about Scientology, because this 'science' has apparently taken a remarkably firm grasp of its members. One should perhaps speak about 'scientocracy', or the power of science. The more unreal the science, the more real the power. This introduces the third problematic: that concerning the role, use and circulation of knowledge in the exercise of power.

To begin with, there was knowledge of the dangers, the possibilities of harm to the existing order that the security authorities said they had achieved on the basis of their experience. This is administrative knowledge on how to maintain peaceful coexistence of populations, a large population in large towns, concentrated in restricted areas. Foreigners, who according to sociologists regularly suffer distressing feelings of alienation in their hearts, are especially risky in such surroundings: statistics show that certain forms of criminal behaviour are peculiar to the immigrant population. This is knowledge about how to keep the population within the limits of peaceful freedom. The worst thing for peaceful coexistence and existing order, as this knowledge has it, would be for people to start taking undue freedoms in the form of demonstrations and political mass meetings. The exercise of public freedoms may turn out to be disastrous for the knowledge of the society and its order.

From the point of view of order and knowledge, democracy is an especially critical element because of the violent potentials inscribed in its history. Democratic convulsions abort the order of society. The danger is that knowledge soon has nothing to know about, as society plunges into complete chaos. This is the first problem of knowledge: the knowledge of society that circulates in the security system, especially in the form of knowledge of the agents of disorder.

The practice of law has a different concept concerning the order of society. This concept is not based on knowledge but on legality. There is really nothing to know about in society itself. States determine what society is in legislation, and the practice of law would rather continue on this basis. However, this turns out to be a problem, because the particular circumstances justifying recourse to the concept of *ordre public* may vary from one country to another and from one period to another, as the judges concluded in *van Duyn*. As far as security and order are concerned, states should be able to work on the basis of their knowledge of the particular circumstances of the country. Community law cannot abstractly determine what could constitute relevant threats to *ordre public*, because dangerous situations are different in different places and change all the time. This is the second problem of knowledge: how does legality, society's legal order, relate to the knowledge of society?

Another kind of knowledge was also involved in the cases, which also escapes normal ways of practising law. This is the individualising mechanism of personal conduct, which requires that cases are decided on the basis of their individuality. This type of decision-making was so unpleasant for the Advocate General in *Bonsignore* that he opined that in future there ought to be a list of offences which could be applied in the normal legal way, in which torts are followed by sanctions.

So there is knowledge of the individual, which also circulates in our cases. This knowledge came about in a special way in the case of *Rutili*, where knowledge of the individual constituted a dispute over the right to information: should individuals be told what the security services know about them? And what else should individuals know about themselves in order to be considered 'safe' persons like the nationals of the Member State in question? According to the immigration authorities, there should at any rate be awareness of the importance of order. Perhaps awareness of order in oneself, too? The knowledge of the individual constitutes the third and final problem of knowledge.

These problems of knowledge will be discussed in the Part III of the book.

Notes

1 Now the Court of Justice of the European Union.
2 Now Article 45 of the Treaty on the Functioning of the European Union, 2008/C 115. See also Article 21.
3 Now Article 18 of the Treaty on the Functioning of the European Union, 2008/C 115.
4 Now Article 45(3) of the Treaty on the Functioning of the European Union, 2008/C 115.
5 Now Article 27(2) of Directive 2004/38/EC.
6 Now Articles 30–32 of Directive 2004/38/EC.
7 'The modern science of mental health' is the subtitle of L. Ron Hubbard's book *Dianetics*.
8 'The principle of the economy of logic, whereby no more logic is mobilised than is required by the needs of practice is at work in any field of practice', according to Bourdieu (Bourdieu 2007: 87).
9 Now Article 27(2) of Directive 2004/38/EC.
10 Interestingly, *Gefährdungen der öffentlichen Ordnung*, or '*des menaces à l'ordre public*', translates, in this instance, as breaches of the peace. The problems of this translation will be discussed below in the context of the *Bouchereau* case.
11 Apparently, Mr Rutili did not submit written observations, but only had a representative in the oral proceedings.

Part I

Human forms

Chapter 3

Homo juridicus and *homo œconomicus*

For a legal reading of Michel Foucault's *Security, Territory, Population* and *Birth of Biopolitics*, the point to start with is the juridical individual, *homo juridicus*, who is a product of the social contract. Humans give up their natural rights to a sovereign and in return receive civil rights in the form of positive legislation. Beyond positive legislation, the social contract, despite serving as a form for many and changing kinds of political criticism, is a pact of subjugation. The juridical form of power established by the social contract is exclusion and inclusion. Excluded individuals are expelled from society, thrown outside its borders into nothingness. Included individuals, in turn, are enclosed by society, confined within its space of order and control that works on the underside of a freely willed contract.

Following Nietzsche, Foucault held that the juridical individual emerged when the 'juridical-moral concept of evil human nature, of fallen nature' (Foucault 2007a: 31) had already been produced by Christianity. For Nietzsche, inculcation of sinfulness and guilt was the way in which the Church made people governable from within their own interiority. According to Nietzsche, the doctrine of free will, together with the idea of responsibility implied by it – both of which one might consider predominantly juridical notions – was at root a ruse contrived by theologians, which they 'invented principally for the purpose of punishment – that is to say, with the intention of tracing guilt. [. . .] Men were thought of as "free" in order that they might be judged and punished'. For Nietzsche 'Christianity' is 'the metaphysics of the hangman' (Nietzsche 2007: 35).

For Foucault, too, the institutions of the Christian church had made Europeans into governable individuals by the time at which the new human form of *homo juridicus* came into being and was imposed on them. This was the time of social contract theories and great revolutions. While others came before and after Rousseau, he seems to have been the sole main source for the elucidation of *homo juridicus* for Foucault. Subjugation by social contract, not only guilt by Christianity, lay at the historical constitution of the juridical individual.

Christianity was still very important for Foucault, but not simply because of its repressive and negative concentration on the individual's 'natural' desires. It was rather because certain practices of the Church had worked out this concentration by a positive mechanism of stimulation and excitement of desire. In mysterious ways Christianity managed to create the historical conditions, not only for the realisation of desire-repressing *homo juridicus*, but also for its opposite: desire-inciting *homo œconomicus*. These mysterious ways, namely the ways in which the ritual of confession of sins developed through the Middle Ages, will be returned to at the end of this book (Chapter 11). The present chapter will only explain the resulting difference between *homo juridicus* and *homo œconomicus* as presented by Foucault.

The logic of strategy

As appears from the above, *homo juridicus* was not the only new human form born at the time of the great revolutions. Social contract theories had an alternative that was in a certain way more radical, namely utilitarian liberalism. The liberalism targeted by Foucault was not a freedom ideology, built for example on the moral concept of human beings as ends in themselves. The home of liberalism is not the enlightenment moral, legal and political philosophy, whose field is the reorganisation of sovereign power so that it represents people rather than God. The home of liberalism is the economic-political field, where it struggled for the liberation of the market.

On the one hand, liberalism was the ideology of the bourgeoisie set against the conservatism of the aristocracy. On the other hand, liberalism was not an ideology at all, but applied social physics – a technology of conducting individual behaviour. This technology and physics instructed an entirely new style of government of humans: the free market. The new technology and physics in the field of the market gave birth to the economic individual, the human form of *homo œconomicus*.

For Foucault, the economic individual of market liberalism is defined by its incompatibility with the juridical individual produced by the social contract. From the beginning, no symbiosis exists between them; these human forms are radical alternatives in their mutual relationship. Despite being born from the womb of the same historical era like twins, they nonetheless possessed altogether different constitutions and qualities. So, two figures appeared in the 18th century, *homo juridicus* and *homo œconomicus*, and they were 'absolutely heterogeneous', according to Foucault (2008: 276).

The disparity and heterogeneity between the rationalities borne by these two creatures does not prevent them from attempting to penetrate, possess and conquer each other: 'heterogeneity is never a principle of exclusion; it never prevents coexistence, conjunction, or connection' (Foucault 2008: 42). The interaction between *homo juridicus* and *homo œconomicus* does not follow *dialectical logic*, whose function is to resolve contradictions by shifting to a higher level where unity and homogeneity may be re-established. No unifying synthesis emerges from overcoming (*Aufhebung*) the contradiction between thesis and antithesis. Instead, the interaction between these two heterogeneous human forms follows what Foucault calls *strategic logic*, whose function 'is to establish the possible connections between disparate terms which remain disparate. The logic of strategy is the logic of connections between the heterogeneous and not the logic of the homogenization of the contradictory' (Foucault 2008: 42).

Kant's text on *Perpetual Peace* is one of the most famous texts showing how history produces such strategic connections: only 'the commercial spirit' – which is egoist, but cannot bear a state of war – can guarantee cosmopolitan right and perpetual peace (Kant 1917: 157). Despite their connections, the rationalities themselves remain disparate; the normative vision of a society of economic liberalism is radically different from a society imagined by law. Whereas according to Kant the society of law should be on its way *zum ewigen Frieden*, liberalism according to Foucault is bound up with the new *culture of danger* emerging in the 19th century. Whereas for *homo juridicus* danger is an evil, for *homo œconomicus* it is something that stimulates:

> First we can say that the motto of liberalism is: 'Live dangerously.' 'Live dangerously,' that is to say, individuals are constantly exposed to danger, or rather, they are conditioned to experience their situation, their life, their present, and their future as containing danger [. . .] everyday dangers appear, emerge, and spread everywhere perpetually being brought to life, reactualized, and circulated by what could be called the political culture of danger in the nineteenth century. (Foucault 2008: 66)

Now, what are these disparate and heterogeneous perspectives, yet capable of strategic connections, casting humans in such different forms and bearing such different prospects for society? For Foucault, the perspective of law is 'the fundamental axiomatic' pertaining to holders of rights, whereas the perspective of economic liberalism is 'the utilitarian calculus' pertaining to independent economic actors (Foucault 2008: 43). The functioning of the fundamental axiomatic in legal practice will be analysed at length in the following chapter. Let us at this point look into the difference between these perspectives, to serve analysis of law with a rigorous conception of its subtext, liberal economics.

Liberalism as normalisation

Liberalism is a style of government that wishes to see things happen in society without intervention. It does not coerce the material reality of society according to some higher order of things like that of the system of inviolable basic rights, principles of deliberative democracy or fundamental values of community life. Liberalism is not the exercise of power from above; it aims not at adjusting society and individuals to externally given standards. The project of liberalism began not as an imposition of liberal rules on society, its members and its governors. Instead, liberalism began when governors started to learn – or at least their advisers learned that they could learn – to play by society's own rules. In an interview from 1982, Foucault estimated the significance of the turn to liberalism as follows:

What was discovered at that time – and this was one of the great discoveries of the eighteenth century – was the idea of *society*. That is to say, that government not only has to deal with a territory, with a domain, and with its subjects, but that it also has to deal with a complex and independent reality that has its own laws and mechanisms of reaction, its regulations as well as its possibilities of disturbance. This new reality is society. (Foucault 2000g: 352)

Having learned what the internal mechanisms of society are, liberal governors should also learn to manipulate society's processes more smartly and sensitively than through juridical prohibitions. It was necessary to find ways to vivify those processes that have beneficial effects, as well as ways to make certain processes cancel out other processes that have detrimental effects. Instead of banning a bad phenomenon by laws, the idea, more generally, was to find 'support in the reality of the phenomenon, and instead of trying to prevent it, making other elements of reality function in relation to it, in such a way that the phenomenon is cancelled out, as it were' (Foucault 2007a: 59).

The simplest way of arranging things in these ways is to refrain from giving people directions on what they should or should not do, and then also letting them suffer the consequences if what they decided to do eventually turns out to be a mistake. This compels individuals to plan their actions and calculate the risks on their own, which also benefits society at large. Liberal government was to follow this path, making – or letting – things happen without the use of juridical prescription and prohibition, commands and bans, in the form of coercive law.

The game of liberalism – not interfering, allowing free movement, letting things follow their course; *laissez faire, passer et aller* – basically means acting so that reality develops, goes its way, and follows its own course according to the laws, principles and mechanisms of reality itself. (Foucault 2007a: 48)

The birth of society in the game of liberalism also gave birth to *homo œconomicus*. In classic liberalism, *homo œconomicus* is defined by his elemental non-governability and independence:

Homo œconomicus is someone who pursues his own interest, and whose interest is such that it converges spontaneously with the interest of others [. . .] *homo œconomicus* is the person who must be left alone. (Foucault 2008: 270)

When first conceived by British empiricists and French physiocrats in the 18th century, *homo œconomicus* was not considered as something produced by the policy of society, but precisely a programme contrary to any policy aiming at producing individuals. It might even be that *homo œconomicus* was considered the very reaction against society's increasing efforts at transformation and betterment of human individuals, that is, as counter-conduct against the procrustean imposition of models on humans. *Homo œconomicus* was anti-disciplinary; his creation was a way of governing humans that constituted an alternative to what Foucault ended up calling 'normation'.

Normation is the work of the disciplinary institutions, practices and techniques of society that ultimately aim at (re)producing standard docile workers for industrial production – people who can be integrated into 'an efficient machine' (Foucault 1991: 164). In 'normation', the norm-humanity is first posited as a model, and concrete individuals are then reformed according to that model in the disciplinary practices of society. Individuals are made normal by way of compelling them towards the pre-given model:

> Due to the primacy of the norm in relation to the normal, to the fact that disciplinary normalization goes from the norm to the final division between the normal and the abnormal, I would rather say that what is involved in disciplinary techniques is a normation (*normation*) rather than normalization. Forgive the barbaric word [. . .]. (Foucault 2007a: 57)

From that point onwards, Foucault reserved the word normalisation (which until then he had used exactly for what he now called normation) for the type of governing that takes factual normality, existing between statistical average and statistical exception, as a basis for construction of its models (norms): 'The normal comes first and the norm is deduced from it' (Foucault 2007a: 63). This turn is the starting point for liberal government.

Liberal government began its project of reconstituting society by liberating the spheres of production and exchange. Clearly, liberal reconstitution of society was not inspired by romantic feelings for the inner and special beauty of each human being that should be allowed to flourish. (In fact, romanticism that spoke so highly of that sort of liberality can be considered an antagonist of the cold rationalism of utilitarian theories.) Nor was it inspired by the moral standard of the inviolability of human dignity. Rather, normation was simply regarded as an inefficient strategy. Its techniques provided no good means to produce what had been set as the goal of politics since the Renaissance: to increase the wealth and strength of the state.

The liberal turn and reconstitution advocated a style of governance where society is allowed to regulate, direct and constitute itself from the inside by way of normalisation. Normalisation is now essentially *normalisation of the norm*, rather than normalisation of the material reality of society and individuals as its members. It is a constant process of empirical induction, readjusting the bandwidth of normality. The norm must better correspond to reality and to the evolution of society and not the other way around. The turn to liberal government is a kind of reversal – indeed, a return to nature – and *homo œconomicus* is what results from this turn and return.

Subject of desire and interest

Unlike *homo juridicus*, who is outspokenly an artificial product of convention (the social contract), the classic *homo œconomicus* is the human being's *natural reality*. That natural reality of the economic individual is desire. Through calculation, desire can be transformed into interest, the human being's *rational reality*. As a result of this process of transformation, *homo œconomicus* is split and doubled: he is at once both the subject of desire and the subject of interest. The immediate consummation of desire may be deferred in the calculation process, but desire nonetheless remains the primitive and absolutely indispensable momentum of the economic individual's activity. The primitive nature and rational nature belong together and form a continuum in *homo œconomicus*, whereas *homo juridicus* breaks with primitive nature: its essence is a second nature produced by convention.

In the second and third of his *Security, Territory, Population* lectures, Foucault explained the views of 18th century French economists, the physiocrats. To begin with according to those views desire is ineradicable. It is entirely futile for governors to try to remove desire from their subjects by installing a civil second nature in its place, or above it to repress it. François Quesnay (1694–1774), the leader of the French physiocratic movement, said: 'You cannot stop people from living where they think they will profit most and where they desire to live, because they desire that profit. Do not try to change them; things will not change' (Foucault's paraphrase). All individuals are different and unpredictable; however, 'there is at least one invariant' which, at the level of the whole population, is also the 'one and only one mainspring of action. This is desire' (Foucault 2007a: 72).

Now, what is the difference between the economic governance of *homo œconomicus* and the sovereign rule over *homo juridicus* with respect to desire?

Jurists, too, presuppose that desire is the one and only invariable present in all human individuals. Yet they assume natural desire only in their negation of it. Negation for Foucault was the basic *modus operandi* of the law overall; legal prohibitions and punishments always work by way of responding negatively to desire. In fact, the juridical sovereign is 'the person who can say no to any individual's desire'. The jurists' part is to find out 'how to legitimize this "no" opposed to individuals' (Foucault 2007a: 73).

The answer is the social contract, whereby negation of the desire of individuals is founded 'on the will of the same individuals'. The social contract is a pact into which the individual enters as a subject of desire, and from which the individual emerges as *homo juridicus*. In exchange for security and civil rights, the juridical individual has given away natural rights, that is, the natural right to fulfilment of natural desire (Foucault 2007a: 73).

Liberal economists have exactly the opposite approach to the desire of the individual. Their 'problem is how they can say yes; it is how to say yes to this desire'. Affirmation of desire is the necessary precondition of liberal government, because its idea is precisely to make use of the individual's desire. Far from expelling desire, liberal economists wanted the opposite: to vivify and stimulate it. In their view, 'this desire is such that, if one gives it free play, and on condition that it is given free play, all things considered and within a certain limit and thanks to a number of relationships and connections, it will produce the general interest of the population'. The task of economists, and of liberal government, is to develop and adopt means by which one manages 'production of the collective interests through the play of desire', a play that must preserve its spontaneity. It is *the free play of desire* that sets the ground for the government of *homo œconomicus* (Foucault 2007a: 73).

In sum, the first fundamental difference between the theory of subject of the law and the theory of subject of liberal economics lies in the way they relate with desire. The one says 'no' to desire, the other says 'yes'. Let us now move from the irrational nature to the rational nature, from desire to *interest*.

In his discussion of classic liberalism in *The Birth of Biopolitics*, Foucault moved his focus from French physiocrats to what he called *English radicalism* or *English empiricism* (Foucault 2008: 40, 271). Foucault contrasted English radicalism, not with physiocrats, but with what he called *Rousseau's approach*, or 'the path taken by the French Revolution' (Foucault 2008: 39). Whereas Rousseau and the French Revolution reconstructed *homo juridicus*, the English discovered *homo œconomicus*, a personhood built on independent and radically self-contained calculation of interest.

Homo œconomicus of English radicalism represented a mutation of the theory of the subject that in Foucault's assessment is 'one of the most important transformations in Western thought since the Middle Ages' (Foucault 2008: 271). Interest, as an exclusively individual point of view and as a principle of one's own atomistic preference, is the nucleus of that theory. This point of view and preference can neither be given away nor taken away; not by coercion nor by persuasion. Even when an individual is threatened with death if not obedient, and thus given no other real choices than either to obey or to cease to exist, it is still a matter for the individual to deliberate on which to prefer: to live or die. As Hume said, anyone can be forced to cut off their little finger and thus spare someone else's life, but no one can be forced to think that losing one's own finger is preferable to someone else's death (Foucault 2008: 272).

The juridical sovereign can cut away its subjects' body parts, and even make it their obligation to perform the cutting by themselves, but the individual's own preference, what one *thinks* is preferable, the sovereign cannot cut away. Exceptional individuals would simply not comply with orders because they would choose resistance in any situation and prefer to bear its consequences, whatever they might be. Yet such exceptional individuals are not what the theory of *homo œconomicus* points at by its notion of the independence of interest. It points at each and every individual, however weak and submissive. Every single individual has an interest of their own, which they ultimately and necessarily choose in every situation. Even the choice unconditionally to obey the orders of a superior in every future situation – for example, an oath of loyalty – is an individual choice for *homo œconomicus* that has nothing to do with obligation. Hence, *homo œconomicus* as the subject of interest is the subject of individual choice, which makes ultimate independence the cornerstone of the utilitarian calculus of economic actors: 'What is important is the appearance of interest for the first time as a form of both immediately and absolutely subjective will' (Foucault 2008: 273).

Subject of right and negativity

The juridical will given by the social contract, the pact of subjection at the foundation of 'the fundamental axiomatic of the rights of man' (Foucault 2008: 43), is not *immediate* and *absolute* in the subject. The juridical will of the individual is *mediated* by and *relative* to the other party to the *pactum subjectionis*, the sovereign. *Homo juridicus* 'becomes a subject of right in a positive system' by agreeing to cede individual natural rights and to transfer them to a sovereign (Foucault 2008: 274).

The sovereign, in turn, emerges from the social contract as a transcendence to which the individual thinks he is subjected, not because of his own interest, but because of the obligation created by the contract. While being originally a subject of natural rights, *homo juridicus* now expresses individual will for the first time – and for the last time as an absolute and immediate will – when subscribing to the limitation of these rights. In strict terms, he would voluntarily accept the transfer of these rights to the sovereign, by which transfer *homo juridicus* leaves behind his original freedom of the will.

This contractual mechanism underlying the juridical field, the juridically conceived field of political power, is what Foucault describes as 'the dialectic of renunciation, transcendence and the voluntary bond of the juridical theory of the contract' (Foucault 2008: 276). While the sovereign is absolutely necessary, the dialectic itself is internal to *homo juridicus*, who:

> [. . .] splits himself, to be, at one level, the possessor of a number of natural and immediate rights, and, at another level, someone who agrees to the principle of relinquishing them and who is thereby constituted as a different subject of right superimposed on the first. (Foucault 2008: 275)

Hence, *homo juridicus* is a split subject 'who accepts negativity, who agrees to self-renunciation' (Foucault 2008: 275). Now, the ensuing fundamental axiomatic of the rights of man, as Foucault calls it, is not mere political philosophy, but also forms the basic underlying parameter of the practice of law, or at any rate of the practice of public law pertaining to the relationship between individuals and public authorities. The way it emerges is this: every time an individual invokes an individual right that limits the power exercised over him, the public authorities may in turn invoke their power to limit these rights.

To invoke natural rights preceding the social contract is to exit the juridical field and the practice of law. Indeed, the relinquishing of rights seems always to take precedence over any individual rights in the legal sense, that is, in the sense of a positive system of law. Yet the same relinquishing of rights also precedes any exercise of public power. This conception, according to which some kind of rights once preceded political power, rights that are not enshrined in positive enactments, brings about what in the theory of the social contract is revolutionary. The pre-existence of rights opens up a remarkable avenue for juridico-political criticism of the exercise of power, an avenue which is an effect of the idea in the background that people can at any time dissolve the social contract and take back their natural rights. The following is from the end of Book III of Rousseau's *Social Contract*:

> I am assuming what I think I have shown; that there is in the state no fundamental law that cannot be revoked, not excluding the social compact itself; for if all the citizens assembled of one accord to break the compact, it is impossible to doubt that it would be very legitimately broken. Grotius even thinks that each man can renounce his membership of his own state, and recover his natural liberty and his goods on leaving the country. It would be indeed absurd if all the citizens in assembly could not do what each can do by himself. (Rousseau 1955: 84)

By contrast, English radicalism's *homo œconomicus* never gives his fundamental position (self-interest) away as *homo juridicus* has given away his natural rights by entering the social contract. This is the second fundamental difference between the theory of subject of the law and the theory of subject of liberal economics (the first being the desire's 'yes' or 'no', affirmation or negation of desire). Interest always remains the interest of the individual and cannot be contracted out of in the way that rights can. The leader of British radicalism, Jeremy Bentham, said: 'every efficient law whatever may be considered as a limitation or exception, grafted on a pre-established universal law of liberty' (Bentham 1970: 119; Hart 2001: 124). The universal law of liberty, as a permissive background principle, is depicted by Bentham as follows:

> [. . .] a boundless expanse in which the several efficient laws appear as so many spots; like islands and continents projecting out of the ocean: or like material bodies scattered over the immensity of space. (Bentham 1970: 120)

It can be in the interest of *homo œconomicus* to enter into the social contract and uphold his existence by law-abiding conduct, for example because of long-standing commercial concerns: stability is good for business. Yet this creates no transcendence that would somehow oblige the subject of interest beyond that interest. Stability and certainty may be beneficial, but nothing more. As soon as the contract – namely, the legal order established by the social contract – is no longer profitable, someone who calculates interests would see no reason to abide by the rules and provisions of this pact. This is the way in which, as Foucault said, the 'subject of interest constantly overflows the subject of right' (Foucault 2008: 274).

Economic independence and legal freedom

Both *homo œconomicus* and *homo juridicus* are split and duplicated subjects. *Homo œconomicus* is split into the subject of desire and the subject of interest. Desire is his ineradicable primitive nature, whereas interest is the outcome of his calculations on what is or is not preferable. *Homo juridicus* is split into the subject of natural rights and the subject of positive rights. Natural rights are given away in order to recover positive rights in exchange. The subject of positive rights breaks completely with the subject of natural rights. The subject of interest forms a continuum with the subject of desire. Desire is the primal momentum for all activity of *homo œconomicus*.

What is the practical meaning of this continuity between desire and interest in *homo œconomicus*? One could say that if the economic individual's supreme desire would for example be to destroy the whole universe – or, more modestly, to create disorder in the universe – use of reason (calculation of interest) would simply consist of finding out the best ways and plans, in the given environment of variables, to achieve this end. No hesitations emerge from the structure of *homo œconomicus*. In other words, no moral or social values mediate the communication of desire into interest in *homo œconomicus*. Therefore, *homo œconomicus* is a pure ideal type of purposive-rational action, comparable with Weber's ideal military commanders who

> [. . .] must know the total fighting resources of each side and all the possibilities arising therefrom of attaining the concretely unambiguous goal, namely, the destruction of the enemy's military power. On the basis of this knowledge, they must act entirely without error and in a logically 'perfect' way. For only then can the consequences of the fact that the real commanders neither had the knowledge nor were they free from error, and that they were not purely rational thinking machines, be unambiguously established. (Weber 1949: 42)

Homo œconomicus, in calculating the means of achieving set goals, is a 'rational thinking machine' like military commanders are. Yet the difference lies in the fact that in place of the determinate, sole and simple 'concretely unambiguous goal' of 'the destruction of the enemy's military power', an indeterminate multiplicity of ambiguous desires sets the goals for economic individuals' pursuits. Hence, *homo œconomicus* is at once both a purely rational thinking machine and a purely irrational emotion. The new precept of economic liberalism, which completely disconnects it from the juridical conception of political power, is that this power must not interfere with the dynamic of desire and interest that is 'naturally inscribed in the heart of man' (Foucault 2008: 280).

Political power is not to interfere in the dynamic of desire and interest in individuals, but governing them is nonetheless carried out entirely through this medium. This approach is radically different from that of the social contract, which suggests civilisation and culture in place of the primitive, bestial dynamic of desire. Rousseau's approach is revolutionary, but nevertheless stays within the framework of juridical constitution of political power, and is contrasted with the radical approach of economic governance that steps outside of the juridical framework.

The revolutionary approach proceeds by reconstructing a social contract that establishes a second nature, which postulates a human form imposing a resounding 'no' to desire: *homo juridicus*. The idea here is that individual wills express and bind themselves (yet at the same time liberate themselves from the vicissitudes of the state of nature) by giving their original rights away to the sovereign to establish a legal order that gives positive rights in exchange.

The radical approach proceeds by way of saying 'yes' to desire, which gives birth to another human form, *homo œconomicus*, whose will is fundamentally independent from political power. To create the conditions in which the self-executing market mechanism (the invisible hand) is capable of unifying the pursuits of self-interested individuals for the common good, the liberty of individuals needs to be protected from state intervention. This task of protection – limitation of the exercise of state power – is allotted in liberalism to the legal order.

It is clear that the conceptions of law and liberty are different in these two approaches. According to Foucault, the first approach has law as a 'system of will-law': collective will is first expressed in the law and then imposed on every individual will. In the second, in turn, 'the law is conceived as the transaction that separates the sphere of intervention of public authorities from that of the individual independence' (Foucault 2008: 41).

Correspondingly, the first approach articulates liberty to the 'juridical conception of freedom: every individual originally has in his possession a certain freedom, a part of which he will or will not cede' (Foucault 2008: 42). According to Rousseau, *homo juridicus* does not cede individual freedom to dissolve the social contract at any time. The other approach, in turn, has freedom 'simply as the independence of the governed with regard to the government' (Foucault 2008: 42). According to Bentham, the pre-established law of liberty is axiomatic in any coercively operating system of positive laws.

> We have therefore two absolutely heterogeneous conceptions of freedom: one based on the rights of man and the other starting from the independence of the governed. (Foucault 2008: 42)

Foucault does not say that the 'two systems of the rights of man and of the independence of the governed do not intertwine' (Foucault 2008: 42); indeed, quite the contrary. Intertwining is precisely the point about his 'strategic logic', a logic that stitches disparate elements together in different social practices.[1] We will see later whether and how this really works in the practice of law, but let us first conclude this chapter.

Conclusion

Why is economic liberalism a technology of governance if *homo œconomicus* is radically independent? Let us return to Nietzsche for an answer to this question. For Nietzsche, an important hypothesis lies behind the idea that an individual can master his or her own conduct and create bonds for the future. Before any of this can come true, a person who is supposed to be free must first become thoroughly something else. An individual will have 'to have power to calculate', which means that an individual must 'have first become *calculable, disciplined, necessitated* even for himself and for his own conception of himself, that, like a man entering a promise, he could guarantee himself *as a future*' (Nietzsche 2003: 35).

For our purposes, the key phrase in the above is between commas: *like a man entering a promise*. Man as a calculating machine is predictable *as if* he had made a promise – *but he does not have to make promises* in order to be calculable. *Homo œconomicus* is calculable for the purposes of governing because that form of humanity calculates. Promises and contracts are superfluous, because individual conduct is streamlined by a much heavier hand, which is invisible.

Clearly, this is a depiction of an ideal *homo œconomicus*, the person that is governable, not top-down, but by way of an anonymous capillary power inscribed in the heart of man, working from the inside. If it works as it should, the end result is normalisation, and a rational individual who has lost the capacity for any kind of surprises. In Nietzsche's words, it means 'the levelling of mountain and valley', which 'makes people small, cowardly and pleasure-loving – by means of them the gregarious animal invariably triumphs. Liberalism, or in plain English, the *transformation of mankind into cattle*' (Nietzsche 2007: 71).

Yet the form of *homo œconomicus* may at any time miscarry in its governing function. Free play of desire is a dangerous game, because nature can make errors in humans. Because *homo œconomicus* by definition does not break with human nature as desire, but establishes a continuum with it, economic governance is powerless when confronted in certain individuals with what could be called, after Georges Canguilhem, 'innate organic errors', or 'bad readings' of the code of one's best interest (Canguilhem 1991: 278). Such individuals are cursed by a malignant abnormality in their procedure of transforming desire into interest. They are *delinquents*, and they constitute the psychological counterpart of *homo œconomicus*. Delinquents as objects of psychological knowledge, as subjects who cannot guarantee themselves a future, will be discussed in Chapter 5.

Note

1   I have dealt elsewhere with the ways in which Foucault saw modern economic liberalism strategically transforming the so-called *Rechtsstaat* principles for its own purposes. See Hurri (2011).

Chapter 4

Royer: rights and decisions

Homo œconomicus as an economic actor clearly belongs to the conceptual fabric out of which the European Community was designed. It was meant to be an economic community, to which only individuals who are economically active belong. Consequently, *homo œconomicus* persists as a background figure in all of the cases analysed in this work. Before any legal discussion on individual rights could start in these cases, a threshold question had to be asked first: is the individual in question an economic actor or not? Only economic actors benefited from the rights entailed by freedom of movement.

The fundamental economic freedoms – free movement of goods, workers, services and capital – were recast in the EEC Treaty after the model of juridical rights, which is an intersection of rationalities as such. In this arrangement, one can see that the economic rationality of liberal doctrines had strategic possibilities ranging much wider than the limited space of the market. The emphasis on individual rights could be a way to connect the liberal vision of society, where freedom of choice is valued more than social security, to its value-neutral analyses of economic processes.

Despite the various possibilities to read utilitarian calculus and economic rationality into the cases at hand, this would ultimately misrepresent them. The discourse of the case files must move within the specifically juridical framework that stands out from practice in the form of legal rights vis-à-vis legal decisions. The economic rationality must really stand aside, first of all because in the juridical framework one needs the figure of a sovereign, an element that cannot be replaced by the market. Like nature, the market can never be in the wrong, because it is the self-sufficient measure of truth. Wrongs as transgressions of limits, which are indispensable for the practice of law, are not possible for the anonymous market.

Secondly, the radical independence of *homo œconomicus* remains a mystery to the practice of law. If an individual does not submit to any rules, the law really has not much to say. Finally, what leaves *homo œconomicus* insufficient is that the concrete individuals of our cases are not rational economically speaking. This last point will be the theme of the next chapter.

Despite the fact that legal practice is steeped in the juridical grammar of rights and decisions, on a broader canvas the cases analysed in this book attest to the dichotomy and strategic amalgamation between *homo juridicus* and *homo œconomicus*. These human forms provide a key to the specific nature and riddle of European efforts at integration more broadly. The political field of these efforts can be seen as an intersection between the juridical social-contract type of integration, on the one hand, and the economic governing type of integration, on the other hand. Regardless of that, however, the key to the cases – especially to the *Royer* case – is *homo juridicus* alone, whereas *homo œconomicus* works at a subtextual level.

Royer is a case that presents an outward special legal problem and an inward general legal problem, both of which have the same basic elements and structure. The special problem is whether the right of Europeans to reside in a Member State pre-exists the decision of the immigration authorities of that Member State to grant residence permits. In turn, the general problem is whether the right, as a fundamental category, pre-exists the decision, as another fundamental category, in the legal system as a whole. Therefore, the two problems come together in the one single question: does right pre-exist decision, or vice versa?

I will begin by presuming that the general problematic is inherent in the special problematic and therefore start with the latter. Following a presentation of facts, the first section of this chapter concerns the relationship between Community law and the Belgian system for controlling the entry of non-nationals in which the power of national authorities to check the security of individuals supersedes the exercise of Community rights until a residence permit is granted.

The second section discusses rights and decisions as a problem internal to Community law. The third section discusses the problem of pre-existence in the relationship between the Community law system and its external legal environment, notably international law on human rights. Focusing on procedural law, the fourth section concludes by discussing the notion of juridical subjectivation, the making of *homo juridicus* in the practice of law.

Facts of Royer

Mr Royer was a French tradesman whose wife, as a salaried manageress, ran a café and dance-hall in Grâce-Hollogne, a small municipality in Belgium near the city of Liège. His wife's contract stated that the 'manageress shall be assisted by the members of her family' which suggests that Mr Royer himself could have been considered an immigrant worker in Belgium. However, this was not significant since Mr Royer had the same rights as spouse of a worker (at 521–22).

Between 1959 and 1966, which was long before the events of the case took place, Mr Royer had been sentenced by a French court to two years' imprisonment for procuring. He had also been prosecuted for, but not convicted of, several armed robberies in France. In January 1972, when Mr Royer had been in Belgium for approximately two months, the Belgian *Police Judiciaire* learned of his residence ('detected' him) in Belgium, and ordered him to 'leave the country on the ground that he was unlawfully resident there'. They forbade him to return and initiated proceedings against him for illegal residence (at 499, 508, 521).

According to Belgian law at that time, no non-Belgian national could enter or reside in Belgium without prior authorisation. As for EC nationals, however, the '"establishment permit' [. . .] shall be issued to them *as of right*' (at 524, italics in the original). Nonetheless, EC nationals too had to be 'entered on the population registers at the local administration of their place of residence within eight days of their entry into Belgium' (at 525). Mr Royer had not declared his arrival to the local administration at all, which is why his residence was considered unlawful.

Mr Royer's failure to comply with the formalities of the population register cannot be regarded as the true reason prompting the Belgian *Police Judiciaire* to take action in his case. Advocate General Mayras, for example, assumed that it was 'solely the information which the Belgian police had on Royer's criminal past which caused them to take the view that Royer's presence constituted a potential danger to *ordre public*' (at 522). Nonetheless, the Belgian authorities considered it to be sufficient to note that Mr Royer's presence was formally unlawful solely because he had not done anything to make it lawful.

Mr Royer left the country, but only for a couple of weeks. He returned in February 1972. The *Police Judiciaire* found him in March, and he was arrested by the *Gendarmerie* in April. At this point, a new dimension was added in the case of *Royer*, which changed its nature significantly: Mr Royer was not only taken into custody so that he could be deported over the Belgian border, but he was 'committed to prison' by the *Procureur Général* (at 499). The 'committal was not confirmed by the judicial authorities', which left the nature of this action (the 'committal') somewhat unclear (at 508). Apparently, the idea was to put Mr Royer in 'preventive detention', that is, to keep him in custody as a remand prisoner to secure a future trial over his earlier illegal residence.

After six days of imprisonment, however, the *Chambre du Conceil* (the judicial council) decided that he should be set at liberty. Execution of this decision, ie the release of Mr Royer, was suspended because it was appealed by the Public Prosecutor in the *Chambre des Mises en Accusation* (the court of indictment). The appeal was denied and Mr Royer was released after 13 days of imprisonment on 10 May 1972 (at 500, 522).

On his release from prison, Mr Royer was again expelled from Belgium, this time by a ministerial decree, on the double ground that 'his personal conduct shows his presence to be a danger to *ordre public*' and that 'he has not observed the conditions attached to the residence of aliens and he has no permit to establish himself in the Kingdom'. At this point, Mr Royer 'apparently did in fact leave Belgian territory' (at 522).

Six months later, in November 1972, the *Tribunal de première instance* of Liège sentenced Mr Royer to suspended imprisonment (probation) for one month and a fine of 3000 Belgian Francs for his original illegal residence (that is, for his stay in Belgium *before* the first expulsion). In the following year, Mr Royer was again summoned before the same court, this time for his second illegal period of residence (that is, for his stay in Belgium *after* the first expulsion). After a further two years, in May 1975, the *Tribunal de première instance* decided to stay these latter criminal proceedings against Mr Royer and requested a preliminary ruling on Community law questions from the ECJ.

The *Royer* case file consists of the contributions of the Commission, the Advocate General and the judges. Thus, all three participants were from within the Community institutional framework. For some reason, neither of the parties to the original conflict – the Belgian State (or its *Procureur Général*) and Mr Royer – made any representations before the ECJ. Compared with the earlier cases, there is a considerable lack of variety in *Royer*. This fact by and large defines the perspective of the whole matter as internal to one band of actors, which will not be true in the cases that follow.

Interspace between nationals and non-nationals

The core question in *Royer* was the relationship between individual *rights*, entailed by the principle of freedom of movement, and their *limitations* justified on grounds of *ordre public*. The Belgian *Tribunal* asks the ECJ: 'Are the limitations provided in Article 48 et seq. inherent in the conceptual content of these rights or are they merely *external and fortuitous* factors [. . .]?' (at 500).

Let us make it clear right away what practical difference it makes to have *ordre public* limitations either as *inherent* in or as *external* to the rights.

What if *ordre public* limitations are 'inherent in the conceptual content of these rights'? Thus interpreted, Community law would allow Member States to uphold a system like that of Belgium. In such a system, prior to affirmation of an individual's right to reside 'the authorities of the host state should first be satisfied that there exists no grounds for objection' (at 503) – in other words, they should be satisfied that the person in question is not dangerous. Only after this check does the person really have the right to enter and remain in that state. The authorities should have pre-emptive powers – prior to realisation of the rights of individuals – to ascertain that immigrants are not dangerous. A decision by the authorities to that effect would be a precondition for the individual to have the right to stay or, at any rate, to exercise it.

Were the limitations *not* inherent in the conceptual content of the rights but '*external and fortuitous* factors', then they would not 'call in question the existence and exercise of a right which is complete in itself' (at 500). The authorities would not have pre-emptive powers, but only the power to make an exception. The immigrant EC national's right exists prior to the decision on his or her residence permit. The immigration authorities could limit the right only in those special and particular cases where they find that the individual in question is dangerous.

The standard procedure under which a check of the immigrant's security or dangerousness is carried out is the grant of a residence permit. Thus, the special problematic on the priority of rights or decisions concretised in *Royer* in the relationship between Community law rights and national decisions on *residence permits*. What is the significance of the grant of a residence permit in relation to the rights afforded by the EC Treaty? 'Does the right based on the Treaty exist independently of the document which proves it', that is, independently of a residence permit (at 501)? According to the judges, in the last instance the Belgian *Tribunal* had asked

> . . . whether this right [. . .] is conferred by the Treaty or other provisions of Community law [or] whether it only arises by means of a residence permit issued by the competent authority of a Member State recognising the particular position of a national of another Member State with respect to Community law [. . .]. (at 510)

The Belgian system for immigration control, but also for control of EC nationals, was based on the priority of the decision. According to Belgian law, 'no alien may enter or reside in Belgium unless he is authorized to do so by the Minister of Justice' and 'no alien may *establish himself* in the Kingdom without obtaining a permit from the Minister of Justice' (at 524 – italics in original). As for shorter stays, the authorisation was delegated to the local population registers. Immigrants were required to report themselves within eight days, upon which they would receive 'registration certificates'.

Without that 'decision' (the grant of a registration certificate) the residence of any non-national in Belgium was illegal. Illegal residence was punishable 'by imprisonment of between one month and one year and by a fine of 100 to 1000 francs' (at 522). The system was no different for EC nationals, albeit for them the registration certificate was to be 'issued *as of right*' (at 524). Nonetheless, the decision was absolutely required, and EC nationals too had to report within eight days to the population register. Mr Royer had not done this, which is why his residence was found to be illegal. And, as we have seen, for this offence he was first expelled, later incarcerated and finally sentenced to imprisonment.

Illegal residence as such is not a valid ground for expulsion because treaty rights pre-exist residence permits, according to all participants in the *Royer* proceedings. The consensus between the Commission, the Advocate General and the judges in this respect can be summarised by the following four points.

First, rights are conferred by the Treaty directly and these rights are complete prior to any decision on the part of Member State authorities, who thus are no longer vested with the power to decide, relative to EC nationals, on who may come and who must go.

Secondly, this means particularly that the rights in Article 48 exist independently of the grant of a residence permit.

Thirdly, the reservation according to which rights are 'subject to limitations justified on grounds of *ordre public*' (Article 48(3)) does not condition the right or its exercise in any other way except by affording the host state the possibility of limiting the right in exceptional circumstances.

Fourthly, mere failure to comply with the administrative formalities of the immigration authorities, such as Mr Royer's failure to report at the local population register, is not sufficiently grave personal misconduct to represent a threat to *ordre public*, and it cannot be penalised by expulsion.

At this level, it is clear that the case affirmed the pre-existence of rights in relation to authoritative decisions. The system of Belgian law was declared to be contrary to EC law in that it 'established a scheme of prior authorization' (at 524); that is, in that it established the priority of decision. The EC Treaty requires priority of rights. This conclusion moves Europeans over the boundary of immigration law, where only permission – a decision – creates rights. This point was made most clearly by the Commission:

> The classic concept in the law relating to the control of aliens, whereby the right of residence depends exclusively on a decision of the competent national authority[,] has been superseded by the intervention of Community law under which the nationals of the Member State possess the right to residence by virtue of the Treaty itself which prevails over any contrary national law. (at 504)

The right of residence, as Advocate General Mayras declares, 'is an individual right attaching to the person of the Community national' (at 524). This is not to say that Europeans had been moved, not only over the boundary of the law regarding non-nationals, but also within the boundary of the law regarding nationals. 'Member States may still expel from their territory a national of another Member State' (at 514), which would not be possible in the case of Belgian nationals.

Conversely, one might also say that nationals are prominent precisely in that they do not need 'a right to reside' and no such thing is 'attached to the person' of nationals. In this day and age, to talk about this kind of right would be inappropriate in their case. A 'right to stay' (*le droit de séjourner*) is the wrong language for nationals who do not 'stay', sojourn, but simply 'live', exist, in their home countries.

Thus the boundary between the law for non-nationals and the law for nationals of a Member State has not been crossed, but a space has emerged within that boundary. What formerly was not a space, but a line, has now become an interspace for Europeans. Europeans remain on the liminal borderline territory between nationals and non-nationals. The emergence of this new conceptual habitat on the threshold between nationals and non-nationals is a legal creation, and the European as a very special form of individuality is split accordingly: half national, half non-national.

In the interspace of Europeans, the authoritative decision on security/danger of the individual is no longer a precondition for the acquisition and exercise of the right of entry and residence. Despite that improvement in their positions, such a decision may in exceptional and individual cases deprive them of that right. Let us say, in a somewhat more complex way, that it is the *exceptionality of the not-right* that marks this new symbolic ground between non-nationals and nationals on which Europeans are placed. There, the authoritative decision is not made on the right, but on the exceptional not-right.

The problem of the priority between rights and decisions provides a window, a vision, on a separation of entire worlds. The first world is this: people have rights unconditionally from the start. For good reasons, these rights can be limited, but only by way of general legislation, under strictly defined conditions and through a democratic procedure that respects minorities. In the second world people have rights only if the ruling power feels gracious enough – or secure enough – and they can be stripped of these rights at any time. The hybridisation of the European individual, as a liminal creature, makes these worlds perceptible and distinct.

Of course, right is not really the same notion in these two worlds. They reflect two different arrangements between the rule and its subject. In the case of *Royer*, the difference appears to lie between fear and trust. In the first arrangement, the assumption prevails that people are *secure*, until proven otherwise, whereas in the other they are always potentially *dangerous*, until proven otherwise. This is the vantage point from which one should approach the dilemma of European individuals and their rights.

Three basic truths: objective, subjective and dialectical

So the interspace is there, rights precede the decisions of immigration authorities, and all this is legal creation. But what does it mean that the interspace, and its priority of rights over decisions, is a legal creation? Does it perhaps mean that the participants in *Royer* and especially the judges themselves created the interspace? Was it somehow their decision? Or does it mean that the Member States, whose representatives once convened to make the Founding Treaty, gave birth to the interspace and the priority of rights? Was it their decision?

To be sure, neither of these would turn out to be a fully satisfactory answer, at least not without reservations. As always in legal adjudication, the *modus operandi* of the ECJ when it gave its *Royer* judgment was that in principle anything (reconstructed as a general norm) in the judgment must have pre-existed the judgment, except its application to this special case. Lawyers clearly regard themselves as lawyers because and insofar as they work on the basis of things-given-before. Turning to the Treaty-making Member States, it is equally clear, however, that the Treaty itself created only some of the framework in which the interspace could later emerge. The direct effect of Treaty rights, for example, came about only with the case of *Van Gend en Loos*.

The simple answer would be that the emergence of the interspace took place somewhere in between these two points in time: that at which the Treaty came into force and that at which the judgment in *Royer* was given. Yet there is a more complex, more intriguing, way to look into the questions how and when the interspace came into being. To get on to that way, let us go back to the beginning, to the point where the puzzle was still there. The participants did not yet know whether rights embraced limitations or whether limitations embraced rights.

In their minds, things were still in a primordial state of non-distinction: no divide existed between limitations and rights, but rather a kind of duplex immanence.

What, after all, created the legal problem in *Royer*? The problem, the dilemma, was neither the concept of right nor the concept of *ordre public*, but the expression that establishes the relationship – the connection – between the two. Quite prosaically, it was the wording of Article 48(3), according to which rights are 'subject to' *ordre public* limitations. The problem is the expression 'subject to'. In the French version, '*sous reserve*' is used; in German it is '*vorbehaltlich*'. The everyday meaning of these expressions is almost the same: rights exist only *if* these grounds do not exist. Nevertheless, all the participants in the *Royer* proceedings insisted that *ordre public* considerations form not preconditions of rights, but mere external and fortuitous exceptions to rights.

Let us turn to the arguments of the participants and see the different ways in which they all establish this conclusion.

The Commission argued that rights are not preconditioned by the *ordre public* limitation because they are fundamental to EC law. This argument implies that *ordre public* derogations are not fundamental, at least not to the same degree. Before considering the consequences of something's being fundamental, it might be worthwhile to consider how it is that one distinguishes fundamental things from things that are not fundamental.

Under the triadic EC law rule-of-thumb of interpretation, one should look at the *spirit*, the *general scheme* and the *wording* of the law in question.[1] Among these, it is most palpably the general scheme that should tell the interpreter what is to be considered fundamental. In order to find out the general scheme of the EC Treaty, one should quite simply take a look at the organisation of the Treaty in its placement of provisions under different headings. These headings should inform the interpreter of how its contents should be weighed. Article 48 was placed under the heading 'Foundations of the Community' in the Treaty, which suggests that rights conferred by this article are indeed fundamental.[2]

So, the rights entailed in Article 48 on freedom of movement are fundamental. On this basis, the Commission submitted two points. First, it said that *ordre public* limitations 'are a derogation from the fundamental principle of freedom of movement and that therefore the concepts of *ordre public*, and of public security, as justification of this derogation, must be strictly interpreted' (at 503).[3] Secondly, as further guidance to carrying out strict interpretation of *ordre public* limitations, the Commission invoked Directive 64/221 that 'limits reliance on this reservation to cases where the personal conduct of the person concerned gives sufficient grounds' (at 503).

Through these two points, the Commission gives a picture that has rights belonging to the texture of the background canvas, the *rasum tabulae*[4] on which any legislation at both national and Community level likewise must be carved. There, the *ordre public* limitation forms a minor figure, a detail. Furthermore, this detail is sharply delineated by the requirements of Directive 64/221. In other words, *ordre public* limitations are mere exceptions that cannot affect 'the right of residence [. . .] as to its nature' (at 503). This picture is in fact a version of Bentham's universal law of liberty (Bentham 1970: 120), depicted as: '[. . .] a boundless expanse in which the several efficient laws appear as so many spots; like islands and continents projecting out of the ocean: or like material bodies scattered over the immensity of space'.

This picture is not the only possible one, however. Exactly the opposite view was presented by the Commission itself in the earlier case of *Bonsignore* (at 303): '*The Commission of the European Communities* recalls that member States are entitled to limit the freedom of movement granted by the Treaty [. . .]. The rules laid down in Article 3 of Directive No 64/221 are thus of an exceptional nature and, in accordance with general principles, they must be interpreted restrictively'.

It appears that in *Bonsignore* the Commission presented a view that would turn Bentham on its head. At that time, it said that Member States' *power* constituted the main rule (the immensity of space) whereas *rights*, as well as the requirements of Directive 64/221, formed exceptions (spots scattered like islands). In this picture, it is not *ordre public* limitations to rights, but the limits to these limitations that must be interpreted restrictively. In *Royer*, the Commission presented new conclusions, but its argument in *Bonsignore* shows that it is possible to imagine a different picture. In that other picture the qualities of 'main rule' and 'exception' are assigned exactly contrariwise.

The *Bonsignore* view of the Commission was a mistake – which, in *Royer*, it admitted and corrected. Should all be clear now? Rights are fundamental and that's it? To everyone's dismay, a nagging question remains. Remember the way in which we established what is fundamental and what is not: the general scheme. That is, in our case, the heading 'Foundations of the Community' under which the fundamentals are enumerated. But *ordre public* limitations are also placed in that same Article 48; they too are under the heading 'Foundations of the Community'. Does it not follow that *ordre public* limitations are also equally fundamental?

At this point one must perhaps reconsider the method of the general scheme. Is there something wrong in our way of establishing what is fundamental and what is not? The method of looking at the 'general scheme', that is, the list of contents of the Treaty, in order to understand what is fundamental is perhaps not entirely appropriate. Fundaments are perhaps not given in the text at all but, as the very notion suggests, go beyond it. Maybe the inner organisation that one should investigate as a 'general scheme' is not as visible as that, but requires a grasp of some higher rationale or deep structure that underlies the visible system of positive legal norms.

As a matter of fact, the Commission made an attempt towards something like this. The Commission seems to have maintained that an invisible inner organisation prevails among the different rights. Accordingly, it said that the rights 'expressly set out by the Article 48(3)' (the rights to accept offers of employment, to move freely, to stay and to remain in a Member State) are *inseparable corollaries* of the 'right of access to wage earning posts' (at 503). What is this new right, a right of access to wage earning posts? Is it a construction of legal principle? Be it a principle or not, it is meant to express the rationale that lies under the rights that are 'expressly set out'. The Commission did not say what this rationale is, but we know what it is anyway: it is the free-play rationality of market and competition for the governing of *homo œconomicus*.

However, legal discourse cannot genuinely spell that out clearly because it has only the language of rights at its disposal, which is why it remains trapped in the fundamental axiomatic between pre-established and positive rights. If the system is based on rights, then any decision is an exception. If the system is an offspring of decisions, then any right must form an exception. A decision that would try to enact a law that says: 'rights are more fundamental than decisions', is a paradox. Fundamental rights, if they exist, can never be based on a decision, a positive enactment, because then that decision is fundamental, rather than the rights it enacts.

Therefore, properly fundamental rights *must be invisible* in texts expressly set out by legislators. In other words, legislators cannot simply *decide* that the system is based on rights. Nor can they decide, for that matter, that the system is based on decisions. Therefore, the foundations, whatever they are, need to be unearthed by someone else. But by whom? Apparently, this must be done by those who apply and interpret, that is, who *practise* the law. Especially, these appliers and interpreters cannot simply rely on legislators' own meta-statements (for example, in preambles and definitions of principles, or in tables of contents) on what they see as underlying their operative statements.

This can be called the first basic truth of law as practice: the fundaments of law are established in, by and through the practice of law. In other words, the foundation of law is the *opus operatum* of legal practice, its spiritual effect, the work wrought. Let us name this truth the objective truth of legal practice.

The Advocate General built his argumentation on the previous practice of the ECJ. Whereas the Commission lingered within the confines of the Treaty, the Advocate General relied on precedents. Any precedent of the ECJ is, of course, in the last instance also an interpretation of the Treaty. Yet with precedents the requirement of consistency in application of the law comes into play. This requirement gives precedents their own normative effectivity, the source of which is not legislation but the general working of the practice of law.

For the Advocate General, the key question – construction of rights vis-à-vis *ordre public* limitations – was 'clearly governed by the case law of the Court', which for him had settled the issue (at 523–24). In *Van Gend en Loos*, the Court had first established the idea of direct effect: on given qualifications, individuals may invoke the rights conferred by the Treaty and the national courts must protect them, irrespective of national legislation. Building on that premise, in *van Duyn*, the Court had then declared that Article 48 fulfils the conditions of direct applicability: rights of free movement are directly applicable.[5]

For the Advocate General, direct applicability of the rights of entry and residence justifies his conclusion that the *ordre public* reservation does not indicate 'a condition precedent to the acquisition' of these rights but only makes it possible 'in individual and properly justified cases' to restrict their exercise (at 524). But how does the given case law (*Van Gend en Loos* and *van Duyn*) support that conclusion? If the argument was only that rights exist because Article 48 is directly effective, we would end up in the same impasse as earlier: the *ordre public* reservation is also in Article 48. Therefore, it should also be applied directly; the rights do not pre-exist it. This way we get nowhere.

However, the Advocate General's argument works if the priority of rights is considered inherent in the concept of direct effect. Only rights are directly effective, not their limitations. Accordingly, direct effect means that individuals may invoke rights, but Member States may not, in the same way, invoke the *ordre public*. Thus it should have been the quality of direct effect that strikes the balance between rights and their limits. If an EC law provision has this quality, then the rights contained in that provision are not 'subject to' *ordre public* in the sense of precondition.

At first sight, this seems to make sense. Should *ordre public* form a precondition to rights, then Article 48 as a matter of fact could not be directly effective. Treaty rights can be directly effective only if these rights are 'unconditional'. Now that one can, after *van Duyn*, safely work on the ground that Article 48 *is* directly effective, it must be presumed that the rights enshrined in it are also unconditional: *ordre public* cannot form a condition to rights.

A watchful reader observes, however, that here is a *petitio principii*. The unconditional nature of rights ought to be the result of argumentation, but it is in fact taken as a premise: rights are not conditional because they are unconditional. Let us presume that the Court was not mistaken in *van Duyn* and rights indeed are directly effective, despite the fact that they are subject to *ordre public* conditions!

All that remains is that the pre-existence of rights was established, and therefore preceded by, the *decision* of the Court in *van Duyn*. That judgment at any event is there and should bind later practice. It had already stated in its headnote that the concept of *ordre public* must be 'interpreted strictly' when it is 'used as a justification for derogating from the fundamental principle of Community law' (*van Duyn* 1338). Furthermore, the 'area of discretion' allowed for Member States in determining what risks *ordre public* and what does not, was confined 'within the limits imposed by the Treaty' (*van Duyn* 1338). It should be clear that the *van Duyn* judgment meant that rights do pre-exist *ordre public*.

Future practice proved that Advocate General Mayras was right: the question of the pre-existence of rights over *ordre public* would be governed by the case law of the Court. But neither *van Duyn* nor other previous cases will govern that question. Instead, it will be the *Royer* case, the very case on which the Advocate General was just now opining. A brief glance at later developments neatly confirms this. Some four years later, another Advocate General, Mr Capotorti, stated in *Pecastaing* on the significance of the *Royer* judgment:

In the said *Royer* case the Court of Justice indeed stated in very clear terms that 'the right of nationals of a Member State to enter the territory of another Member State and reside there . . . is a right conferred directly by the Treaty or, as the case may be, by the provisions adopted for its implementation' and accordingly 'independently of the issue of a residence permit by the competent authority of a Member State' [. . .]. *That statement today constitutes without doubt the key* to a proper understanding of the legal situation of a national of a Member State who moves to another country in the Community. *(Pecastaing* at 720 – emphasis added)

It is, of course, a well known fact that case law contributes to development of legal norms. Yet the practice of law admits this only retrospectively, that is, with respect to *previous* cases, but not with respect to the case upon which this practice is working at the time. Someone who makes new law is not a lawyer but a politician. The difference in the statements of the Advocate Generals in the two cases – first in *Royer* that previous case law governs the question, and then in *Pecastaing* that in fact *Royer* governs the question – is reminiscent of the notion of the lawyerly 'double language' that entertains an 'inconsistent set of ideas', succinctly observed by Henry Sumner Maine in his *Ancient Law*:

When a group of facts comes before an English Court for adjudication, the whole course of the discussion between the judge and the advocates assumes that no question is, or can be, raised which will call for the application of any principles but old ones, or of any distinctions but such as have long since been allowed. It is taken absolutely for granted that there is somewhere a rule of known law which will cover the facts of the dispute now litigated, and that, if such a rule be not discovered, it is only that the necessary patience, knowledge, or acumen is not forthcoming to detect it. Yet the moment the judgment had been rendered and reported, we slide unconsciously or unavowedly into a new language and a new train of thought. We now admit that the new decision *has* modified the law. The rules applicable have, to use the very inaccurate expression sometimes employed, become more elastic. In fact they have been changed. (Maine 1920: 35–36)

Until the case is closed, lawyers must keep quiet about its law-making qualities. Yet Advocate General Capotorti seems to have broken this *omertà* of legal practice. In his opinion on *Pecastaing*, he conceded in a compromising explanatory note that legal application is law-making at once, because he could not make that invisible in *Royer*. Courts 'are required to interpret the provisions in force', but at the same time, he said, courts are required to endeavour 'to adapt them to the developments in the system and the changing requirements of the Community' *(Pecastaing* 721).

Remarkably, even this confession is given in the form of an obligation: courts are *required* to do this! Action is even here designated as merely fulfilling pre-given obligations. This is the way lawyers define themselves as lawyers; it is their conceptual and apodeictical truth, their rule of existence, further confirmed by Mr Capotorti: 'The Court of Justice has already adopted this method in its judgment in the *Royer* case and there is no reason to depart from it' (*Pecastaing* 721). The funny thing is that the adopted 'method', from which one should *not* depart, is that one *should* depart (nay, one is *required* to depart) from what is adopted previously, if only the 'requirements of the Community' have changed.

We have arrived at the second basic truth of legal practice. Whereas the *opus operatum* of legal practice is to establish the law (the first truth), the *modus operandi* of that practice is always to look for something pre-established that determines all practice of law. Let us name this the subjective truth of law as practice.

The judges again adopted a different approach, and perhaps the most interesting one. They took certain pieces of *secondary* legislation, regulations and directives, as their support for an interpretation of primary legislation, the Treaty. Yet they did *not* search for what the secondary legislators, ie the Council and the Commission, had set out explicitly. Instead, they wanted to explore their state of *awareness* that their text shows indirectly. What is this peculiar method of interpretation?

To begin with, one should not confuse this with one of the usual methods of legal interpretation, namely construction of legislative intent. Legislative intent, in our case, should have targeted the ideas that the makers of the Treaty would have had in connection with Article 48. Instead of those ideas, the judges were trying to induce the tacit understandings that prevailed within the bodies established by the Treaty, the Commission and the Council. These bodies only operate the Treaty system that is a system which was not their initiative; with respect to that system they are not legislators, but institutions endowed with a function.

The judges began by stating that Article 48 has the effect of conferring rights directly on EC nationals, which is something that the Court had established from before, just as the Advocate General had stressed (at 510). But curiously, the judges neither referred explicitly to the earlier cases, nor did they reproduce from those cases the reasons supporting this conclusion. Instead, the judges prepared their argument in the somewhat extraordinary way already indicated: with the help of a survey and discussion of Community secondary laws issued for the purposes of implementing Article 48. The contents of the provisions in the secondary legislation in question are in themselves immaterial for our purposes.[6] What is interesting, however, is the use the judges made of these provisions for the purposes of interpreting the Treaty. To begin with is the following observation by the judges:

> These provisions show that the legislative authorities of the Community were aware (*avaient conscience*) that, while not creating new rights in favour of persons protected by Community law, the regulation and directives concerned determined the scope and detailed rules for the exercise of rights conferred directly by the Treaty. (at 512)

Thus the judges invoke the awareness (*conscience*) of the Commission and the Council, which are, to repeat, bodies endowed with a function whose authority depends on the Treaty, that is, bodies that work inside the framework of the Treaty. Why did the judges choose this awareness to justify pre-existence of rights in the Treaty? Maybe they did not have many choices left. The Treaty itself contained no clear answer, because rights and *ordre public* are there positioned symmetrically. It was also not entirely appropriate for the judges to refer to themselves only (their *Van Gend en Loos* and *van Duyn* judgments), because it would stand out as a strange kind of self-indulgence in a form of *fiat*: this is the law because we have said so. The judges had to invent something else to support their conclusion: the priority of rights. This conclusion followed immediately the above invocation of the awareness of Community legislators:

> It is therefore [ie because of the awareness] evident that the exception concerning the safeguard of *ordre public* [. . .] must be regarded not as a condition precedent to the acquisition of the right of entry and residence but as providing the possibility, in individual cases where there is sufficient justification, of imposing restrictions on the exercise of a right derived directly from the Treaty. (at 512)

This method is not unproblematic. The judges invoked legal materials that expressed 'awareness' of an *inferior* authority, the Community legislator, to explain the meaning of a *superior* authority, the Treaty legislator. What if the Community legislator's comprehension of the Treaty was wrong? As a matter of fact, it is the job of the ECJ to watch out for Member States that such mistakes are corrected. The ECJ should act as master in its interpretation of the Treaty, whereas the Community institutions are subjects that in principle cannot inform how this mastery should be carried out. Even if the master adapts to the comprehension of his subjects, are the Member States then under an obligation to bear this, if it is not right?

Through a detail in the discussion of the judges one can see how significant in fact is the way in which the judges' method breaks away from the methods of the Commission and the Advocate General. The Commission and the Advocate General had also discussed the significance of secondary legislation for the case. For them, the directives and regulations implementing freedom of movement had *confirmed* the rights set out in the Treaty. This choice of words accords with the rest of their discussion, and it also accords with the basic, preconceived views of legal practitioners more generally on the normative structure of their field. Upper level norms measure lower level norms; lower level norms must conform to upper level norms. The lower level can only confirm the upper level; if it does not, the upper level norms in themselves are not affected in any way.

The judges, in turn, did not use the term confirm, but said that the secondary legislator had *recognised* the fact that the rights are there (at 511). Saying 'recognise' instead of 'confirm' is not really a matter of choice between interchangeable words.

The difference might otherwise pass unnoticed, but it does not this time because of the very specific use the judges made of secondary legislation. Generally speaking, the idea behind 'recognise' is the following. For a piece of law as a positive enactment to be real and existing, its practice (interpretation, application and enforcement) needs to recognise it in action. In relation to the Treaty, the secondary legislators (the Commission and the Council) were not only practising, but recognising the Treaty.

The law is what its practice (interpretation, adjudication, enforcement) recognises. In this sense practices, which from the point of view of norm-hierarchies are considered to be lower and confined by the overall system, master the system. Usually this remains implicit in the materials produced by the practice of law. Unlike the Commission and the Advocate General, however, the judges worked on this basis explicitly. When they looked at the secondary legislation, they looked for presumptions prevailing in practice, for the self-enclosed constitution of practice in its own *pragmateia*. Whereas 'confirmation' indicates something that is mere supplementary proof, something unimportant as to the nature and existence of rights, 'recognition' is quite another matter: only recognition by legal practice completes the discourse (mental production, ideological work) on legal ideas such as rights. Ideas that remain unrecognised simply are not there.

It is now possible to discern the third basic truth of legal practice: legal practice finds out and reproduces what is pre-given to it *through self-reflection*. Legal practice reflects its own implicit presuppositions and makes them explicit. In fact, the Advocate General lends us the words to express this: according to him, one must find out what the law 'postulates by implication, but beyond all doubt' (at 523). Let us call this final basic truth the *dialectical truth of law*.

After this rather brief but informative digestation of certain juristic techniques, the results, the three basic truths of legal practice, can be summarised as:

- the first truth (objective): the law, its foundations included, is the *opus operatum* of the discursive practices of law (interpreting, applying, implementing)
- the second truth (subjective): the *modus operandi* of the discursive practices of law is to work on the basis that the law is always pre-given
- the third truth (dialectical): *self-reflection* is the crucial and critical discursive resource to legal practice; it foregrounds the implicit postulations of pre-existing conditions, reflects upon presuppositions.

We can see that the dialectical third truth in fact closes the gap, the misrecognition, between the objective first truth (that law is produced by practice) and the subjective second truth (that law is pre-given to practice). The critical thing here is that one who practises law discursively does not have to confine discussions to a given law, ie to what the law-giver has explicitly given or intended to give, but the additional resource of *the conditions presupposed* is available.

These are the conditions of law-making practice which are implicitly presupposed – 'by implication, but beyond all doubt'. These conditions are, again, objects produced by retrospective reconstruction carried out by law-applying practice. The practice of law drags itself up by the bootstraps: it produces the conditions of its own existence, not only by simply acting on their basis, but also by reflecting on the bases of their action. This is one of the ways in which practice of law is discursive.

In this section, certain mysteries of the practice of law were analysed through the *Royer* participants' argumentation. This has moved us away from the rules that regulate the relationship between individuals and public authorities. It has also moved us away from the rules that regulate the relationship between Community law and national law. We have been observing techniques of argumentation and interpretation, something that is absolutely internal to the law as practice. Insofar as these techniques are rules, they are rules addressed to *lawyers*, calling them to their post in maintaining the symbolic order of the legal system.

When thinking about the law as practice, maybe one should not begin by posing the question of the ways in which the legal system comes to handle conflicts between the powers it affords to authorities, on the one hand, and the rights it endows to individuals, on the other hand. A better question perhaps would be whether the legal system as a whole, as it is constantly reproduced in the practice of law, can commit itself to rights from the beginning. That is, in such a way that rights are to be considered as something that were already there: not retroactively, not through ex post facto recognition of a constitutional moment, but because of the eternity of the rule of law, so to speak.

Thus prioritised, rights could precede all possible decisions by the mysterious, fuzzy logic of legal practice. Depicted by Bourdieu, fuzzy logic is 'the logic of practice', which 'is logical up to the point where to be logical would cease being practical'. It is the logic of 'woolly reality' in which one is immersed and in which one gets by perfectly without ever really knowing how (Bourdieu and Wacquant 1992: 23). Ultimately, this practice ignores – or at any rate does not depend on – the chronology of the linear time-concept implied by such questions as 'what pre-exists?' Practice happens in the now-time that wraps up and enacts both the past and the future in its present action.

External legal constitution: hybrid, interpretation and division of labour

The rights discussed above, rights whose pre-existence the participants argued for and postulated, were nonetheless rights enshrined by the Treaty. Despite the interesting variation in their reproduction of the idea of the rights' pre-existence, all the participants could still work and remain within the confines of the framework of the Treaty. The rights entailed by free movement of course did not pre-exist the Treaty. In their attempts to find standards or measures by which to strike a balance between rights and their limitations, they did not have to move outside that framework, but to the different corners inside it: inner structure and rationality (the Commission), previous case law (the Advocate General) and apparatuses for secondary legislation (the judges). In principle, all of it was interpretation of the Treaty, which by implication stood out as a system of self-contained closure.

Something needs to be said about this hermetic cocoon. As a matter of course, in an interpretation of any text one brings in elements (words that explain other words) not referred to by the text itself, either explicitly or by implication. Despite the connectedness of the text to the open universe of signification, the points at which that open universe has to be connected remain fixed in the text. (In terms of signs: the *signifier* is fixed and the *signified* changes.) As for legal texts, I take for granted the following two things that represent the elementary dilemma of legal interpretation.

First, there are no fixed and self-evident rules for demarcating between what can serve interpretation and what cannot serve it. The legally relevant elements that can be brought up from without the legal system (to explain and determine the contents within this system) do not carry with them a label separating them from other elements that are altogether irrelevant and foreign to law and therefore not to be smuggled within the system in the guise of its interpretation. In principle, one is free to present any argumentation. The scarce resources of formal reasoning – 'a symbolic system, a set of axioms, rules of construction' (Foucault 2008: 269) – are not all there is: legal reasoning is an elastic and open-ended way of thinking that has the lavish and extravagant resources of language and culture at its disposal.

Secondly, however, everyone knows that the possibility of this demarcation is at the same time the very possibility of making judgments altogether. Moreover, any judgment-making begins to produce this fundamental condition of its own reality at the same time as it begins to work under this condition – namely, in the case of legal judgments, the condition that the line between right and wrong can be drawn. The essence of the activity of judgment-making, however rigorous or however inexact its methods of construction, is precisely to draw a line that separates. A judgment-maker must uphold those that are right and cast aside those that are wrong and distinguish between the appropriate and the inappropriate.

Those two aspects make up the elementary dilemma of legal interpretation. Once again, thus far the participants of *Royer* have been able to proceed by way of interpreting the Treaty; that is, by way of trying to determine what is right and what is wrong in terms of the text of the Treaty through an explanation of its meaning. However, the *Royer* case enables us to shift from the framework of the Treaty towards what can be called its *external legal constitution*, that is, the legal constitution outside of the text of the Treaty. This shift opens up in the scarce but nonetheless existing discussions the case presents on the relevance of human and basic rights in Community law.

At the time of *Royer*, human and basic rights were still not Community statutory law at any of its levels. In the Community law context, one had to go beyond explicit legal provisions and bring in elements that are no longer second-order words explaining the first-order words present in the Treaty. Fundamental human rights were elements that had to be docked with the Community law system without anything to hold on to in the text of the Treaty. These rights can be seen as forming part of the external constitution of the Community law system (that is, the legal constitution external to the Treaty). To arrive at this constitution, the hermetic cocoon of the Community system has to be penetrated and brought into contact with the constitutional law of the Member States and with international law on human rights.

There we have a new level at which to discuss our question: how should one conceive the priority question between rights and decisions at that level? If it were the Treaty that is the final source and foundation of all individual rights that can be relevant, then we would perhaps have to say that it is ultimately the decision that forms the deepest fundament. As a decision, the Treaty would be definitive, not only of all relevant rights, but also of its own general concept of right pertaining to Community law. If, however, the Treaty is not the final source, there can be both individual rights external to and pre-existing the Treaty, as well as a concept of right that the Treaty did not invent from scratch but merely utilised.

The discussion on fundamental human rights in Community law was prompted by Mr Royer's deprivation of liberty. Recall that Mr Royer 'was put under arrest for having disobeyed the order to leave the country and the prohibition on returning, and was handed over to the office of the *Procureur Général* and committed to prison', apparently *not* for the purpose of deporting him, but for securing future trial of his offence against immigration legislation. When that trial occurred six months later, he was convicted of illegal residence by the Tribunal of Liège and sentenced to suspended imprisonment for one month. The following year he was again charged with the offence of illegal residence, this time committed by having re-entered Belgium against an explicit order to stay away. In this trial, there was a strong possibility that, had Mr Royer been convicted, his sentence would also have activated his earlier suspended imprisonment.

At this point, the question of Mr Royer's basic right to liberty was brought up by the tribunal in relation to Mr Royer's arrest, detention and even the tribunal's own earlier sentence of suspended imprisonment. Reflecting on the grave consequences of Mr Royer's rather negligible offence of failing to report at the population register, the tribunal asked whether 'such a failure in itself constitute[s] a lawful ground for depriving an individual provisionally of his liberty', taking into account 'the principle of the protection of basic rights in the application of Community law' (at 499–500).

These were the facts that hurled the *Royer* proceedings before the ECJ to the boundaries of the Community law system. Here is our question: was there, at these boundaries, anything that lay beyond the Treaty – if not something altogether ineradicable, at least something that could be, must be, or is inevitably invoked *not* in interpreting the Treaty *but* in interpreting Community law through its external legal constitution? Or is Community law indeed a *sui generis* entity, an autochthonous son of the soil, beyond which there is legally nothing?

Despite the momentum towards an external constitution, the point to start with must still be the Treaty, not because it was the supreme transcendence, but simply because it affords the ECJ as a court its jurisdictional powers. So we must imagine and reconstruct the *conception* of the Treaty. That conception is not the signing – the historical act of the Treaty-makers in Rome in 1957 – and the gradual entry into force of the Treaty, its formal consummation after all the transitional periods. Instead, the conception is the mental arrangement that continuously apprehends and generates the Treaty anew. In other words, conception is the endless rebirth given to the Treaty through its discursive practice.

I will not attempt to recite the story of the formation of the ECJ doctrine of human and basic rights, a process that had already been catalysed before the *Royer* case. However, a rough picture of the very basic parameters, insofar as they had already taken form by the time of *Royer*, is necessary for any understanding of the discourse in the case of *Royer*.[7]

First, the starting point for the ECJ had been that it should have no authority to carry out constitutional review on the basis of national constitutions. This is for national systems to regulate and for national courts to implement. The ECJ interprets and applies only Community law, a task which it attempts to perform in a way that does not infringe 'fundamental human rights'.[8]

Secondly, Community law constitutes a *sui generis* legal system. While that system was established through the procedures of national constitutions for making international treaties, Community law nonetheless is, and has been since its establishment, an autonomous and independent 'new legal order'.[9]

Thirdly, the Community had limited and conferred powers (*compétences d'attribution*). The meaning of this was that Community institutions may act, and Community law applies, only in areas defined specifically in the Treaty. In every Community Act, an indication of its legal basis (*base juridique*) is to be found in the Treaty. The ECJ should be the only authority to examine *ultra vires* claims.[10]

Fourthly, in areas where Community competence was established, Community law should be supreme. In practice, this should mean that insofar as Community law exists, this will ultimately be the only law applicable. National laws are regarded as measures implementing Community law, and if the former do not conform to the latter, this should be corrected either by way of interpretation or regarded as void. National courts were expected to recognise this and carry out their practice accordingly.[11]

Fifthly, if a national law or other action of the Member States infringes fundamental human rights in an area that is unconnected to Community law, it is not for the ECJ or other Community institutions to get involved in any way. It is for the national systems and for other possible supranational and international systems to settle the issue.[12]

Sixthly, if Community law, or the national action implementing it, was alleged to be in breach of fundamental human rights, it is exclusively for the ECJ to examine its validity. This examination is not to be considered as an application of international human rights law or national constitutions, but application of Community fundamental rights.[13]

Seventhly, Community fundamental rights were not incorporated into Community law as enacted provisions, but were integral to it as general principles of law.[14] In the construction of these principles, the ECJ drew inspiration from constitutional traditions common to the Member States, and was guided by international treaties for the protection of human rights.[15]

This doctrinal background was developed by the ECJ. A more complete view would require a discussion of the responses of other relevant courts. However, this *précis* is sufficient for our purposes: Community law tells us that enquiry into the rights/decisions structure in its external constitution has two avenues to follow: guidelines given by international human rights treaties and inspiration drawn from the constitutional traditions common to all Member States.

The *Royer* judgment is silent on the latter, but discusses the former. Before examining that discussion, let us briefly assess international human rights prior to the *Royer* judgment. Needless to say, the right to liberty or, rather, against its arbitrary deprivation, is a right granted by all important human rights instruments.

Initially, the General Assembly of the United Nations had adopted and proclaimed the Universal Declaration of Human Rights (1948). The problem with the Declaration is its legal nature. It is nothing more than a declaration: it contains no monitoring mechanisms whatsoever and infringements of the Declaration do not involve legally regulated consequences. In principle, this fact does not constitute an obstacle for the ECJ to invoke the principles enshrined in the Declaration as an argumentative aid to its own construction of basic and human rights, if it elects to embark in that direction. The strictly legalistic argument from binding law is, however, excluded.

A remarkable body of international law on human rights was already in place, which was intended to be legally binding and on which a broad variety of conventions could be listed. Looking at the treaties made under the UN framework, the International Covenant on Civil and Political Rights (1966) is the most relevant. This Covenant includes a monitoring apparatus and infringements of the Covenant can lead to legal cases; there is even a procedure established for complaints by individuals.

However, the first problem with the Covenant is that it had entered into force only on 23 March 1976. The date of the *Royer* judgment was 8 April 1976, which was only two weeks later. The Covenant was not valid international law at the time of Mr Royer's detention (April–May 1972), and thus was not applicable as such to this particular case.

The second problem was that, despite its having entered into force (by the 35th instrument of ratification/accession), the Covenant was far from being valid in all Member States of the EC. Belgium had signed the Covenant in 1968, but would ratify it only in 1983. Ireland ratified it in 1989, Luxemburg in 1983, France in 1980 accession, the Netherlands and Italy in 1978 and the United Kingdom on

20 May 1976, this last ratification being only 12 days after the date of the *Royer* judgment.

The third problem was that the monitoring apparatus (the Human Rights Committee) was present in the Covenant (Article 40), but the procedure for infringement claims would only enter into force on 28 March 1979 (Article 41). This fact somewhat compromises the practical, if not the formal, validity of the Convention.

Despite all these problems, at least for the future the Covenant was already relevant and effective international law at the time of the judgment. In principle, it could have been open to the ECJ to invoke the Covenant as argumentative support in its construction of basic and human rights as general principles of Community law, or at least the idea of them. In practice, however, it would perhaps have been rather awkward to refer explicitly to the Covenant as it was not valid in Belgium or, indeed, in any other Member States save Germany and Denmark.

Let us turn from the UN framework to regional arrangements. The European Convention for the Protection of Human Rights and Fundamental Freedoms (1950) was signed by the Member States of the Council of Europe, which included all of the Member States of the EC at the time of the *Royer* judgment. Within this framework a court is also established for examining infringement claims.

The problem with the European Convention was that, at the time of the material facts of *Royer* (April–May 1972), the European Convention was not valid law in all of the Member States of the EC. Although France had signed the European Convention in 1950, it was only as late as on 3 May 1974 that it had ratified it. At the time of the *Royer* judgment, however, the European Convention had been in force for two years in France, and it was possible for the ECJ to take the European Convention into account as part of the body of the international human rights law in force.

Initially, EC law and the European Convention constituted two different regional systems that had different but overlapping Member States. Over time, as we know, this changed and all the EC Member States became parties to the European Convention. With its ratification by France, the time of *Royer* happened to be precisely the time at which the process of convergence was going through one of its crucial turning points.

One should take note that international law, be it in the form of a UN treaty or of regional arrangements in Europe, does not necessarily mean that its territorial scope of application would be broader than that of EC law, not to mention anything of its universality. International law is by its main substance the law embodied in treaties between two or more states, that is, it consists of positive enactments. Hence the body of international law emerges not from reason beyond history, but from the decisions of sovereign states, subjects of international law. Even if international law in some situations recognises the validity of human rights *erga omnes*,[16] its baseline is normally the sovereignty of states.

With regard to our basic question of whether rights or decisions are pre-existing, any international treaty is certainly a decision before – or at the same time as – it is an expression of a commitment to rights. This is inescapable and irrespective of the way a treaty describes the nature of the rights it prescribes in its preamble (International Covenant: 'rights derive from the inherent dignity of the human person') and irrespective of the indicative mode it might use in its paragraphs (Universal Declaration, Article 1: 'All human beings are born free and equal in dignity and rights. They are endowed with reason and conscience [. . .]').

Finally, after all these preliminaries, let us move back to our case. Let us ask, to begin with, what would be the consequences for our problem, the problem of pre-existence of rights or decisions, if the participants took the view that international law on human rights is binding as Community law? Would it not mean, insofar as international law consists of decisions by states, exactly that *decisions* pre-exist? Only now these would be decisions that are made, not within the framework established by the Treaty, but somewhere else.

Yet it was precisely the very fact that at the time of *Royer* human rights were only just becoming – it was foreseeable that they would be, but they were not quite yet – binding as international law in the Member States. This fact gave the participants an exceptional chance to *deny* the primacy of the decision and *affirm* the opposite. Namely, if they were to declare that *despite* or *irrespective of* the transitional stage at which human rights law was placed at the time, it nonetheless expresses what should be considered the foundation of Community law beyond any positive law: the pre-existence of rights.

What did the participants in *Royer* think of all this? Recall the essential factual background: Mr Royer was deprived of his liberty without a judicial decision, ultimately because he had not reported to the population register. Recall the question put to the Court (at 500): 'Taking into account [. . .] the principle of protection of basic rights in the application of Community law', should the circumstances of the case 'constitute a lawful ground for depriving an individual provisionally of his liberty'? On this issue the views of the participants were considerably more divided than previously.

In the view of the Commission, 'the rules of Community law' addressed to national authorities as binding legal norms 'embrace fundamental human rights, including individual freedom. Therefore, a national of a Member State may not legally be deprived of his liberty in another Member State, albeit temporarily, merely because he makes use of his right under the Treaty to reside there, if no reason of *ordre public* or public security enables this right to be withdrawn or restricted' (at 504). As we already know, according to the assessment of the Commission there were no threats to *ordre public* present in the circumstances of *Royer*. Hence, according to the Commission, deprivation of Mr Royer's liberty was illegal.

At this point, the Commission did not individuate the right to individual freedom in the body of Community law in any other way other than by making a general reference to 'the rules of Community law' which embrace human rights. Later, namely in the oral proceedings, the Commission added something crucial. First of all, the Commission pointed out that deprivation of liberty 'comes within the sphere not only of the right of residence guaranteed by the Treaty but also protection of fundamental rights of the individual' (at 506–507).

So a distinction is made between Treaty rights and fundamental rights. In the *Royer* case, the Belgian authorities had invoked the *ordre public* provision in order to justify their derogation from 'the principle of freedom of movement' – not right, but principle. 'The invoking of the exception of *ordre public*', the Commission said, 'is subject to supervision by the Court of Justice' (at 507).

Secondly, in order to carry out this task of supervision appropriately, which means 'determining the bounds to be observed by Member States', it is not sufficient for the ECJ to consider the EC Treaty alone. According to the Commission, 'the Court must also consider the Convention for the Protection of Human Rights and Fundamental freedoms', that is, the Convention belonging not to the framework of the EEC but to that of the Council of Europe. Why should the Court consider the European Convention? Perhaps it should do so because this Convention, as the Commission notes, 'is ratified by all the Member States of the EEC'? Moreover, and yet more critically, it should do so because this Convention, according to the Commission, 'is an integral part of Community law' (at 507.)

At this point, the Commission individuated the right to individual freedom as a rule of Community law: it is enshrined in the European Convention on Human Rights.[17] As a result of this blending carried out by the Commission, there emerges something that must be regarded as a hybrid, belonging not to either of the two systems but to the point of contact between these systems. This hybrid is 'the fundamental right of freedom of movement' (at 507). It is no longer a 'principle' entailing specific Treaty rights such as that of residence. It is in itself a 'fundamental right' born from a merger with the human right to liberty.

The Commission had already referred to the case law of the ECJ, according to which 'respect for fundamental rights must be ensured within the legal system of the Community'. According to the Commission, in cases such as *Royer* where the ECJ has jurisdiction, this means not only that fundamental rights 'be protected against infringements caused by the institutions of the Community but also against the actions of Member States and their authorities' (at 507).

This was basically the way the Commission saw the situation: the system of Community law and the system of international law not only work in tandem, but embrace each other in the process of signification.

Advocate General Mayras started out on a different basis from that of the Commission. According to the Advocate General: 'Community law does not prevent Member States from imposing penalties for failure to comply with national provisions relating to the control of aliens'. However, he added that: 'these penalties must not be in excess of those applicable to nationals of the Member State in question where they do not comply with the administrative requirements prescribed for cases of change of residence'. In other words, it should be possible, according to Belgian law, to arrest a Belgian citizen who moves from one town to another without reporting this at the population register. Indeed, it would be contrary to Article 7 of the Treaty (requiring non-discrimination) to arrest a European individual doing the same thing (at 525).

Thus the Advocate General needed neither the construct of Community fundamental rights as non-statutory general principles nor the invocation of international law on human rights. In fact, formal equality between Belgian nationals and Europeans before Belgian law is sufficient in the case of Mr Royer. It was solely on the basis of the Treaty (Articles 7 and 48) that the Advocate General could lay down his conclusion: 'so serious a measure as arrest, detention for the purpose of removal or expulsion from the national territory appears to be out of proportion with the infringement with which Royer is charged'. This conclusion, the Advocate General thought, 'is inescapable' (at 525).

In the view of the Advocate General, in contrast with that of the Commission, the European Convention on Human Rights 'cannot be regarded as a Community measure whose direct application must be ensured by the national courts, under the supervision of this Court'. In spite of this positioning of the Convention outside Community law, the Advocate General nonetheless said that 'it should be noted that [its] Article 5(1)(f) serves, if it were necessary, to confirm the conclusion'. In other words, international human rights can be used as an argumentative aid to interpretation of Community law.

In sum, the Advocate General did not reject reference to international law on human rights, although neither did he regard it as indispensable. For him, the effective Community law in any case is the Community law of the Treaty.

According to the judges, it seems at first sight that the conclusion of the Advocate General (according to which the change of residence of nationals and other Europeans should be treated on the basis of formal equality) was not at all inescapable. The 'temporary deprivation of liberty of an alien', the judges said, is not 'permissible if a decision ordering expulsion from the territory would be contrary to the Treaty'. However, if the alien in question 'was unable to prove that he was covered by the terms of the Treaty', or if it was legitimate 'for reasons other than failure to comply with the formalities concerning the control of aliens' to expel him or her, 'Community law as such does not yet impose any specific obligations on Member States' with respect to deprivation of liberty. Dangerous individuals, who may be expelled, may also be arrested (at 514).

What is the meaning of this from the perspective of decision-making by the policemen and immigration authorities? Surely the legality of an arrest will depend on an estimation of the individual's dangerousness for the purposes of deciding upon one's residence permit/expulsion? Both of these actions – the assessment of dangerousness and arrest – need to be done simultaneously. If an individual is dangerous, then it is also possible to arrest him or her; this is clear enough.

However, the Court's reasoning seems to imply that, until the danger that the individual poses to society is established, he or she must remain at liberty. The legitimacy of the arrest could never be transparent prior to the decision to expel or not to expel is made. If the arrest is made before that decision and it then transpires that the person was not inherently dangerous, the damage could no longer be undone: the arrest would be contrary to Community law.

However, the special problem in the case of Mr Royer is that at the time of his arrest he had already been expelled by the decision of a competent authority. He was arrested only when he *returned* to Belgium. It transpired, however, that this particular decision to expel had been contrary to Community law: Mr Royer was not dangerous, but only somewhat indolent. Yet it is perhaps not reasonable to require that the police should have understood this; after all, there was already an expulsion order in place. Therefore, it would not have been possible for the police to know that the earlier decision by the immigration authorities was flawed and that the residence of Mr Royer was and continued to be lawful at all times. When works come in line, it is not for the machine to reason why. The special puzzle of *Royer* as to deprivation of liberty seems to remain unresolved by the Court: was it wrong to arrest Mr Royer or not?

As a matter of fact, according to the Court the settlement of that issue 'depends on the provisions of national law and the international obligations assumed by the Member State concerned' (at 514). Hence, Community law remains silent and leaves national and international laws to resolve the problem on their own. This conclusion has significant consequences with respect to our problem of the external constitution of Community law. Very much unlike the Commission, but also unlike the Advocate General, the Court keeps the systems separate. It declines the invitation to interpret them together, that is, it draws no inspiration or guidelines from outside Community law. Instead, the Court leaves it for other systems to care for matters that belong to them.

So far so good. With the help of contributions from the Commission, the Advocate General and the Court, we can construct definite ideal types of relaying an external legal constitution. The Commission's submission stood for the genuine *hybrid type*: the systems embrace each other and germinate things that come into being only in the nexus between those systems. The Advocate General lingered within Community law, but allowed it to be entertained with international human rights – that is, he allowed it to be interpreted with the help of external elements (affording them the status of second order words explaining the meaning of primary words). Let us call this the *interpretation type*. Finally, the judges kept the systems separate and trusted in their independent functioning, which made up what can be called the *division-of-labour type*.

Is it now possible to consider the question of the pre-existence of right at the level of external legal constitution? Let us concentrate on the division-of-labour type, not because it is conclusive and overrides the others, but because it is also the most revealing as regards the other two types. The question to be asked is: how would the systems function if they all had to do so separately? This can be illuminated by looking into the provision in the European Convention on Human Rights referred to by both the Commission and the Advocate General, namely Article 5(1)(f):

> Everyone has the right to liberty and security of the person. No one shall be deprived of his liberty save in the following cases and in accordance with a procedure prescribed by law: [. . .] (f) the lawful arrest or detention of a person to prevent his effecting an unauthorised entry into the country or of a person against whom action is being taken with a view to deportation or extradition.

In Article 5(1), a right is followed by a list of cases where a limitation of that right is justified. One of these cases is the one indicated by sub-section (f): *lawful* deprivation of the liberty of a person whose entry into the country is *not authorised*. Now, can this provision function without reference to systems other than that of the European Human Rights Convention? Clearly it cannot. Whether an arrest or detention is lawful or not is determined by laws other than the Convention itself. The Convention merely requires *legality*; it says that there must be a law.

We already know that the arrest and detention of Mr Royer was lawful according to the Belgian legal system. The Belgian system required prior authorisation of the residence of a person, a system which is also the presumption of Article 5(1)(f) that speaks of 'an unauthorised entry into the country'. But was there an infringement of Article 5(1)(f) in the case of *Royer*? If the facts are assessed solely on the basis of Belgian law as it stood at the time, then clearly no infringement arises. There was a law and Mr Royer had been treated according to that law. All is in conformity with Article 5(1)(f). Had the other courts operating the other legal systems (national and international) adopted the division-of-labour approach, they could not have established the unlawfulness of the arrest. On that basis, the arrest and detention of Mr Royer would have been regarded as perfectly lawful.

So, in order to establish the unlawfulness of the arrest, what do these other players need? They need *Community law*. It is Community law that tells them that, with respect to European individuals, Belgian law is contrary to the EC Treaty. This is the only way – by crossing the boundaries between systems – in which the lawfulness of deprivation of Mr Royer's liberty can be impugned. Only in connection with, and because of, Community law is there unlawfulness and consequently an infringement of the human right to liberty.

At this point we can see the way in which the division-of-labour approach eventually leads to an impasse or lacuna. The Liège Tribunal had indeed requested the ECJ to specify what Community law says on the matter, and the latter court had explained to the former court that the system of prior authorisation of residence is contrary to Community law. However, with respect to the deprivation of liberty, the ECJ threw the ball back: on this one look to your own laws, the Court said. Yet ultimately the court in Liège – and for that matter the Court in Strasbourg alike – simply could not confine itself to its own system. Community law clearly belonged to the effective external constitution of these systems.

In conclusion, does the right exist prior to a decision at the level of external constitution? To begin with, none of the systems *taken on its own* seems to say that a right to liberty is applicable in cases such as *Royer*. Hence, it seems that insofar as there is nonetheless a right, it somehow exists *externally* to the positive enactments of each system taken separately. Yet it is equally clear that the right would not exist without these positive enactments, albeit none of them seems to establish it definitively. The right lingers in the network created between them, in the relays that connect these systems to each other. At last, it is not for the legislators of each system, but for the practice of these systems dealing with concrete cases to set up these relays. What is more, it is for private individuals who assert their rights to get things right. This last point leads our discussion to the fourth and last dimension of the rights/decisions problematic.

Conclusion: juridical subjectivation

In the previous sections, the question of the pre-existence of rights/decisions opened up in different dimensions, common to which all, in one way or another, was the postulation of presuppositions of a normative system through its discursive practice. In the words of the Advocate General, these presuppositions are contained in the system *by implication but beyond all doubt*. At any event, the rights-decisions mechanism belongs to the legal corpus in ways that are not exhaustively explained in its positive enactments. Let us say that that this mechanism belongs to the ways of thinking and acting in the field of law.

We are moving now to the last dimension, the dimension of procedural law that opens up a wholly new avenue to our inquiry. Here, rights are no longer presuppositions of lawyers who act in the field of their own practice, but crucial elements in the mechanics of that field, something without which the whole apparatus would not only not function, but also not exist in the reality of society. What exactly do the legal field and apparatus need in order to exist in the reality of society? To put it shortly, they need subjects, who insert their actions into the rituals and practices of the law (exactly those rituals and practices that this chapter has been discussing). By inviting individuals to act in the field of law through ascription of rights, the whole regime pins its hopes on their accepting this call by asserting their rights.

Thus, the legal form of subjectivity, *homo juridicus* – the embodiment of the law in human individuals – enters into individuals at the same moment as they enter the field of law. This is *juridical subjectivation*, the work of legal rituals and practices on individuals: inculcation of the juridical form of existence in them.

The avenue of juridical subjectivation opens through a tiny window in the *Royer* judgment: its discussion of what appears to be an unimportant detail. In its question put to the ECJ, the Belgian tribunal had asked what, in the case where an individual appeals against the decision of one authority to expel him, should be done while awaiting the review decision of another authority. Can the Member State nonetheless deport the individual in question, or should it hold back and wait? In other words, does an appeal suspend execution of the expulsion decision? On this question, the opinions of the participants diverged.

The Commission submitted that Community law provides only that the authorities should 'grant a certain time for leaving the territory' (at 505). This requirement, derived from Article 7 of Directive 64/221, which stated that the period allowed for leaving the country 'shall be not less than fifteen days if the person concerned has not yet been granted a residence permit and not less than one month in all other cases'. Additionally, the Commission's view was that a Member State of the EC had no obligation to tolerate 'the continued presence in its territory of a national of [another] Member State against whom the exception of *ordre public* or public security has legitimately been invoked for serious reasons' (at 505). In other words, while awaiting review the individual may be deported, said the Commission.

The Advocate General disagreed. In his opinion, the individual must in all cases be able to 'exercise his right of defence', and before that 'the decision ordering expulsion may not take effect' (at 527). A European enjoys freedom until the case is reviewed and deportation may not be executed before the review decision. The judges agreed with the Advocate General, stating that: 'all steps must be taken by the Member States to ensure that the safeguard of the right of appeal is in fact available' (at 516). This safeguard would become 'illusory' if Member States could execute the expulsion order immediately. The minimum criterion is that the individual has 'the opportunity of lodging an appeal and thus obtaining a stay of execution before the expulsion order is carried out' (at 516).

For the Advocate General and the judges it was crucial that the individual should have the chance to lodge an appeal and to make representations before a review authority, preferably a court. Without that possibility, they said, the individual's rights of defence and appeal would become 'illusory'. However, there is more to be said about this risk of illusion. In a certain way, the whole business of legal practice and legal discourse relies on individuals asserting their rights and what procedural law actively cares about is that courts will have cases to decide. Otherwise, the law as a whole is in danger of becoming 'illusory'.

This is why the court must impose a moratorium, arrest the material flow of events and order a stay of execution, if not until it has given its judgment at least until the individual has asserted his or her rights before it. What this means is not only that a space is created for the individual to make legal claims but that the practice of law must also create a space for itself in the reality of society. This is a space for individual struggles, but all the same the law lives out of these struggles. Hence, when a court of law protects individuals' procedural rights, it in fact safeguards its own reality.

This rather elementary insight into the conditions of existence of law in society gives the basis on which to proceed to a conclusion. Let me do this by elaborating on the problem of rights and decisions through a classical text of jurisprudence, Rudolf von Jhering's *Struggle for the Law* (*Der Kampf ums Recht*), written as long ago as 1872. In German law, the same word *Recht* is used for the law as a legal system (*Recht* in the objective sense), as well as for individual rights (*Recht* in the subjective sense). In Jhering's words, the objective *Recht* 'embraces all the principles of law enforced by the state; it is the legal ordering of life', whereas the subjective *Recht* is 'the precipitate of the abstract rule into the concrete legal right of the person' (Jhering 1897: 5–6).

Jhering's thesis is that the objective legal system as a whole relies on concrete individual rights: 'In defending his legal rights the individual asserts and defends the whole body of law' (Jhering 1879: 68). When individuals from their own point of view struggle for their own subjective rights only, from a point of view external to their subjective interests they struggle for the law in the objective sense as well: 'Whether the person himself looks upon it in this way, is a matter of no moment' (Jhering 1879: 72). Maintenance of the law is carried out not only by the functionaries of the system but also by individual persons asserting their rights: 'the person with legal rights returns to the law the service which he receives from it' (Jhering 1879: 72).

Every time an individual right is asserted, the individual in question gives objective law its 'life and strength' (Jhering 1879: 65). Reproduction by way of these vivifying individual struggles for rights is absolutely necessary for the law's existence. Clearly, the distinction between objective and subjective *Recht* reflects our distinction between authoritative decision and individual right. This is the way Jhering (1879: 66) illustrates our problematic: '[. . .] the relation of objective or abstract law and subjective or concrete rights is the circulation of the blood, which flows from the heart and returns to the heart'.[18]

Individual rights reinvigorate the law as a whole each time they are asserted. Hence, the action of the individual has effects that 'extend far beyond his own person', in that 'the established order of social relations is defended and assured' (Jhering 1879: 68–69). Assertion of rights is not a mere possibility left open to the individual. On the contrary, the assertion of rights is a duty. On the one hand: 'resistance to injustice, the resistance to wrong in the domain of law, is a duty of all who have legal rights to themselves' (Jhering 1879: 27).

On the other hand: 'the assertion of one's legal rights is a duty which he owes to society' (Jhering 1879: 64). The result is something more than mere defence and assuring of the established order: 'The power of a people is synonymous with the strength of their feeling of legal right. The cultivation of the national feeling of legal right is care for the health and strength of the state' (Jhering 1879: 99).

If rights are not asserted, the moral order will break down, and out of this feebleness the nation will lose its vitality. Eventually the nation will be plunged into 'lawlessness' and 'universal indolence and cowardice': 'The responsibility for this state of things falls not upon those who transgress the law, but on those who have not the courage to assert it' (Jhering 1879: 70). Further: 'Law and justice cannot thrive in a country simply because the judge sits always ready on the bench, and the agents of the police power are ever at its command. That they may thrive, every member of society must cooperate with these' (Jhering 1879: 72).

Therefore, that people make use of their legal rights is not only absolutely necessary as a *condition* of the factual existence of law, but there is also a *command* addressed to individuals to make use of law and its rights – to struggle for the law. One might in the last analysis situate this command in the realm of political morality rather than that of law, but all the same, for Jhering it is a duty imposed on every member of the nation: 'each of us, in his own place, is called upon to defend the law, to guard and enforce it in his own sphere' (Jhering 1879: 68) and: 'Every one is called upon [. . .] to crush the hydra-head of arbitrariness and lawlessness, whenever they show it. [. . .] Every man is a born battler for the law in the interest of society' (Jhering 1879: 72).

So this is required of individuals: to struggle for their rights, which is at once reproduction of the legal regime on the whole. But what kind of subject emerges out of this struggle? In other words, what is the legal form of subjectivity, *homo juridicus* – the embodiment of the law in human individuals – that enters them as they enter the field of law. A few succinct lines in Jeremy Bentham's *Of Laws in General* may be taken as guidance to clarify this problem of the effects of juridical subjectivation on human individuals.

'The idea of the law', Bentham says, 'is the idea of an object which may be purely intellectual existing nowhere but in the mind of him who speaks of it' (Bentham 1970: 12). In other words, it 'is what must previously be formed' in the mind of a subject 'in order to serve as a pattern to which the contents of a statute or any number of statutes may be reduced' (Bentham 1970: 12). An idea of the law must be formed *previously* to any specific legal norms. This idea is not one of the norms binding on the subjects, but a *pattern* inculcated in the minds of those who thus become capable of thinking and acting in legal terms, and thus may also invoke the law.

What then is the reductive pattern that constitutes the idea of law that a legal subject should internalise? For Bentham, it consists of two elements that belong to the same weave; if one of them comes loose, the whole idea of the law falls apart. At first, the idea of the law involves the element of command given in the form of 'an assemblage of signs declarative of a volition'. Whose volition is this? It is the volition of 'the sovereign in a state' who wields legislative power. The sovereign's prospect is that this declared volition 'should act as a motive upon' subjects addressed by the command (Bentham 1970: 1).

Therefore, properly juridical subjects are not those who may feel a need to abide by commands because they would in any event be externally forced to so. Instead, the subjects must have internalised the idea of the law in such a way that commands given in the form of legislation would thenceforth act as, or in the place of, these subjects' own motives. For that reason, the point is not that any particular piece of legislation has managed to convert the subject's will at some particular point. Rather, the point is that the subject's whole mental set up, the faculty of willing, has been transformed so that the subject's own volition will fuse with the volition expressed in general legislation. In other words, the sovereign's volition permanently forms the subject's volition.

However, mere command in the above sense of internalised volition of the sovereign is not sufficient and complete, but only one part of the pattern. The pattern is completed only when the second element, that of 'countermand', is included in it (Bentham 1970: 10). If there is no possibility of countermand – defence – then there is no law according to Bentham. So what is a countermand? My view is that it stands for a possibility of resistance, but what kind of resistance is this? Perhaps it springs directly from the requirement that these commands should be given in the form of general legislation (Bentham 1970: ch IX). The requirement of generality opens these 'signs declarative of a volition' to a variety of interpretations as soon as they are made public or, at the latest, as soon as they are applied to a concrete case. Indeed, it is an old principle deriving all the way from Aristotle that the sovereign legislator must step back and not intrude in the business of the application of law: 'what is most important of all is that the judgement of the legislator does not apply to a particular case' (*Rhet.* I.1: 1354b).

In this way the effective meaning of the legal declarations of volition escapes the power of the sovereign who promulgated them in the first place. What is more, the fusion between sovereign volition and subjects' volition may even start working backwards. Having internalised the idea that the will of the sovereign should be identical to one's own will, the subject may turn the whole power-relation on its head. On the basis of the identity of wills, *homo juridicus* may very well start interpreting the law's 'signs declarative of a volition' in the light of their own volition! Insofar as laws must be given in a general form and legislators must step back from individual struggles, the countermand element is always potentially there and the law a strategic instrument always available to struggling subjects. This way, the law may eventually turn from a vehicle of subjugation into a means of resistance.

Plainly, Bentham's two elements of command and countermand reflect our problem of decisions and rights. The command element stands for the decision quality of the law, which is the perception that in the last resort law is a declaration of volition. The countermand element stands for the resistance made possible by the law, which is the perception that the law may even turn against its progenitors. To put it in the context of the previous analyses of *Royer*, Bentham's idea of the law belongs to the objective structure of the legal field – as fundamental categories of the practice of law – but also to the habitus of *homo juridicus*. Consisting of elements that seem to cancel each other out like magnetic fields, this idea amounts to what Judith Butler designates as *the psychic life of power*, in our case, the juridical subjectivation as 'the process of becoming subordinated by power as well as the process of becoming a subject' (Butler 1997: 2).

Finally, let us go back to the beginning. In light of the duplex structure of the idea of law, the significance of the personal conduct of Mr Royer can perhaps also be reassessed. If he did not care enough about his rights to bother to show up at the office and perhaps fill in a form, he certainly neglected his duty to assert his right. His inactivity prevented the idea of the law from constituting him as a subject. He was in any case not doing what he was expected to do as a reasonable man, and moreover could have done fairly easily. This makes him appear as a strange man from the point of view of the functioning of the law. If there were too many odd people like him, legally generated social order would soon dilute or become 'illusory'.

But what, according to Foucault, happens to humans entering the *pactum subjectionis* by asserting their rights? There will be a process of identification, in which the individual: 'splits himself, to be, at one level, the possessor of a number of natural and immediate rights and, at another level, someone who agrees to the principle of relinquishing them and who is thereby constituted as a different subject of right superimposed on the first' (Foucault 2008: 275).

Mr Royer was indulgent enough not to care for this legal subject-position that awaited him in the population register. In effect, he refused to be a man of the law, a subject of rights. Instead of receiving that identity, he stayed in the underworld, declined to enter into the social contract – the legal communion. While all of this is evident, his failure to respond to the calling of the law to assert his rights was not what was ultimately wrong in Mr Royer's conduct. In fact, not asserting one's rights can be regarded merely as a consequence or symptom of something generative in his person; something that lies beneath. The participants in the *Royer* proceedings were well aware of this. As the Advocate General points out, it 'appears then that it was solely on the information which the Belgian police had on Royer's criminal past which caused them to take the view that Royer's presence constituted a potential danger to *ordre public*' (at 522).

For the police, Mr Royer's criminal past was presumably indicative of such 'gangsterism' that the Liège authorities had wished to suppress. Despite having noted that an enquiry on 'Royer's behaviour in Belgium had disclosed nothing discreditable', the Advocate General inferred anyway that there was something guileful in Mr Royer: 'his personality and his convictions in France can hardly be said to operate in his favour' (at 522). What does the Advocate General mean by 'his personality'? Maybe it is here that we are touching the subtextual heart of the problem. Recall what the Advocate General in *Bonsignore* had said with respect to the 'personal conduct' upon which exclusions justified by *ordre public* must be based: 'The concept of personal conduct must be examined not only in light of the offences committed, but also in view of the "potential criminality" of the offender, to use the language of the criminologists' (*Bonsignore* 316).

On that basis, one finds that Mr Royer having been a *law-breaker* is not decisive. So what is decisive? Maybe Mr Royer was the kind of person in whose personality something is more fundamentally wrong. This fundamental fault is without the grasp of normal juridical reason, which always focuses on acts instead of character. If there is a more constant tendency to deviant behaviour, the person in question is not a law-breaker but a *delinquent*.

Notes

1   The triadic rule of thumb was introduced by the Court in Case 26/62 *Van Gend en Loos*, judgment of 5 February 1963.
2   At the time of *Royer*, the EEC Treaty was organised so that the free movement of persons appeared both in Part 1 as 'Principles', and in Part 2 as 'Foundations of the Community'.
3   In fact, the doctrine of strict interpretation of derogations from fundamental principles, such as the principle of freedom of movement for workers, had already been applied in earlier judgments. Advocate General Mayras had said in *Bonsignore* that the *ordre public* limitation 'constitutes an exception to the rights conferred by Article 48 on EC nationals, [and] must be strictly construed in the light of Council Directive No 64/221/EEC' (*Bonsignore* 311). The judges declared in *van Duyn* and subsequently in *Rutili* that the concept of *ordre public*, where 'it is used as a justification for derogating from the fundamental principle of freedom of movement for workers, must be interpreted strictly' (*van Duyn* 1350; *Rutili* 1231).
4   '[. . .] the light stratum of wax on which the pen inscribed characters' (Agamben 1999: 215).
5   In fact this was affirmed even before *van Duyn*, in Case 167/73 *Commission v France*.
6   The pieces from Community secondary legislation discussed by the court (at 511–12) stipulated, among other things, that family members of an EC national should also have the 'right to install themselves' in Member States (Article 10 of Regulation 1612/68), and that the 'Member States shall grant [*reconnaître, gewähren*] the right of residence in their territory' and 'as a "proof" of this right an individual residence permit shall be issued' (Article 4 of Directive 68/360). Relative to freedom of movement in the form of the right of establishment was a directive declaring in its preamble that freedom of establishment can be fully attained only 'if a right of permanent residence is granted to the persons who are to enjoy freedom of establishment', and furthermore, relative to free movement of services, that persons receiving services should also have the right of residence (Directive 74/148). In passing, it may be noted that this last point anticipates the important judgment of the Court of 31 January 1984 in *Luisi and Carbone*, Joined Cases 286/82 and 26/83, where the rights of the recipients of services, including services connected with tourism, were affirmed.
7   The following points rely directly on cases. Piling them up, one can use any well resourced textbook in the field. I have relied on Clapham 1991, Craig and de Búrca 1998, Arnull 1999, and Kumm 2010.
8   *Stork* (1/58) paras 26–27; *Stauder* (29/69) operative part para 7.
9   *Van Gend en Loos* (26/62) summary pt 3; *Costa v ENEL* (6/64) summary pt 3.
10   See Opinion on Accession by the Community to the European Convention for the Protection of Human Rights (2/94) paras 23, 27.
11   See *Costa v ENEL* (6/64) summary pt 3. In truth, the division of power between the Community and national systems is not a zero-sum game. It is customary to distinguish between exclusive powers, concurrent powers and shared powers; see for example von Bogdandy and Bast 2002.
12   This was clear at the time of *Royer* and still the situation about 10 years later in *Cinéthèque SA* (60 and 61/84) and then again five years later in *Grogan* (C–159/90).
13   *Internationale Handelsgesellschaft* (11/70).

14 In *Stauder* (29/69) the ECJ had already held that fundamental human rights are 'enshrined in the general principles of Community law and protected by the Court'.
15 Internationale Handelsgesellschaft (11/70); Nold (4/73) para 13.
16 The Convention for the Prevention and Punishment of the Crime of Genocide (1948) is typically given as an example. See Koskenniemi 2007: 193–206 (paras 380–409).
17 Article 5(1) provides that no one shall be deprived of his liberty, save in cases specified in that same provision (sub-sections a–f) and in accordance with a procedure prescribed by law.
18 Jhering 1879: 66. I have modified the translation slightly to preserve the accuracy of the German original: 'das Verhältnis des objectiven oder abstrakten Rechts und der subjecktiven konkreten Rechte ist der Kreislauf des Blutes, das vom Herzen ausströmt und zum Herzen zurückströmt' (Jhering 2003: 25).

Chapter 5

Law-breaker and delinquent

At this point, we must return to the beginning, namely to the reading of Foucault on liberalism presented before entering into analysis of *Royer*. There we had the two human forms of *homo juridicus* and *homo œconomicus* that had different concepts of law and different concepts of freedom. Recall that while these human forms presented 'disparate terms' for everything, there nonetheless was a perceptible strategic logic, the function of which was 'to establish the possible connections between disparate terms which remain disparate' (Foucault 2008: 42).

In the last resort, for Foucault strategic logic means conjoining or cross-breeding *power* and *knowledge* in practices and apparatuses of governing. Returning later to the more extensive notion of 'knowledge-power' (Chapter 9), I shall now present yet another reading of Foucault, another instance of cross-breeding of power and knowledge. This time it is not about the connection between juridical power and economic knowledge, but between juridical power and psychological knowledge. Corresponding to the human forms of *homo juridicus* and *homo œconomicus* presented earlier, this chapter deals with another two human forms: the *law-breaker* and the *delinquent*.

However, the link between these two readings of Foucault lies not only in these analogies of structure. There is a real and material link as well. Their connectedness belongs to the anatomy of the two non-juridical human forms: *homo œconomicus* and delinquent are similar in their nature, or rather, they are similar as to the relation they establish with nature, with desire. As will be seen, in the background of this connection is the way in which Foucault saw economic liberalism somehow as part of what he called 'the political culture of danger'. Indeed, for him the motto of liberalism itself was: 'live dangerously'.

> In short, everywhere you see this stimulation of the fear of danger which is, as it were, the condition, the internal psychological and cultural correlative of liberalism. There is no liberalism without the culture of danger. (Foucault 2008: 66–67)

Now, to discuss this 'internal psychological correlative' more directly, I will have a look into Foucault lecturing in early 1975, that is, three years before he started talking about liberalist governmentality. It was also the time of the publication of his *Discipline and Punish*, which was in February 1975. (It so happens that this was also the time in which the events of the *Royer* case were developing.) His lectures of 1975, given under the title of *Abnormal*, present one stage in his exploration of the European history of the subject, of its formation in the exercise of power that intermingles with knowledge.

The materials that Foucault there works with may seem irrelevant to understanding the exclusion of Europeans on the basis of *ordre public*. However, the conceptualisations Foucault develops on the basis of those materials are not only illuminating but strike at the heart of the problematic of our legal cases: the dangerous individual.

The following analysis will concentrate mainly on the first session of the lecture course of that semester, in which Foucault set out a very basic analysis of the specific strategic logic of normalisation. (At this point, 'normation' and 'normalisation' were not yet differentiated in Foucault's mind.) In order to make that perceptible, he discussed a selection of concrete expert psychiatric opinions delivered in criminal cases before French courts. These opinions meshed medical discourse in a peculiar way with juridical power, which made them for Foucault an instance of what he then called the 'truth-justice relationship', a relationship that has at least since the times of Plato been 'one of the fundamental themes of Western philosophy' (Foucault 2003a: 11).

Expert opinions on suspects of crime were interesting to Foucault because they were two things at once. On the one hand, they have the 'power to determine, indirectly or directly, a decision of justice'. On the other hand, they 'function as discourses of truth within the judicial system' (Foucault 2003a: 6). This is penal psychiatry's special truth-justice relationship, and it was because of this relationship that Foucault was interested in it. From the standpoint of the present work and the ECJ cases on excluded Europeans, these expert opinions discussed by Foucault are most interesting because in them a 'certain character has appeared': '[. . .] a man who is incapable of integrating himself in the world, who loves disorder, commits extravagant or extraordinary acts, hates morality, who denies its laws and is capable of resorting to crime' (Foucault 2003a: 17).

It is this same character, in other words the character whose personal conduct constitutes a danger to society's *ordre public*, who also appears in our cases. Apart from Western philosophy, on which Foucault managed to provide a strange perspective with his materials, his discussion of expert psychiatric opinions and their 'certain character', the dangerous individual, was about normalisation as a specific 'technology of power' designed to secure society from the 'man who is incapable of integrating himself' (Foucault 2008: 65).

Normalisation, therefore, belongs to governmental reason consisting of 'strategies of security, which are, in a way, both liberalism's other face and its very condition': 'The game of freedom and security is at the very heart of this new governmental reason [. . .]. The problems of what I shall call the economy of power peculiar to liberalism are internally sustained, as it were, by this interplay of freedom and security' (Foucault 2008: 65).

So, normalisation and liberalism stand for a new governmental reason. Juridical and medical reasons, in turn, represent something older. Expert opinions show how the technology of normalisation makes strategic use of judicial and medical discourses, tries to put them to work for its own purposes (Foucault 2003a: 25–26). Foucault's discussion gives a perspective not only on the modern battle between the human forms of law-breaker and delinquent. Moreover, it illuminates the nature of juridical power against the background of its more recent subtext, normalising power. Just as it will be shown that things exist in common between *homo œconomicus* and the delinquent, so it will also be shown that things exist in common between economic liberalism and normalising power of psychology.

Expert opinions

The basic idea of the use of expert psychiatric opinions in criminal cases is well known. They determine whether for the purposes of criminal law adjudication a person accused of an offence was mentally in such a condition as to be accountable for what he or she did and therefore open to sanction. If owing to a diagnosable mental malady a person lacks sufficient self-control, then no legal guilt (*culpa*) arises and the courts will acquit the person. An expert psychiatric opinion '*should* make it possible', in Foucault's words, 'to distinguish clearly between pathological causality and the freedom of the legal subject, between therapy and punishment, medicine and penalty, hospital and prison' (Foucault 2003a: 31). What belongs to doctors gives courts a release: 'It is the principle of the revolving door: In terms of the law, when pathology comes in, criminality must go out. In the event of madness, the medical institution must take over from the judicial institution' (Foucault 2003a: 32).

Foucault's point was that, in truth, expert opinions are not about the simple distribution of cases between judges and doctors, but something quite different. Although penal psychiatry 'makes possible an exchange between juridical categories [. . .] and medical notions' (Foucault 2003a: 33) and indeed works by way of stitching together these areas of practice, the meaning and purpose of its own practice is completely foreign both to law and to medicine. Its concerns emerge neither from the field of law nor from the field of medicine. It disregards the basic principle of law (legality) just as it disregards the basic principle of medicine (cure) (Foucault 2003a: 41).

Expert opinions move in the 'sublegal' area. That is, they analyse behaviour and personal histories that always stay below any threshold of legally defined crimes. Legality in the criminal law sense plays no role in the expert's analysis of the person. This is so despite the fact that experts are called for by the legal system to fulfil a legal function. Legally, a perpetrator's sanity is a condition for criminal responsibility, and expert analysis is meant to examine whether the perpetrator was in 'a state of dementia' in such a way as to rule out criminal responsibility. Following its own logic, however, penal psychiatry eventually turns out to be an analysis of the person's *character*, not only in ways completely alien to criminal law, but in ways that offend against the important principle of criminal law according to which only materialised acts of crime are punishable.

Expert analysis does not meet the standards of medicine either. It falls back to the level of what Foucault calls 'parapathological' (Foucault 2003a: 20). The moral wretch, typical of the constructions of penal psychiatry according to Foucault, has nothing that proper medicine can apprehend as an illness. These are not medical problems, and are more aptly dealt with by educational institutions concerned with the upbringing of children.

The subject of expert opinions is neither the sick body of medicine, the patient, nor the transgressor of criminal law, the law-breaker. Instead, it is the *disorder-loving subject*. That subject is illustrated by the following quote from one of the expert opinions Foucault had in his materials:

> In short, individuals of this kind never feel well integrated into the world in which they find themselves; hence their love of paradox and of everything that creates disorder. They feel less out of place in a somewhat revolutionary climate of ideas [I remind you that this is 1955 (MF)] than in a more settled environment and philosophy. (Foucault 2003a: 2)

Love of disorder is neither crime nor illness, and expert opinions are not about choosing between these categories. The game played in these opinions is not about substitutions, replacements of one discourse by another, by way of the principle of the revolving door, through which juridical reason must go out as medical reason comes in. Rather than substitution and replacement, certain 'doublings' take place in expert opinions. 'In other words, for these psychiatric discourses on penal questions it is not a question of installing, as people say, another scene, but, on the contrary, of splitting the elements *on* the same scene' (Foucault 2003a: 15).

Foucault gives three different doublings that take place in expert opinions: first, the act of crime is doubled by the characteristic of *criminality*; secondly, the legal form of offender (law-breaker) is doubled by the normalising form of *delinquent*; and, lastly, the judge and the doctor are doubled by their twisted combinations: the *judge-doctor* and the *doctor-judge*.

First doubling: crime and criminality

The first doubling provides the legal notion of crime with 'its moral and psychological double' – criminality (Foucault 2003a: 17). In the beginning, the legal notion of crime is constituted and confined by the criminal law principle of legality. As Foucault notes: 'Since the end of the eighteenth century, one can be sentenced only for breaches of law that have been defined as such by a law that was in force prior to the action in question' (Foucault 2003a: 15). Unlike in criminal law, the target of expert opinions is not the actual offence, but rather something in the offender's inner life that can be projected as 'the crime's cause and point of origin and the site at which it took shape' (Foucault 2003a: 17).

For the moral and psychological double to emerge from the individual's concealed interiority, 'a whole series of other things that are not the offence itself but a series of forms of conduct' must be placed in the foreground (Foucault 2003a: 15). Expert opinions work on the basis of trivial biographical elements ('little scenes of childhood'), which they turn into 'kinds of miniature warning signs' of the individual's potential dangerousness (Foucault 2003a: 33).

The expert opinions that Foucault discussed refer, for instance, to the suspect's 'passion for reading comic strips and the books of *Satanik*' (Foucault 2003a: 23), to the fact that, as a child, one had 'bullied his parents' or had a 'taste for firearms and a passion for gambling' (Foucault 2003a: 19) or 'is a cynical and immoral individual' or a person 'for whom it is evidently less tiring to change records and find clients in a nightclub than it is to really work' (Foucault 2003a: 5). All of these are quotes from expert opinions.

These quotes belong to the special semiotics of the criminal tendency, with which penal psychiatry 'tries to establish the antecedents below the threshold, as it were, of the crime' (Foucault 2003a: 19). They point out signs that stand for such criminality, which have not yet materialised as transgressions of law, but will most probably do so in the future. In expert opinions, criminality is talked about not as something that *follows* acts of crime, but as something that *precedes* these acts, as '*laziness, pride, stubbornness* and *nastiness*' in a character that is in need of social orthopaedics and discipline, rather than legal atonement of wrongdoing (Foucault 2003a: 33). Attuned to this kind of vocabulary, the focus of expert opinions seems at first sight completely irrelevant for the purposes of criminal adjudication. There is, however, relevance.

The focus on these little things 'allows one to pass from action to conduct'. That is, one may shift 'from an offence to a way of being'. The dimension of action and offences is not disengaged altogether, however. Quite to the contrary, the level of tendencies of conduct as one's 'way of being' is the reality and the source of acts of crime on another plane – the plane of appearances. What this level of the 'way of being' shows beyond appearances is 'nothing other than the offence itself, but in a general form, as it were, in the individual's conduct'. Expert opinions after all do not abandon the criminal offence and replace it with something else. Crime subsists; only its *reality* is shifted with its general form (criminality) from the level of single acts of a responsible subject to the level at which one may speak, for example, of a subject's 'being affectively unbalanced or having emotional disturbances' (Foucault 2003a: 16).

One no longer moves on the level of acts committed by a responsible subject, but on the level of the dangerous individual. The dangerous individual is by definition not someone who has done something terrible in the past – this is mere data to be taken into account in assessing the personal conduct of an individual. A dangerous individual is someone who might do something in the future.

This shift of focus from the level of crimes committed to the level of crime-generating imbalances and disturbances should not be confused with the age-old idea according to which offences committed by individuals should be interpreted as signs of 'a disease of the collectivity, of the social body' (Foucault 2003a: 91). 'Criminality' as the psychological and moral double for the legally defined offence is not a matter of crime-generating social structures that can be cured by means of political welfare reforms. Instead, the disease is one of the individual alone. Its diagnosis detects and marks the man or woman who 'hates morality' (Foucault 2003a: 17).

Second doubling: law-breaker and delinquent

One who hates morality is not a law-breaker but a *delinquent*, whose nature is not characterised by singular acts of crime but by a constant tendency to deviant behaviour. Corresponding to the first doubling – 'the twinning of offence with criminality' – is the second doubling where 'the author of the offence', the law-breaker, is doubled 'with this new character of the delinquent' (Foucault 2003a: 18). The silly misdeeds discussed in expert opinions are the fabric for construction of the delinquent-subject. Through these silly things – that is, in the language of our cases, through the individual's *personal conduct* – expert opinions create a view of the person as the individual that he or she is.

What then is the 'individual that he or she is' from the point of view of the human form of dangerous delinquent? The individual is a subject 'present in the form of desire' (Foucault 2003a: 20). More accurately, this individual is a subject defined by a criminal desire, a desire 'closely connected with transgression of the law' (Foucault 2003a: 21); a bad desire that for some reason or other reigns over the individual. The idea of a delinquent as the subject of bad desire is something constitutive of the whole practice of penal psychiatry: it 'makes it possible to fix what could be called the fundamental position of illegality in the logic or movement of desire' (Foucault 2003a: 20).

This fundamental position replaces the juridical fundamental position, which always imposes on individuals the juridical construct of subjectivity – the subject of rights and obligations, and of freedom and responsibility. However, along with the juridical subject, the medical subject of mental malady is also abandoned. The function of that was to disqualify the subject – to lift the burden of juridical responsibility – but it transpires that this function is no longer there. Instead, the aim is to chart, register and diagnose the individual as a 'crater full of evil desires' (Nietzsche 2007: 14) that the delinquent individual is in his or her more intimate reality. What ultimately is so evil in these people is not so much that they commit crimes, but *hubris*: 'In these people we find Alcibiadism', stated the expert opinion on a certain Mr A, and continued:

> [. . .] they sometimes allow themselves to be corrupted by hatred of bourgeois morality to the point of denying its laws and resorting to crime in order to inflate their personality, especially when this personality is naturally insipid. Naturally, in all of this there is an element of romantic daydreaming (*bovarysme*),

of man's ability to imagine himself other than he is, and especially as more beautiful and great than he is by nature. This is why A could think himself a superman. (Foucault 2003a: 3)

So from below the threshold of illegality, one finds the movement of desire that leads to antisocial *hubris*. This was so in the case of Mr R, who according to the expert looking at his case 'wanted to know every pleasure, to enjoy everything in a hurry, to experience strong emotions. [. . .] R could not tolerate any obstacles to his goals and whims' (Foucault 2003a: 20). In other words, R could not say 'no' to his desire.

In the end, this free reign of an unbearably bad desire – love of disorder and paradoxes – 'is always the correlate of a flaw, a breakdown, a weakness or incapacity of the subject', in other words, a 'deficiency of the subject' (Foucault 2003a: 21). What lies at the root of this deficiency is the fact that the person in question is not willing or capable of entering or renewing the social contract. The criminal, emerging from gazing into inner delinquency, has made a return to nature:

> So, when the criminal takes up his egoistic interest, withdraws it from the legislation founded by the contract, and makes it prevail over the interest of everyone else, does he not restore nature? [. . .] As a result of this, do we not encounter in the criminal a character who is the return of nature within a social body that has given up the state of nature through the pact and obedience to laws? (Foucault 2003a: 90–91)

The correspondence between the delinquent and *homo œconomicus* is more than clear. Moreover, *homo œconomicus* is always potentially a dangerous individual (recall the motto of liberalism: live dangerously). *Homo œconomicus*, too, is independent from the juridical symbolic order, defined by non-acceptance (or rather: *impossibility*) of any obligation transcending private and personal interest. However, in the case of *homo œconomicus* it is precisely one's interest that checks and domesticates one's conduct.

In the words of Foucault, '*homo œconomicus* is someone who accepts reality' (Foucault 2008: 269). While *homo œconomicus*, too, is a 'natural individual' (Foucault 2003a: 91), it is one's interest that instructs one to integrate one's plans and actions to the prevailing environment. In so far as one calculates one's interests rationally, one will not embark in one's actions on anything untoward. In one's independent estimation of one's best interest, *homo œconomicus* 'appears precisely as someone manageable', and indeed and ultimately: '*Homo œconomicus* is someone who is eminently governable' (Foucault 2008: 270).

Yet all of this works only if *homo œconomicus* does not become 'deficient'. A delinquent – as a defective subject contaminated by 'a flaw, a breakdown, a weakness or incapacity' – is not so much a malformed *homo juridicus*, but a malformed *homo œconomicus*, who 'is unaware of the necessary tendency of interest and that the supreme point of his interest is to accept the game of collective interest' (Foucault 2003a: 91). A delinquent is *homo œconomicus* without the ability to transpose desire into interest, which the invisible hand may then turn into collective interest. A delinquent is someone who remains in the sphere of his or her irrational nature, where desires remain unchecked. Foucault asks: 'Is this not the monster?' (Foucault 2003a: 91). We might add the question whether or not *homo œconomicus*, too, is nearby. Is *homo œconomicus* not a dweller, if not of the very same danger zone, then at least of the vicinity of the no-go area of human monsters?

Reverting to expert opinions, the ultimate aim of penal psychiatry 'is to show how the individual already resembles his crime before he has committed it' (Foucault 2003a: 19). In the guise of the threshold problem of determining lucidity or madness, expert opinions manage insidiously to transfer their probings into the petty, infracriminal spheres of an individual's conduct closer to the heart of the forensic exercise. Eventually, not only the subject but the whole scene of law is split when the delinquent-double of legal subject, the cuckoo's egg in the nest of legal practice, is given a role to play. This leads us to Foucault's third and last doubling.

Third doubling: doctor-judge and judge-doctor

The point at which the game of psychiatric expert opinion in criminal proceedings becomes truly interesting is when it begins to have a more serious impact on the structures of the juridical field, that is, when it affects the very constitution of criminal law adjudication. At this point, the expert opinion extends its diagnostic logic from the borderline spheres of procedural thresholds and forensic exercises into the very core of punitive power. Judges no longer punish exclusively for actual offences; instead, punishment is based on the criminal's underlying morale (Foucault 2003a: 17).

This imaginable turn in the ways of practising criminal law – or, in Foucault's terms, in the ways of exercising punitive power – brings us to the third doubling. This one is not directly about individuals who are the objects of diagnosis or subjects of the imputation of sentences. Instead, this third doubling is about the mesh of roles, an exchange of certain elements pertaining to these roles, between the doctor and the judge. This brings about a subordinate blur and mutation in the thought-regimes defining these professional carriers of rationalities.

First of all, the doctor becomes a *doctor-judge*. The split role of the doctor-judge, being a double of the doctor-proper, is to tell 'whether the subject analyzed has traits or forms of conduct that, in terms of criminality, make it probable that there will be a breach of the law in the strict sense' (Foucault 2003a: 22). In other words, the doctor-judge gives a judgment on the individual's 'potential criminality'.

There is more to this potentiality than mere speculation: 'The purpose of describing [the person's] delinquent character, the basis of his criminal or paracriminal conduct since childhood, is clearly to facilitate transition from being accused to being convicted' (Foucault 2003a: 22).

Although real judges will in time make the final decision formally, in reality the doctor-judge has by that time already shown the judge what this decision must be. This is of course wrong; psychiatric analysis should not be a part of the forensic evidence, but only about the sanity of the person in question: the doctor should not try to find out whether the suspect has done something or anything, but only whether he or she is or has been in 'a state of dementia'. Against this background, assessments such as the following on a certain Mr X are not appropriate: 'Three thousand years ago he would certainly have been an inhabitant of Sodom, and the heavenly flames would have justly punished him for his vice.' (Foucault 2003a: 5)

There is no irony. The above is a quote from an opinion given in all seriousness on Mr X who was accused of blackmail. In statements such as these the 'psychiatrist really becomes a judge'; Foucault asserted that the penal psychiatrist 'really undertakes an investigation, and not at the level of an individual's legal responsibility, but of his or her real guilt' (Foucault 2003a: 21–23).

As for judges, in turn, a corresponding doubling is effected by the expert opinion. Pleased by the emerging possibility of softening the rather gloomy image of their profession, judges assimilate surreptitiously with the medical profession, which is revered rather more highly than their own. At least in judges' own subconscious make-believe, they become *judge-doctors*. Dealing now with delinquent-subjects rather than plain and simple transgressors of the law, the judge-doctor may 'allow himself the luxury, the grace, or the excuse, as you like, of imposing a set of measures of correction, reform, and reinsertion of the individual. The sordid business of punishing is thus converted into the fine profession of curing' (Foucault 2003a: 23).

Hence, the third type of doubling: doctor-judges and judge-doctors. As a result of these conversions, a metamorphosis of the penal activity ensues, without judges really ever being aware of it: 'Penal sanction will not be brought to bear on a legal subject who is recognized as being responsible but on an element that is the correlate of a technique that consists in singling out dangerous individuals' (Foucault 2003a: 25). This is no longer a matter of responding to crime juridically ('since for this punitive institutions would suffice'). Instead, it is 'a response to danger' (Foucault 2003a: 34).

What happens is a fundamental change in the form imposed on individuals by legal practice. This change is the same change that is present in our cases where one needs to prove and examine, on the basis of the personal conduct of an individual (Ms van Duyn, Mr Bonsignore, Mr Rutili and, finally, Mr Royer), that he or she is dangerous to the *ordre public* of society. So what, in the end, is this fundamental change, this metamorphosis, perceptible in the transformation of law-breaker into delinquent before the eyes of magistrates and jurors in law courts? Foucault (2003a: 21) posits that: 'Magistrates and jurors no longer face a legal subject, but an object'.

In *Discipline and Punish*, Foucault said that at this point criminal adjudication became a 'scientifico-juridical complex' (Foucault 1991: 19), where 'the notion of the "dangerous individual" is formed' (Foucault 1991: 252). The complex of power passing through dangerous individuals played two registers: 'the legal register of justice and the extra-legal register of discipline' (Foucault 1991: 301). The law was entrapped by this play because it 'was able to introduce the criminal justice system into relations of knowledge that have since become its infinite labyrinth' (Foucault 1991: 249).

Part II

Power

Chapter 6

Law and war

All the law in the world has been obtained through strife. Every principle of law which obtains had first to be wrung by force from those who denied it; and every legal right – the legal rights of a whole nation as well as those of individuals – supposes a continual readiness to assert it and defend it. The law is not mere theory [*Gedanke*], but living force [*Kraft*].

(Jhering 1879: 1; 1872/2003: 5)

'The end of law is peace. The means to that end is war [*Kampf*]', said Rudolf von Jhering to start his essay *The Struggle for Law (Der Kampf ums Recht)*, and continued: 'So the life of law is a struggle, a struggle of nations, of the state power, of classes, of individuals'. Insofar as law is politics, it is a very special kind of politics. Upright and heroic: 'so long as the law is compelled to hold itself in readiness to resist the attacks of wrong – and this it will be compelled to do until the end of time – it cannot dispense with war' (Jhering 1879: 1).

Insofar as the law is an instrument, it is not an instrument available and malleable for any end. A teleology exists, but this is the ancient type of teleology that involves a development towards the one and the only *telos*, a struggle for consummation of a preconceived inner nature. This *telos* and inner nature, which must be practised relentlessly, is not reason but *fight*: the splendid, frantic fight against wrong – *das Unrecht*.

Let us compare, or rather elaborate on, these views of Jhering on law as war, fight and struggle with the views of Foucault, for whom, too, it was clear that 'right, peace, and laws were born in the blood and mud of battles':

The law is not born of nature, and it was not born near the fountains that the first shepherds frequented: the law is born of real battles, victories, massacres, and conquests which can be dated and which have their horrific heroes; the law was born in burning towns and ravaged fields. It was born together with the famous innocents who died at break of day. (Foucault 2003b: 50)

Throughout the 1970s, Foucault's works and talks presented a continuous problematisation of the triad: politics, law and war. His conviction seems to have been that prior to anything else the law should be dismissed: 'we must break free' of the law as the frame for understanding politics and 'construct an analytics of power that no longer takes law as a model and code' (Foucault 1998b: 90). In a programmatic text from 1971 entitled *Nietzsche, Genealogy, History*, he started out from the view that in fact the legal system is a depository of wars and violence: 'humanity instals each of its violences in a system of rules and thus proceeds from domination to domination' (Foucault 1998a: 378). Ten years later, in an interview from 1981, he indicated that the problem of war and law still troubled him and that he would like to return to it:

> And if God grants me life, after madness, illness, crime, sexuality, the last thing that I would like to study would be the problem of war and the institution of war in what one could call the military dimension of society. There again I would have to cross into the problem of law [. . .]. (Foucault 2007b: 143)

The following piece from an interview conducted in 1976 sums up his stance during his so-called genealogical phase:

> This is the problem I now find myself confronting. As soon as one endeavours to detach power with its techniques and procedures from the form of law within which it has been theoretically confined up until now, one is driven to ask this basic question: Isn't power simply a form of warlike domination? Shouldn't one therefore conceive of all problems of power in terms of relation of war? (Foucault 2000b: 123–24)

In his lectures of 1976 under the title '*Society Must Be Defended*', Foucault presented the most elaborate variety of this theme and problem. Nowhere else does one find Foucault so obsessively fighting against the juridical model of understanding politics. In order to create once again a new perspective for an analysis of power, he started out by inverting Carl von Clausewitz; Foucault declared that 'politics is the continuation of war by other means' (Foucault 2003b: 16). He proposed this dictum as a radical alternative to what he regarded as the prevailing juridical conception.

The juridical conception of power was for Foucault a specific scheme for understanding politics, a scheme based on the distinction between legitimate and illegitimate exercise of power. This scheme he would now rival with another scheme: that of war. Setting out from the basis that 'power is indeed the implementation and deployment of a relationship of force', Foucault wanted to lay bare a system of forces that does not implicate standards for distinguishing between the legitimate and illegitimate exercise of power. Foucault proposed that power should be analysed 'first and foremost in terms of conflict, confrontation, and war' (Foucault 2003b: 15). Struggle is the fundamental and permanent condition of political society and human life, which is something that juridical theories shy away from recognising.

Law's conception of power is a misconception, but at the same time it has been 'the language of power, the representation it gave of itself' (Foucault 1998b: 87). This language is a modern phenomenon: 'since the Middle Ages, the exercise of power has always been formulated in terms of law' in Western societies (Foucault 1998b: 87). According to Foucault, 'power is tolerable only on condition that it mask a substantial part of itself. Its success is proportional to its ability to hide its own mechanisms' (Foucault 1998b: 86). The law has no grasp of these mechanisms, but it hides them well and has therefore lasted as their language. Juridical language should be mistrusted more than other languages, but for Foucault any language is in principle under suspicion.

> Here I believe one's point of reference should not be to the great model of language [*langue*] and signs but, rather, to that of war and battle. The history that bears and determines us has the form of a war rather than that of a language – relations of power, not relations of meaning. (Foucault 2000b: 116)

Historically speaking, the law has not always been relegated to the sphere of mere talk and removed from the sphere of real power. This started to happen with the break of political modernity; only then did the law begin to lose its grasp of the reality of power.

> We have been engaged for centuries in a type of society in which the juridical is increasingly incapable of coding power or of serving as its system of representation. Our historical gradient carries us further and further away from a reign of law that had already begun to recede into the past at a time when the French Revolution and the accompanying age of constitutions and codes seemed to destine it for a future that was at hand. (Foucault 1998b: 89)

Thus, Foucault's overall goal was to create for politics a framework of analysis that grasps its reality and replaces the juridical schema of the legitimate and the illegitimate that is deceptive language. In his '*Society Must Be Defended*' lectures, this alternative framework would be war.

One problem arises, however. If the law as a mere language of power was an outcome of modern developments, then what was the law in medieval times? Perhaps surprisingly, before modernity and before the historical gradient started to work, it was precisely the law that provided Foucault with an understanding of power as struggle and contestation. Medieval law appears to be nothing but war for Foucault: 'In the medieval world there was no discontinuity between the world of right and the world of war' (Foucault 2007a: 300–301). 'Law was thus a regulated way of making war', said Foucault, it was nothing but 'the ritual form of war' (Foucault 2000a: 35).

The idea of the following reading is to reconstruct the juridical principle of intelligibility – the one which distinguishes between the legitimate and the illegitimate – in terms of struggle and contestation. In other words, the idea is to reinsert the medieval form of battle into the basic structures of legal practice, to be able to see how strategies are formed and wars waged in its field. However, the distinction between legitimacy and illegitimacy inscribed in the juridical model of power remains as its principle of intelligibility. For Foucault, this principle is absolutely different from the principle of war and struggle. For me it is not: the prospect is to unite what Foucault separated. The peculiarity of legal practice lies in that it indeed proceeds by justifications. However, they are strategies played against an adversary, not communications of understandings that in the end should be genuinely shared by an interlocutor. Justifications are about legitimacy and illegitimacy in law, but it does not forestall seeing their production as what indeed it is: a form of battle.

The goal of this chapter is a conceptual reworking of juridical practice as a form of battle. It also pays homage to Jhering but, unlike him, it does not leave the cardinal enemy of the law unexplained as some indeterminate 'wrong' only. This chapter suggests that insofar as the notion of law as a battlefield is taken seriously, its real enemy can be identified: it is 'the military dimension of society' as depicted by Foucault (2007b: 143). Constituted by the principle of order, this dimension is upheld not only by special institutions such as the army and police forces, but it disseminates and works throughout society. The principle of order aims to make societies safe; it promotes docility and immediate obedience in individuals, who should be persuaded to repulse and repress all kinds of mutiny that may swell around them, as well as within themselves.

These purposes and goals – understanding the law as a battlefield and military order as the law's enemy – have guided the following reading of Foucault. However, before continuing, let us pause for a moment to ask what ultimately drove Foucault himself in his 'Society Must Be Defended' lectures. It seems to have been the problem of the nature of historical knowledge.

Historical knowledge

In 'Society Must Be Defended', historical knowledge was interwoven in a special way with political power. Foucault looks for a point at which people started to use history for political purposes in a new way, that is, as a critical weapon against the royal house, or against the juridico-administrative apparatus that de facto governed that house. The birth of these 'counter-histories', the new politics of history, was to replace what Foucault called 'Jupiterian' political history – the traditional form of history – the function of which was to narrate the feats of sovereign power for the purposes of justifying its public right. Jupiterian history had been 'the discourse of power, the discourse of the obligations power uses to subjugate; it is also the dazzling discourse that power uses to fascinate, terrorize and immobilize' (Foucault 2003b: 68).

The new histories that emerged in early modernity were not intended to justify sovereignty. On the contrary, they were undermining it and trying to generate resistance. They tried to mobilise those people who until then, as was realised only at this point, had been kept down by their oppressors. Foucault claimed that history was inserted into the strategies of the subjugated groups who struggled against their rulers. This history recounted events from the perspective of the vanquished; it was 'the history of subjects' that looked 'at power from the other side' (Foucault 2003b: 168).

However, power and history are also interwoven in a general way throughout Foucault's work. For him, the practice of exploring and writing history is a special political activity. For Foucault's own histories, the commanding objective is radically political: 'It is a matter of making things more fragile through this historical analysis'; it proceeds by way of placing 'strategic logic inside the things' coming from the past and taken as granted in the present, so that 'finally what appears obvious to us is not at all so obvious'; finally, if one can show that something 'is historically constituted, it can be politically destroyed' (Foucault 2007b: 139).

As knowledge, history is special because 'relations of force and the play of power are the very stuff of history' (Foucault 2003b: 169). Other forms of knowledge, comprising merely neutral facts, are suspicious because they would hide their effects of power. Insidiously, they rule and regulate people's lives in the guise of scientific or quasi-scientific objectivity. In Foucault's mind, history is different because of its deeply political baseline: this knowledge is from the start inserted into the power games of society. In 'Society Must Be Defended' Foucault wanted to discuss the political nature of historical knowledge and clarify the way in which the practice of writing history is his political practice.

However, 'Society Must Be Defended' was not only political but also theoretical self-reflection for Foucault. He seems to have embarked on something resembling a general methodology for his overall projects that were running in the background. The nature of these reflections can perhaps be called historical ontology: anything that exists must exist in history, and anything that exists in history must have a genesis in human struggles. Historical struggles and changing power relations generate every new thing and uphold every old thing that exists.

> History exists, events occur, and things that happen can and must be remembered, to the extent that relations of power, relations of force, and a certain play of power operate in relations among men. (Foucault 2003b: 169)

In 'Society Must Be Defended', the central topic was the new historiography developed for political purposes of resistance from the 16th century up until the time of the great revolutions. The new counter-history would now fabricate a discourse about a 'struggle that goes on within nations and within laws', instead of the pacifying, justifying and order-constituting discourse of old Jupiterian history (Foucault 2003b: 69). Foucault tells of an historical discourse that 'tears society apart and speaks of legitimate rights solely in order to declare war on laws' (Foucault 2003b: 73).

Foucault's view on the nature of historical knowledge can be summarised in three points. First, it is knowledge that 'takes the form of the interpretation and analysis of forces'. Historical events take place in historically changing relations between forces. Secondly, it is knowledge that not only describes struggles, but 'becomes an element of the struggle'. In other words, historical knowledge is a weapon. Last but not least, historical knowledge gave Foucault 'the idea that we are at war; and we wage war through history' (Foucault 2003b: 172).

War: a general analyser

In '*Society Must Be Defended*' Foucault discussed two cases of counter-history: the English and the French. A crucial similarity as well as a crucial difference existed between these two cases. Both in England and in France, historical knowledge was drawn on for the purposes of justifying attacks on the regimes of the rulers. In the political struggles of England these would climax in the 17th century Civil War and Glorious Revolution. To overthrow the king's regime, the English politics of history was to condemn it as illegitimate. Whereas the Norman Conquest of 1066, in which the Saxons were defeated, had in former Jupiterian histories justified the Norman rule, the same historical fact would now in the counter-histories justify the very fight against 'Normans' and their regime. The strategy of the struggling groups was to identify themselves with the old 'Saxons' and thus to assert their rights as the rights of the genuine English nation. Nevertheless, in England counter-history remains in the juridical framework of illegitimate and legitimate. In this case, the new historical discourse is still about wrongs committed by the one group and about the violated rights of the other group.

This was not the case in France. There the strategy – or at least the strategic outcome – of the new historiography was the replacement of the juridical framework of the legitimate and illegitimate by another framework. This new framework pins down a new idea: any system of public right will not stop the struggle: struggle is constant, it was there before the law and it is more fundamental than the system of law. The war is 'going on within all the institutions of right and peace' (Foucault 2003b: 171). Plotting, conspiracies and machinations between and amongst the different power groups are incessant.

Moreover, unlike in the English case, in the French case the struggle was not set up between the ruling monarch and his oppressed subjects. It went on between the different groups – clergy, nobility, bourgeoisie – who all tried to increase their influence in the royal house. These groups constitute the 'nations' in French counter-histories. Each of them desired power and no system of public right – natural or rational – would have gone beyond the constitutive power game.

For Foucault, the most central figure in the formation of French counter-histories was Henri de Boulainvilliers (1658–1722), who defended the cause of aristocracy, the 'Nobles of the Sword'. Linking this group with the ancient Frankish warriors, Boulainvilliers embarked on a project of analysing the French society's power structures through their changes in history. His problem, however, was not the juridical problem of who had the right to sit on the throne and what the extent of his or her power was. Examining first how Romans defeated Gauls, secondly how Franks defeated Romans and, finally, how the bourgeoisie and clergymen were about to defeat the 'Frankish' aristocrats, Boulainvilliers's problem was instead 'to discover how the strong became weak and how the weak became strong', which required 'understanding the internal reasons for the defeat' (Foucault 2003b: 160). These internal reasons for defeat were Boulainvilliers's entry point to society as a domain of knowledge, producing an overarching generalisation of the notion of war in an analysis of that domain.

The first way in which war becomes a general analyser of society came about through Boulainvilliers's coupling of the military system with the economic system. History shows that wealth and prosperity of the realm is bound up with the ways in which the government arranges and produces its military strength. Boulainvilliers saw that the Romans' use of mercenary armies had necessitated heavy taxation, which led ultimately to the ruin of Rome's economy. This is why the Romans lost their strength and could no longer defend themselves against Franks who, in turn, were all warriors.

One of Boulainvilliers's points was that a social stratum responsible for fighting was clearly the better way to organise a country's defence, but that was not all. One group takes over another by force – not by right – and the strength required for that is a matter of economic resources. However, this does not mean that economy is the most fundamental structure of society, thereby determining who becomes weak and who becomes strong. On the contrary, the point made by Boulainvilliers was that in fact the organisation of a country's military strength underlies its economic performance. This way, war became generalised with respect to economy: a country has to be wealthy because it has to be strong, and improvements of its system of production sprout from military needs in the background.

The second way in which war becomes an analyser of society is that through historical knowledge it becomes generalised with respect to the legal system. For Boulainvilliers, this was not a matter of victories as constitutional moments that overthrow old legal regimes and establish new ones, as in the English case. Rather, history shows that an insatiable thirst for power and brazen trickery always infiltrates the legal system. The law is not the sacred constitution of political life, but merely one of the elements deployed in the plots, strategies and intrigues of those who either wield power or harbour conspiracies. In Boulainvilliers's history, society's internal wars, struggles and violence stand on the foundation of any legal system – not only at the time of its formation, but these things constantly form the basis of the law as it operates in any given political society.

However, for Foucault, the generalisation of war by Boulainvilliers with respect to the system of law concerns not only the uses and abuses of law in hapless power games. In truth, more important were the political and ethical conceptions of the ancient Frankish warriors that still underlay the values of the Nobles of the Sword. These are truer to history than the juridical values and they do not pretend to constitute a code of decency and respect for others. Frankish warriors had no morals in the modern sense of the term. The ethical-political life of the Franks was founded on war alone:

> The freedom enjoyed by these Germanic warriors was essentially the freedom of egoism, of greed – a taste for battle, conquest, and plunder. The freedom of these warriors is not the freedom of tolerance and equality for all; it is freedom that can be exercised only through domination. (Foucault 2003b: 148)

According to Foucault, there were three ways in which Boulainvilliers argued this 'generalization of war with respect to right and the foundations of right'. The first of these is plainly historical: 'you can study history as long as you like, and in any way that you like, but you will never discover any natural rights. Natural rights do not exist in any society'. All that one finds is 'either war itself [. . .] or the inequalities that result from wars and violence' (Foucault 2003b: 156).

The second way was theoretical. Even if one could imagine a society where all are free and equal and no domination exists, the freedom of the people living in such conditions would 'be something that has no force and no content'; it would be 'weak, impotent and abstract' freedom (Foucault 2003b: 157). In fact, it would not be real freedom at all, because real freedom is quite something else. What is real freedom? 'The first criterion that defines freedom is the ability to deprive others of their freedom. What would be the point of being free and what, in concrete terms, would it mean if one could not trample on the freedom of others?' (Foucault 2003b: 157).

The third way for Boulainvilliers to argue for the generalisation of war with respect to the legal system was a combination of the above two. Namely, even if at one point a state of natural right had existed, it would have been 'defeated by the historical force of a freedom that functions as nonequality' (Foucault 2003b: 157). What the state of natural right, real or imaginary, would be unable to resist is *the law of history*:

> [. . .] the law of history states that freedom is strong, vigorous, and meaningful only when it is the freedom of the few and when it exists at the expense of the others, only when a society can guarantee an essential nonequality. (Foucault 2003b: 157)

So far war has become a general social analyser in two ways. First, the economy of weapons underlies the economy in general. Economy is needed for the purposes of rearmament, and the way in which rearmament is organised affects the economy. Secondly, war underlies every system of law, in the last resort because of 'the law of history' that takes care that any system of right cannot stay on the basis of justice, because the tough and strong will always triumph over it. The law is rather an element in the political wars that go on, where it is an element of different strategies of domination.

However, these two generalisations of war were not all. The most important generalisation was in fact *internal to* the war-model, namely that war will be generalised with respect to the *form of battle*. This means that war is extended beyond battles and not limited to periods where situations of confrontation take place. With this, Boulainvilliers turns to 'war as an internal institution, and not the raw event of a battle' (Foucault 2003b: 159–60). War as an internal institution consists, in the first place, only of the military institutions of society. But when Boulainvilliers drops the form of a battle, he would in fact start to look at society as a whole through its military institutions. It transpires that these institutions have 'general effects on the civil order as a whole' (Foucault 2003b: 158–59).

As a general analyser of society, war is no longer a disruptive battle – a conquest that leads to an invasion and then to a change of regime – which would then 'leave its mark on the social body' in the form of new rule and new laws. Instead, war is the military organisation and order that will 'put the seal of war on the entire social body'; only military institutions 'make it possible to articulate society as a whole' (Foucault 2003b: 159).

This internal transmutation of the war-model completes the war-schema so that it now makes society intelligible in an entirely new way. At the same time, however, this transmutation devours the former war-model, that of battles. Unlike battles, the military version of the war-model is constitutive of *order*. Whereas battles meant transient disorder in society, war as a military institution is internal to society and becomes an element of order and discipline within it. Military institutions are not established for the purposes of protecting society against external enemies only, but against its own formlessness, the surge and chaos that goes on inside it if left alone.

Battle forms and military order

We can now try to clarify Foucault's war-model of power, and finally try also to deal with his so-called expulsion of the juridical model of power. Let us begin with the war-model of power. Where we started, the war-model was a principle of intelligibility that one should put in place of the juridical principle of intelligibility, that of the illegitimate and the legitimate. This war-model is one model. With the generalisation of war, however, the war model is doubled. The original *battle-form* depicts all social relations, the fight that we all fight against each other and the fighting that goes on within each of us. Fight is what makes things exist in reality, and battle-form is the principle of intelligibility that makes things perceptible in reality. From within this war-model another model emerges, which in fact is an anti-battle form: the *military order*. The reality of battles is not what the military order as a generalised social analyser makes perceptible. The reality made perceptible by this second war-model is the reality of political power exercised over society and subjects as an incessant rearmament, that is, as if everything in society was a preparation for war. This is the reality of military institutions, which Foucault saw as working for Boulainvilliers as a *pars pro toto* – a single institution that stands for all institutions.

This concept was initially Foucault's own idea. In his book *Discipline and Punish* (1975), Foucault had already explained the changes and transformations revolving around war as real historical developments. 'Docile bodies', the central section in *Discipline and Punish*, explained how the birth of so-called disciplinary techniques occurred and what the broader effects of that were.

These techniques first emerged in isolated disciplinary institutions: monasteries, hospitals, factories, schools, orphanages, prisons and, above all, in the army. From these institutions, all of which were a type of military institution in a generalised sense, disciplinary techniques extended and spread throughout society by disseminating their specific rationality, so-called panopticism: the organisation of a minute, omnipresent and permanent control and surveillance of individuals (Foucault 1991: 133–69).

The point is not only to explain the change that happened in human life when military order was disseminated throughout society. Prior to that, a change had happened within the military institution itself, which corresponds to the internal transmutation of the war-model discussed above. The crucial elements of war – soldiers and armies – changed radically during the course of the 17th century. The military techniques of regimentation and discipline developed entirely new kinds of armies. The early 17th century warrior (*homme de guerre*) still bore 'the natural signs of his strength and his courage', so that he 'could be recognized from afar'. By contrast, in the late 18th century soldier (*militaire*) there was nothing natural: 'out of formless clay, an inapt body, the machine required can be constructed' (Foucault 1991: 135).

The military production of soldiers sought a totally docile individual, an instrument that can be commanded and programmed like a robot. This production of individuals is what 'war' stood for in *Discipline and Punish*. It meant not the 'noise of the battle' but the 'order and silence' of perfectly constituted troops (Foucault 1991: 168). What Foucault had written about military institutions in *Discipline and Punish* was certainly also in his mind when he gave his next year's lectures on Boulainvilliers.

In *Discipline and Punish*, one spots Foucault once again contrasting war, now in the sense of military order, with law. There is 'the dream of a perfect society' of the 'philosophers and jurists of the eighteenth century', a dream that referred to the social contract, fundamental rights and the *volonté general*. Let us say that it was Rousseau's dream. On the underside of that juridical dream, however, another dream existed. This was 'a military dream of society.' (Foucault 1991: 169)

Its reference, in turn, was the order of 'the meticulously subordinated cogs of a machine'. Society should be a machine, a war-machine, whose individual elements are as society's soldiers. This necessitated 'permanent coercions' carried out as in the army. It also necessitated 'indefinitely progressive forms of training' that took their models from the army. The objective of coercion and training was to install 'automatic docility' in the individual – the dream individual of the military order (Foucault 1991: 169).

On the face of it, the military and the juristic dreams of a perfect society are apprehended as completely disparate and incommensurate visions. However, in the practices that created the modern world they were coeval, both taking place at the same point of history, as if being special cooperating parts of the same general development:

> And although the universal juridicism of modern society seems to fix limits on the exercise of power, its universally widespread panopticism enables it to operate, on the underside of law, a machinery that is both immense and minute, which supports, reinforces, multiplies the asymmetry of power and undermines the limits that are traced around the law. (Foucault 1991: 223)

This would finally make sense of the way in which war broke its continuum with law and created another with politics. It was really that the change happened in *war*. This was the shift from the noisy battle of *la guerre* to the silence of a military order. That change broke the medieval continuity between law and war, and marked the beginning of the modern world.

Law against order

What was the significance of the doubling of the war-model into battle-form and military order with respect to Foucault's overall project of historical ontology? The above depicted turn, the turn from the battle-form to the military order, is certainly an important episode in Foucault's overall work. As an episode, it is crucial for the historical formation of the modern subject: a soldier, a cog in a big machine, and so on. But as an episode, I think it is even more crucial to the understanding of Foucault's own standpoint, in two ways. First, historical knowledge, the production of counter-histories, was what he considered his own personal battle-form. This is where he took Boulainvilliers as his own forerunner. His own histories were his ways of fighting. Secondly, the other side of the turn – the military order – provides what Foucault needed as a fighter, the enemy. Foucault directed his historical attacks against society as a military order, the military ordering of society – or, quite simply – *against the order*.

This also helps to understand Foucault's expulsion of the juridical representation of power that has lost its grasp of reality. One realises that the changing or unchanging of the law is not the key to clarifying Foucault's analytics of power. For him, the law – with its misleading problematic of legitimacy and illegitimacy – stands for something that needs to be dismissed, in order to be able to fight against order. And he dismissed it time and time again. In spite of that, his war model can serve our attempt at rendering the law as a battlefield. There is a position that the law might take *within the war-schema* in its doubled Foucauldian sense. The first part of the following sketch on this position is about legal *battles*, and the second part is about the law's eternal *enemy*.

As early as 1971 (that is, at the beginning of his so-called genealogical phase) Foucault wrote in *Nietzsche, Genealogy, History* not about medieval law, or about modern law, or about liberal law, but about the law most generally. At that general level, the law seems first to be the repository for what social and political contestations produce:

> It would be wrong to follow traditional beliefs in thinking that total war exhausts itself in its own contradictions and ends by renouncing violence and submitting to civil laws. [. . .] Humanity does not gradually progress from combat to combat until it arrives at universal reciprocity, where the rule of law finally replaces warfare; humanity installs each of its violences in a system of rules and thus proceeds from domination to domination. (Foucault 1998a: 377–78)

So the law seems to be a mere record of victories. While produced by a history of battles and struggles, the law itself is a dead book of domination. At most, it is 'the calculated pleasure of relentlessness', which means that in laws the victors can secure, not the pleasure of fighting, but the pleasure they have won by fighting: domination. It seems that the law is not the scene for *battle*, but the scene for the *order* that ensues from battling (Foucault 1998a: 378).

As 'promised blood', the law 'permits the perpetual instigation of new dominations and the staging of meticulously repeated scenes of violence'. What is the meaning of this? It could be that the victors repeat the original violence that had brought them victory, but only now in the legal framework of domination. It could also mean that there will always be new wars and at the end of those wars new victors will take over the law. Then the law allows 'the resurgence of new forces that are sufficiently strong to dominate those in power'. Yet again, the law would still not be a scene for battles, but a record, only now the record for these new victors. They would again install an order of domination in laws (Foucault 1998a: 378).

'Rules are empty in themselves', Foucault continues, 'they are made to serve this or that, and can be bent to any purpose'. This is not new, but what then follows is more interesting: 'The successes of history belong to those who are capable of seizing these rules, to replace those who have used them, to disguise themselves so as to pervert them, invert their meaning, and *redirect them against those who had initially imposed them*' (Foucault 1998a: 378, empasis added).

It seems to be that at this point Foucault no longer speaks about the law as a record of victories, but as the actual scene of battles. And so it is in the end. One must introduce oneself 'into this complex mechanism' of law and 'make it function in such a way that *the dominators find themselves dominated by their own rules*'. Is this nothing less than a presentation of the law as a scene for resistance? In this scene, war is waged by way of 'substitutions, displacements, disguised conquests, and systematic reversals' – that is, by way of changing prevailing interpretations and making new ones, *by practising the law* (Foucault 1998a: 378, emphasis added).

If interpretations were the slow exposure of the meaning hidden in an origin, then only metaphysics could interpret the development of humanity. But if interpretation is the violent or surreptitious appropriation of a system of rules, which in itself has no essential meaning, in order to impose a direction, to bend it to a new will, to force its participation in a new game, and to subject it to secondary rules, then the development of humanity is a series of interpretations. (Foucault 1998a: 378)

In that light, the practice of law is not only a surreptitious appropriation of a system of rules, but the scene where the history of the development of *humanity* discloses itself. That is: 'the history of morals, ideals, and metaphysical concepts, the history of the concept of liberty' and so on. All of these 'stand for the emergence of different interpretations'. That is, legal interpretations. Morals, ideals, concepts and so on 'must be made to appear as events in the theatre of procedures'; that is, in the theatre of legal procedures. In the end, the law is not only a scene for battles, but a scene for the history of humanity: 'The role of genealogy is to record this history': that is, the history of the practice of law (Foucault 1998a: 378–79).

For the analyses that will follow, the import of the above revision of legal practice is twofold: first, the practice of law is a form of battle and, secondly, its field is not only a battlefield but is also a field that can be conquered. This field can be conquered by those who practise resistance, but it can also be conquered by those who practise domination.

At the start of his genealogical projects, Foucault was certain about the centrality of the law as a form of battle for his own historical undertakings. However, the expulsion of law is visible there too, but it concerns only the problematic of the legitimate and the illegitimate. The juridical field as such was not uninteresting from the point of view of struggles and battles. By the mid-1970s, however, Foucault seems to have stopped thinking that the law was about battles, and started thinking instead that it was about domination and order only.

The system of right and the judiciary field are permanent vehicles for relations of domination, and for polymorphous techniques of subjugation. Right must, I think, be viewed not in terms of a legitimacy that has to be established, but in terms of the procedures of subjugation it implements. (Foucault 2003b: 27)

At this time, the law seems to have been for Foucault one of the vehicles of order. Therefore, the law really was not only a principle of intelligibility that one must dismiss in order to fight order – to make the real enemy visible, so to speak. Insofar as law belongs to the side of order, law forms part of the enemy's forces. The law must be fought. However, in the end, the law does not belong to the side of order, as we shall see.

In 1982, Foucault gave a talk at the University of Vermont on *The Political Technology of Individuals*. This can be considered the last piece of his work that belongs to what is generally considered his genealogical phase exploring the history of power and domination over individuals and the social technologies and mechanisms this history had produced. Whereas in his discussion on Boulainvilliers the law was depicted as an integral part of the administrative machinery of the royal house, it now transpires that there is an 'antinomy between law and order', that is, between the juridical system and the system of the state (Foucault 2000c: 417). In Vermont, Foucault depicted the relationship between law and order as follows:

> Law, by definition, is always referred to a juridical system, and order is referred to an administrative system, to a state's specific order, which was exactly the idea of all those utopians of the beginning of the seventeenth century and was also the idea of those very real administrators of the eighteenth century. I think that the conciliation between law and order, which has been the dream of those men, must remain a dream. It's impossible to reconcile law and order because when you try to do so it is only in the form of an integration of law into the state's order. (Foucault 2000c: 417)

The implications and background to this will be revisited in Chapter 8, where the notion of 'reason of state', a notion that connects directly to what in this chapter has been depicted as military order will be discussed. At this moment, suffice it to say that law and order were eventually considered by Foucault as *enemies* or antagonists. In *Lemon and Milk*, a short text written in 1978, Foucault put this enmity and antagonism aphoristically: 'Just as people say milk or lemon, we should say law *or* order. It is up to us to draw lessons for the future from that incompatibility' (Foucault 2000e: 438).

Chapter 7

Bouchereau: public good and the rule of law

There are two basic levels in the following analysis of the *Bouchereau* case. At the first level, the standpoint consists of an unholy alliance between the battle-form and the juridical schema of legitimacy and illegitimacy. The field of law is depicted as a field for confrontations between adversaries, where the means for clashing with others is discourse on justification, discourse on legitimacy and illegitimacy.

At the second level, this standpoint undertakes to make perceptible the permanent antagonism between law and order. This is not an antagonism between different actors, but between different systems and regimes. At this level, the field of law incorporates stable mechanisms that have a specific legal nature, but these mechanisms can be made use of by other apparatuses, notably the apparatuses of order and security. However, these legal mechanisms also provide the possibility for individuals to resist the apparatuses installed for their control. Let us clarify these two levels a bit more.

First level: law as battleground

Justification distinguishes the legal field and its struggles from other fields and struggles. Legal battles are waged by way of constructions of justifications, and legal knowledge and skill consists of one's capability to produce such constructions. Mastery of this is what the field of legal practice demands from actors engaging in the practice of law. Distinction-making between the illegitimate and the legitimate – precisely the schema banished by Foucault from his force system – is an imperative demand in the legal field. Legal practice cannot dispense with the problem of the legitimate and the illegitimate.

The discursive practice of justification enacted in the legal field reproduces that field's normativity. Albeit justifications can be styled in many ways and they can be used selectively, normativity is there before the strategic actors enter the field. Normativity and justification are a *real* part of the constitution of the legal field, in that they are materialised by its core mechanisms. What makes them real, however, is not their would-be extra-historical givenness, but precisely their omni-historical presence in each and every battle waged within the field of legal practice.

They belong to the elements of the field by which the strategies of the litigants must be planned and carried out.

Seen from the vantage point of strategies, justification discourses of law appear as consisting of tactical choices between different conceivable ways of arguing. Passing through strategic filters, the different ways to justify one's normative propositions (one's defences and attacks) are not chosen with a view to common normative understanding, but with a view to a victory. The discourse of justification is a game of power relations played in the form of communicative action: 'Whether or not they pass through systems of communication, power relations have a specific nature' (Foucault, 2000e: 337).

Concrete tactical decisions taken by actors provide both material and form to theoretical analysis of the strategies of these actors. In other words, there is no radical distinction between practical schemes of action and theoretical schemata for understanding. An analysis that takes the point of view of strategies is not in this regard different from a normative or systemic analysis; both get under way by looking at the same basic stuff: justifications. However, insofar as strategic analysis is applied to the law, justifications do not unfold as if stemming from an original or ideally constructed unity of the system. Systemic reasoning is regarded as merely one of the effective tactics in the practice of law. Justifications themselves stem from elsewhere, they are the roar of legal battle.

In *The Subject and Power* (1982) Foucault made a note on the ways the word 'strategy' is commonly used. Accordingly, the notion of strategy (Foucault 2000e: 346) designates:

- the means employed to attain a certain end
- the way in which a partner in a certain game acts with regard to what he thinks should be the action of the others and what he considers the others think to be his own
- the procedures used in a situation of confrontation to deprive the opponent of his means of combat.

These means, ways and procedures pertain to situations of confrontation between adversaries who have different objectives. Being a field for confrontations, the law provides a variety of means, ways and procedures for strategic action. The following analysis tries to capture a general structure underlying this variety by way of focusing on what will be called the ultimate principles of justification in the practice of law. What surfaces in the *Bouchereau* case as ultimate principles are the principle of the *general good* and the principle of the *rule of law*. General good and the rule of law are schemes of action that belong to the permanent arsenal of legal strategies, and at the same time they make the practice of law intelligible for theory.

It is significant that this pair of principles is not a *binary* one, in the way the pair of illegitimate/legitimate is. The general good and the rule of law may form different combinations. Different tactics may present these principles, for example, as complementary, mutually constitutive and even identical, but also as standing for opposing values that undermine and devour each other.

By contrast, the distinction between legitimate and illegitimate is an either/or type of distinction: justified, not justified. To reconstruct a living thing out of it, the juridical principle must be reconstructed in such a way that one can see how it generates and facilitates action. One must recover the schemes of action that work within the juridical principle. In other words, one must insert into the juridical principle such elements that one can tactically – through different strategic filters – either combine and conjoin in order to make them intensify each other, or dissociate from each other in order to make the one displace the other. One must insert the principles of the general good *and* the rule of law.

The following analysis of *Bouchereau* presents the tactical choices and combinations made by the participants between these different principles of justification during the course of their argumentative manoeuvres. At the general level, it should be noted that the obligatory reference to the principles of justification in the field of legal practice produces a very real effect that extends beyond the effects sought by strategically oriented actors. This real effect realises objective interests of justice, perhaps not with respect to so many particular substantive points under dispute, but at the very least with respect to the requirement of justification as such – as the compulsory mode of action of legal practice – imposed on actors.

It is another matter that, with the obligatory production of justification, the actors' engagement in discourse may even have an effect on the goals and morale of the actors themselves. Even where these remain intact, the field of law at any event traps the actors entering it in an exclusive space of transparency. In legal practice, one works on and takes into account only what the participants have made visible in the proceedings. In a space of transparency, any hidden agenda often fails insofar as it must remain hidden.

Second level: antagonism between law and order

The level at which Foucault made his expositions on the functioning of strategic logic – 'the logic of connections between the heterogeneous and not the logic of the homogenization of the contradictory' (Foucault 2008: 42) – was that of historically interconnecting fields and practices. He tried to show how social practices are stitched together in that they combine different types of power and different types of knowledge. Foucault focused on the ways in which practices hold together and conjoin disparate rationalities and institutions, disparate theoretical types of knowledge and applied sciences (Foucault 2008: 42–43). Between these his genealogical analyses reconstruct 'a whole network of alliances, communications and points of support' (Foucault 2007a: 117). For Foucault, taking the 'point of view of power is a way of identifying intelligible relations between elements that are external to each other' (Foucault 2007a: 215).

The meaning of this is that Foucault's treatment of his materials was always *transversal*, crossing through the boundaries of different discursive practices and different social institutions. In *The Will to Knowledge*, Foucault had the juridical mechanism of power provisionally as something that gives importance 'to the problem of right and violence, law and illegality, freedom and will, and especially the state and sovereignty'. With respect to this mechanism, Foucault's claim is that 'it has gradually been penetrated by quite new mechanisms of power that are probably irreducible to the representation of law'. Therefore, one must add to the so-called expulsion thesis (according to which 'the historical gradient' has made the law lose its hold on the reality of the exercise of power) another thesis: the *penetration thesis*. Mechanisms and strategies foreign to law can work through legal institutions (Foucault 1998b: 89).

In the following analysis, the penetration thesis will be conceived on the basis of the foregoing reading of Foucault's theory of the generalisation of war, on the one hand, and his final conviction about the irreconcilable antagonism between law and order. In the *Bouchereau* case, the penetration into legal discourse of elements pertaining to keeping order can be made perceptible. But not that alone: the case file also makes visible the reverse penetration of the mechanisms of law into mechanisms of order. This is not a confrontation situation between individual adversaries, but the permanent antagonism of regimes that goes on beneath these battles between individuals.

In what follows, these regimes will be called the legal system, on the one hand, and the security system on the other hand. Immigration administration and control, whatever the institutional arrangement within which they are carried out, belong to the security system. These apparatuses house the rationality and mechanisms of security. In the antagonism between order and law (or between the state's order and the juridical system) immigration administration and control stand for order, the state's order. In the case of *Bouchereau*, that antagonism is activated when the state's order enters the other house, the ECJ as an apparatus for the practice of law, an apparatus that houses the juridical system.

'Heats' in the legal contestation on Bouchereau

The following analysis of *Bouchereau* will be organised into three different 'heats', demonstrating confrontation situations between three sets of pairs. The possibilities for carrying out this kind of demonstration with *Bouchereau* are much better than they were with *Royer*. In *Royer*, each of the three participants came from the Community institutional structure and played a role only in the procedural stage of the preliminary ruling. It was a perfect setting for dialectical logic, that is, for 'the homogenization of the contradictory' that 'promises their resolution in unity', to use Foucault's terminology (Foucault 2008: 42).

By contrast, in *Bouchereau* there are six different perspectives that, first, represent a variety of interests and come from all the different stages of the life-cycle of the case. Secondly, they present sharply opposing views, but in a way that conjoins elements from the disparate systems of law and order, and deploy the principles of justification in a way that the one is made to intensify the other. *Bouchereau* is a perfect setting for making perceptible the strategic logic that 'establishes the possible connections between contradictory terms', by the deployment of which the litigants make these 'connections between the heterogeneous' serve their strategic aims (Foucault 2008: 42).

Pierre Bourdieu has noted that the 'practical meaning of law is really only determined in the confrontation between different bodies (e.g. judges, lawyers, solicitors) moved by different specific interests' (Bourdieu 1987: 820–21). The analysis of *Bouchereau* that follows will be a presentation of this kind of confrontation, which determines the practical meaning of law. This will be carried out by presenting the strategies and tactics of the different participants in three pairs, so that each pair forms 'a heat' (a round, a set) in the following manner.

First, there will be the dispute between the parties to the main proceedings, that is, to the criminal case before the Marlborough Street Magistrates' Court in London that originated the request for a preliminary ruling. There are the two litigants: Mr Bouchereau, the defendant, and the Metropolitan Police that conducted his prosecution. The interests of these parties were simple: the Metropolitan Police wanted to have Mr Bouchereau expelled, while Mr Bouchereau wanted to stay in the UK.

Secondly, there will be the dispute between the Commission and the UK Government. The interests represented at this level, the 'national interest' of a Member State and the 'Community interest' of the Commission, are more general and overlapping than the particular and antagonistic interests of the prosecutor and the accused person at the previous level. The Community and the Member States, insofar as the latter form any kind of unity, are of course not in all matters against each other. With differing emphases, both still care for the legitimacy and functionality of the EC system as a whole.

As for the case at hand, however, we know that the UK, at the time at least, had among the political actors of the EC the most critical attitude towards European integration. Among other things, the UK was of the opinion that it was paying too much of the Community's expenses and demanded 'renegotiation' of their distribution. In Britain there had been, at least since the Labour Party victory in the elections of 1974, serious consideration of the UK's possible resignation from the Community. Furthermore, one of the political historians of the Community observes that the 'continuing saga of Britain's "renegotiation" epitomised the Community's malaise' that prevailed throughout the 1970s (Dinan 1994: 90). For the Commission, of course, this malaise and British recalcitrance was something to be overcome, as progression of European integration was for the Commission the only and the ultimate goal – the very purpose of its existence.

Thirdly, there will be the dispute between the Advocate General, on the one hand, and the judges on the other. While designation of this round as a 'dispute' might be somewhat misleading, it is perhaps true that advocates general, whose task it is to assist the judges, also play their game in certain senses against the judges.

Maybe it is not entirely wrong to presume that an internal game goes on over the *orthos doxa* of Community law – a game played by displays of symbolic capital, wit and erudition – between the holders of these two offices. It is a fact, however, that advocates general and judges always have the last word, in which they can embrace the arguments of previously performing participants. Therefore, someone might say that it is better not to depict their contributions as belonging to the contest at all, but constituting the final stage of refereeing at which winners are chosen.

However, there is confrontation here too, albeit not in the same way as in the earlier heats. This heat is the point of junction at which the permanent antagonism, the permanent controversy, between *order and law* becomes most clearly visible. The word 'permanent' should be taken seriously: the Advocate General and the judges cannot stop this antagonism, because there they are not the referees, but only standing on one side of a fundamental conflict. Therefore, it is not one's part at this point to be as objective and neutral as possible; one's part is to be 'willing to remain at his post and to defend himself against the enemy without running away'; we are no longer witnessing a legal trial, but a trial of the law itself, where its 'endurance of the soul' is contested through the performance of the Advocate General and the judges (Plato, *Laches*: 190e, 192c).

Facts of *Bouchereau*

Mr Pierre Roger André Bouchereau was a French national, who worked as a motor mechanic in the United Kingdom. In December 1975, at the age of 19, he was caught in possession of amphetamine and cannabis. For this offence, he was 'conditionally discharged' for 12 months in January 1976. This kind of sentence means that the offender is released, but if another offence is committed during the time of conditional discharge, the offender will be sentenced for both offences at once. Very soon, in March 1976, Mr Bouchereau was again caught in possession of drugs: this time it was LSD and amphetamine. This offence was dealt with before the Marlborough Street Metropolitan Stipendiary Magistrate in London, a regular court for criminal matters. He was found guilty in June 1976, but sentence was deferred because questions of EC law were raised (at 2001, 2016).

The questions of EC law did not concern the criminal proceedings themselves but were the consequence of the fact that, in the UK, criminal courts had a role in carrying out the administrative control of immigrants. In this instance, the criminal court had powers to recommend to the Secretary of State that an offender it had found guilty of crime should be expelled from the country. By its formal nature, this measure was of the type of consultative opinion in an administrative matter, rather than part of the judicial decision in the principal criminal matter; as a recommendation it was not formally binding. The recommendation had not yet materialised in *Bouchereau*, but the criminal court was merely 'minded' at the end of the proceedings, presumably by the prosecutor, to make such a recommendation (at 2001). At this point, Mr Bouchereau claimed his rights under Article 48 of TEC, and submitted that his deportation, as well as the recommendation to that effect, would be illegal (at 2022).

The Marlborough Street Magistrates' Court in London decided in November 1976 to request a preliminary ruling from the ECJ and, after the question concerning the grant of legal aid for Bouchereau before the ECJ was sorted out, the request was finally received at the ECJ registry in March 1977 (at 2001–2002). Interestingly, during those couple of months, namely in January 1977, Mr Bouchereau was in fact granted his first residence permit in the United Kingdom (at 2026).

The first of the three questions posed by the Marlborough Street Magistrates' Court in London concerned its own function in the administrative expulsion procedure, which I will not discuss. Let us note, however, that the mesh of the two systems (security and law) was already present at that level: a juridical court was integrated in, and put in the service of, the immigration administration in the UK. I will concentrate here on the other two questions put forward by the Marlborough Street Metropolitan Stipendiary Magistrate. They are, once again, about the concepts of personal conduct and *ordre public*. The first question asked (at 2001):

> Whether the wording of Article 3(2) of Directive 221/64/EEC, namely that previous criminal convictions 'in themselves' shall not constitute grounds for the taking of measures based on *ordre public* [a] means that previous criminal convictions are solely relevant in so far as they manifest a present or future propensity to act in a manner contrary to *ordre public*; [b] alternatively the meaning to be attached to the expression 'in themselves' [in the said provision].

The second question asked (at 2001):

> Whether the words '*ordre public*' in Article 48(3) of the Treaty Establishing the European Economic Community upon the ground of which the limitations to the rights granted by Article 48 must be justified, are to be interpreted:
>
> (a) as including reasons of state, even where no breach of the public peace or order is threatened; or
> (b) in a narrower sense in which is incorporated the concept of some threatened breach of public peace, order or security; or
> (c) in some other wider sense?

Let us make these questions a bit simpler. The first question was centred on *personal conduct*: what is the relation of immigration administration to penal power? The second question concerned *ordre public*: what is the scope and width of the powers of the security system?

Tactical reversals

In Mr Bouchereau's and the Metropolitan Police's choices one perceives operations that will be called *tactical reversals*. To begin with, Mr Bouchereau places his discussion of the notion of personal conduct entirely in the context of the state's order and security system, where the principle of the general good supports him negatively: no general good would follow from him being expelled, because he would not behave badly in the future. Turning to the notion of *ordre public*, Mr Bouchereau reverses his former tactics. *Ordre public* must be articulated to and confined by the juridical system of strictly defined powers, which narrows down its scope. This time the principle of the rule of law supports Mr Bouchereau and replaces the principle of general good. The Metropolitan Police, in turn, perform the same tactical operations but exactly the opposite way. Personal conduct is referred to the juridical system and the rule of law where it is equivalent to criminal acts that must be punished. Coming to the notion of *ordre public*, however, the reference for the Metropolitan police will be the security system, where the principle of general good justifies the wide powers this system affords to authorities.

Looking at the confrontation situation between Mr Bouchereau and the Metropolitan Police as a whole, there are four different problematisations altogether, all of which operate by separation of the juridical system from the security system. In this separation, one or the other of the principles of justification can be inserted, but not both, it seems. As far as it goes, the one principle may be used only if it excludes the other. A rule of law argument is never a general good argument, and vice versa. Let us see in a little more detail how the parties develop their tactical turns.

Mr Bouchereau's view on the question of personal conduct with respect to previous criminal convictions was somewhat different in the representations he made before the criminal court in London and later before the ECJ. In London, Mr Bouchereau had stated that previous criminal convictions 'were solely relevant in so far as they manifested a present or future intention to act in a manner contrary to *ordre public*' (at 2022). The immigration authorities should examine his *intentions*, upon which they would find that he does not intend to continue drug use and possession in the future. Before the ECJ, Mr Bouchereau dropped the notion of intention and replaced it with propensity, which accords to the wording of the preliminary ruling request of the London criminal court. Not intention, but propensity must be evident. As evidence of propensity, a person's past criminal conduct is only one aspect in the overall assessment of the probabilities about his future conduct. Past conduct and future conduct are separate, which also separates the two systems: legal systems assess past conduct, whereas security systems assess future conduct (at 2007).

Having made this distinction between the two assessments, between past and future, Mr Bouchereau would now insert his argument from the principle of general good: the security system must look into the 'likelihood of present or future propensity to act again in a harmful manner'; past action alone can no longer be harmful. The mere 'fact of criminal conviction' in the past cannot be 'sufficient to justify deportation'. One must distinguish between the two systems, because otherwise Member States could 'use *ordre public* for the punishment of criminals rather than for the protection of the State' (at 2007).

Punishing is one thing and protecting the state is another. Expulsions pertain to protection of the state and cannot be used for the purposes of punishment. Otherwise individuals could be punished twice for the same thing. However, the tactic was not to invoke the traditional rule of law argument of *ne bis in idem* (ban on double punishment). Instead, Mr Bouchereau emphasised that it is not at all in the nature of the security system to punish. His change of vocabulary makes this even clearer. 'Intention' would have been a notion of penal law, while 'propensity' belongs to the security administration. Unlike in its common usage, where intention refers to future potentialities, in the criminal law context intention is a phenomenon of the past. On the basis of a reconstruction of past intention, culpability can be retrospectively ascribed to the perpetrator of an offence. Moreover, intention implies agency, whereas propensity really does not. Individual agency and its absence is one of the things that marks a difference between the legal system and the security system.

The Metropolitan Police disagreed strongly. They maintained that 'there is nothing in Community legislation' to support the views of Mr Bouchereau. While it is true that criminal convictions 'in themselves' do not form grounds for taking security measures, it is not true that both systems could not operate at the same time and in a similar way. The idea of the personal conduct requirement is simply to 'ensure that the facts or actions giving rise to the conviction are examined'. In other words, the security authorities must re-examine the case, revisiting personal conduct from the point of view of *ordre public* (at 2004).

What is this point of view from which personal conduct must be assessed? It transpires that it is exactly the same as the point of view of penal law: punishments will have to follow past offences, however harmless the person will be in the future. The penal system and the security system are not mutually exclusive, but must work alongside each other. In both systems, past conduct alone must form the basis on which security measures are to be taken. At this point the Metropolitan Police inserted the rule of law as a principle of justification by making it clear that the ultimate reason behind their interpretation was *justice*.

On the one hand, if general good would apply exclusively, Member States would be prevented from expelling any perpetrator, even one who had committed 'the most heinous breach of *ordre public* or public security as long as it has not been shown that the individual concerned may commit a future breach' (at 2004). On the other hand, in the view of the Metropolitan Police it would moreover not stand to reason that the perpetrator of a crime may not be deported, while: '[. . .] a person who has not previously been convicted of a criminal offence but whose personal conduct nevertheless infringes *ordre public* or public security may be deported without any need to consider the future danger which he represents' (at 2004).

For the Metropolitan Police, offences against criminal law and offences against *ordre public* are not different by quality, but only by gravity. Lesser offences violate *ordre public*, while graver ones violate the law. In any event, the Metropolitan Police would have accepted neither the argument of double punishment, nor any radical functional separation of the two systems. Both function at the same time and in the same way, which is the juridical way. The Metropolitan Police did not consider future propensities at all, not even in the absence of criminal convictions: offenders against *ordre public* could be deported by the juridical logic of pure retribution. The Metropolitan Police did not endorse what Mr Bouchereau purported to be the special nature or the essential and exclusive attribute of the security system – namely, fear for future safety.

In their discussion of the notion of personal conduct, both parties have now established their initial tactical positions. One party (Mr Bouchereau) wanted to play by the rules of the security system and inserted there his principle of the general good. The other party (the Metropolitan Police) wanted to play by the rules of the criminal law system and inserted there the principle of the rule of law. In the practice of law it seems that different parties can actually play entirely different games. The game of law is about succeeding in imposing one's own game upon the other players.

Moving now to the second question, that of *ordre public*, one will see how both parties reverse their initial tactical positions and switch to another position. At the heart of the question of *ordre public* is the balancing between the powers of Member States and the protection of EC nationals. The wider the scope of the notion of *ordre public*, the more are powers vested in Member States and consequently less in the protection of EC nationals. Therefore, Mr Bouchereau's tactic had to be to argue for the narrowest possible meaning of *ordre public*, whereas the Metropolitan Police would argue for the widest possible meaning.

Mr Bouchereau began by submitting that the concept of *ordre public* incorporates 'the concept of a threatened breach of public peace, order or security'. His own past possession of drugs should first have to be considered as constituting a threat sufficiently grave to society in order to have him removed from the country. Mr Bouchereau's conclusion would be that no threats existed, or at least they were not grave enough. This conclusion emerges, Mr Bouchereau continued, from the case law of the ECJ. That case law had established the doctrine of strict interpretation of derogations from the rights entailed by freedom of movement, because those rights are fundamental to the system (at 2008).

One perceives that Mr Bouchereau at this point no longer referred to the system of security, but to the juridical system. Strict interpretation of derogations means wide interpretation of rights. The wider the rights, the more confined the powers and the narrower the scope of *ordre public*. In other words, Mr Bouchereau inserted the rule of law as a principle of justification to *this* question, which excludes the principle of general good that he had used in the *earlier* question. The rule of law requires, among other things, that the powers of the authorities are determined and limited substantially.

Unlike the rule of law, the general good would merely instruct the authorities to act in whichever way that served the public interest. Unsurprisingly, justification by general good was endorsed by the Metropolitan Police. On that basis, the Metropolitan Police maintained that the scope of *ordre public* is much wider than Mr Bouchereau suggested. 'Member States cannot determine unilaterally the scope', the Metropolitan Police admitted, but 'nevertheless they are not bound to restrict it to the concept of public security or to the criminal law'. Having thus stepped out of the space limited according to the rule of law, the Metropolitan Police inserted the other principle: Member States may give *ordre public* 'a meaning approximate to the concept of public good' (at 2005).

So it is public good, *salus populi*, not because this is the fundamental rule of governing, but because thereby *ordre public* is in this situation given the widest possible scope of application, to the extent that the powers of the Members States would remain almost unrestricted. Taken as a political philosophical concept, *salus populi* does not bind authorities in the way that legal rules and principles do but, on the contrary, legitimises their action when it would otherwise be legally dubious. Even without these Ciceroan pretensions, drugs would certainly fall under the concept of public good, and thereby under the concept of *ordre public*.

Clearly, the parties are again playing different games. Mr Bouchereau drew on the principle of the rule of law and juridical system, whereas the Metropolitan Police wished, to say the least, to minimise its consequences by invoking the principle of public good. Mr Bouchereau invoked strict interpretation of *ordre public* and hence strict limits on powers, whereas the Metropolitan Police invoked public good as the supreme law in the area of security administration. Mr Bouchereau played the game of the legal system, while the Metropolitan Police played the game of the security system.

Regarding the first heat as a whole, the remarkable point is that when moving from the first question – personal conduct – to the second question – *ordre public* – both parties switched to another game, or rather exchanged games with each other. As for the first question Mr Bouchereau played the game of the security system and the Metropolitan Police that of the legal system, but coming to the second question it was the other way around. The choice between principles of justification was filtered according to these tactical reversals.

Two strategies: juridification and purification

The above discussion presented certain tactical combinations that worked on the basis of an analytical distinction between the juridical system and the security system. Turning to the confrontation between the Commission and the UK Government, it will be possible to analyse movements in somewhat deeper layers. By using principles of justification in a certain way, the logics of the two systems can penetrate each other. These penetrations will be called the strategy of juridification and the strategy of purification. Juridification of the security system was the strategy of the Commission, whereas purification was the strategy of the UK Government.

The Commission conceded that 'it has so far not been possible to define any Community concept' of *ordre public*. All the same, it 'emerges' from the case law of the Court that *ordre public* is a 'restricted' concept when it is brought to bear on expulsions. This restrictedness appears in the first place by certain exclusions of areas from the scope of the concept of *ordre public* (at 2003).

National interests in the area of economic policy are explicitly prohibited by EC law as *ordre public* grounds (Article 2(2) of Directive 64/221). For example, Member States cannot deport Europeans because there are many unemployed nationals, irrespective of the disturbance that this fact may cause to *ordre public*. Next, the area of 'undisclosed reasons of state' must be prohibited by implication: the security system must not operate in secrecy because this would shield it against all substantial legal control. Lastly, also excluded are 'areas in which *ordre public* can be adequately protected by the application of criminal sanctions'. The criminal justice system must prevail over the security system: the legal consequence for transgressions of law should not be expulsion, but penal sanction passed by the same standard that applies to nationals (at 2004).

These exclusions mean juridification in a specific sense. They purport to move Europeans under the protection of the principle of the rule of law by liberating them from the security system. That is, policy-making governed by the principle of the general good (which moreover is not the general good of non-nationals, but the general good of nationals) is no longer possible with respect to Europeans.

The idea of this juridification strategy is to move people from one system to another, but another strategy was also applied by the Commission. The Commission made the juridical system penetrate the security system itself, by inserting the principle of the rule of law into its very entrails. To carry out this juridification strategy, the Commission employed the derogation doctrines developed in human rights law and in the constitutional adjudication of basic rights. These doctrines explain not what must in particular be excluded, but what the concept of *ordre public* may only include: '[. . .] enacted, or otherwise clearly defined, measures which are necessary in a democratic society for the protection of public order or safety or for the protection of rights and freedoms and where a substantial and present threat to *ordre public* exists through the anti-social personal conduct of a particular individual' (at 2004).

This strategy of juridification strikes at the heart of the security system by confining its room for manoeuvre by the requirements of the principle of the rule of law: (1) *clearly defined measures*, (2) *necessary in a democratic society*, (3) *protection of rights and freedoms*. The objective of this juridification strategy is that the security system, when it deals with Europeans, should be subjected to the principle of the rule of law. In effect, the reign of the principle of the general good should be over.

The response of the UK Government to this was a counter-strategy of purification. This strategy was not to invoke the special nature of the security administration, but rather to undermine the juridical system within its own essence, where it invoked elements of legal practice that always resist the force of the rule of law. The strategy of the UK Government can be reconstructed as proceeding by three steps: a plurality argument, a singularity argument and, finally, insertion of the principle of the general good.

The concept of *ordre public* is not restricted, but open. Reiterating what the ECJ had said in its judgment in *van Duyn,* the UK Government stated that circumstances in which *ordre public* may be threatened are always particular circumstances, and they vary from one country to another. This kind of pluralism is inherent in the concept of *ordre public* for the UK Government, and the effect of pluralism is that 'the Member States have an area of discretion when invoking the concept of *ordre public*'. No wall-to-wall definition is possible at the level of legislation, which is why the principle of the rule of law has no rigorous application in the assessment of what sort of things may come into question (at 2007).

The next turn is the argument of singularity, which is carried out by tactically reversing the function of the personal conduct requirement. In Article 3 of Directive 64/221, the function of this requirement is to *limit* the powers of Member State authorities so that expulsion measures cannot be taken because of some general policy-making objectives (such as deterrence of the immigrant population living in the country; see the discussion of *Bonsignore* in Chapter 2).

In the treatment of the UK Government, this requirement is subjected to total conversion: it *widens* the area of discretion and relieves the authorities from legal bounds. The personal conduct requirement in fact justifies handling each individual on a case-by-case basis, and therefore it not only undermines, but rules out the rule of law. Consequently, any 'greater precision in defining the concept of *ordre public* is neither possible nor necessary, since each case must be looked at in the light of its own circumstances'. The rule of law – that is, the command of generally applicable and unambiguous norms – is not possible because the law itself excludes this by demanding singularity (at 2007).

Having established plurality and singularity, the UK Government could complete its manoeuvre by inserting the principle of the general good. It transpires that 'the concept of *ordre public* must be understood in the wide sense as including measures adopted to counteract activities which are merely socially harmful without amounting to an actual breach of public peace, order or security' (at 2007). While for the Metropolitan Police it was public good, for the UK Government it is *social harm* that defined the meaning of *ordre public*. If possible, this definition is even more destructive to the principle of the rule of law: not only drugs, but indeed anything can be socially harmful under the conditions of plurality and singularity.

In conclusion of the foregoing, there is again a selection of tactical choices; this time, however, in somewhat more complex combinations. For the Commission, *ordre public* excludes considerable areas from the operation of the security system, and where it still operates, the principle of the rule of law is inserted. This is juridification, penetration of juridical reason into the administration of immigration.

For the UK Government, in turn, *ordre public* is an open concept that allows wide powers to be exercised on a case-by-case basis. In this strategy, it should be noted, the UK Government was actually working with structural elements that belong to the field of legal practice itself. On the one hand, any legal concept is in principle semantically open to the plurality argument, because the meaning of words cannot be totally fixed. On the other hand, fairness to the facts of the case can always be invoked in the practice of law. Generally speaking, the UK Government fought the law with the law itself, to counteract the Commission's strategy of juridification and to cleanse the field from the principle of the rule of law. The strategic objective of the one was to paralyse the security system; the objective of the other was to paralyse the juridical system.

Deep public revulsion

The foregoing presented attempts to force one system's principle of justification inside the other system, which can be called strategies of penetration. In the next, some more subtle amalgamations take place. These amalgamations emerge in a discussion that still revolves around the two systems, immigration control and penal power. To begin with, we must ask: What do we need to know about penal power?

Penal power is exercised through criminal law, which both constitutes and confines that power. In criminal law there are two absolutely elementary requirements: the principle of legality (*nulla poena sine lege*) and the principle that there has to have been an act (*actus reus*). Without a provision in law, on the one hand, and an act of offence, on the other hand, there is no criminal case. The basic argumentation tactics of the litigants and prosecutors in a criminal law case is to interpret the definitions of offences in penal laws and to describe the factual acts and omissions. Crimes are actual transgressions that must lead to penalties.

For the Commission, the difference between the security system and the system of criminal law lies in that offences committed do not automatically lead to security measures. The conduct of the individual will have to manifest 'a present or future propensity' in the person in question. Past conduct 'can only be relevant in so far as they provide supplementary proof that the personal conduct of an individual constitutes a grave and existing danger to *ordre public*' (at 2003). There is nothing new about this, because it was all established in the previous case law of the ECJ.

The UK Government presented a different reading of the previous case law, which leads to something that could be called the archaeology of penal power. Unlike the Metropolitan Police, the UK Government concedes that future threats to *ordre public* and public security are the issue. Therefore, the type of assessment pertaining to the security system, not the criminal law system, will have to be the basis. Despite having set out on this basis, the UK Government's strategy was to make certain elements movable between the criminal law system and the security system. The first of these movements comes about in the UK Government's development of standards for assessing the relevance of conduct – criminal or otherwise – from the future-oriented point of view of *ordre public*.

> The nature and gravity of the offence, the circumstances in which it was committed and how recently it has been committed, may be a guide to the future behaviour of the individual and, in particular, to the likelihood of his committing further offences. (at 2006)

The standard suggested by the UK Government for assessing future behaviour sounds very much like the standards for measuring punishment in criminal law. These latter standards explain the circumstances that mitigate or aggravate the sentence. This would show that the security system may very well borrow certain things from criminal law, but it also shows that security considerations pertaining to the future are not entirely foreign to criminal law either. Future threats and dangers to the security system have their counterpart in criminal law assessment of the probability of recidivism. This does not yet imply that the two systems function in the same way: they would just borrow elements from each other, but there is no convergence at this point.

The second move by the UK Government, however, invoked a novelty that would eventually suggest, in rather strange way, a profound convergence between the two systems. The UK Government had carefully studied the wording of the Court in *Rutili* and found that, according to the text of that judgment, personal conduct is not absolutely necessary at all. The judges in *Rutili* had stipulated that restrictions cannot be imposed on an EC national 'unless his *presence* or conduct' constitutes a threat to *ordre public*.[1] Leaning on this wording, the UK Government explained that there 'may be circumstances in which the threats to *ordre public* or public security are not committed by the person concerned but are caused or occasioned by his presence in the State' (at 2006). In such cases even the existence of the individual, the UK Government explained, may be a source of 'such deep public revulsion that *ordre public* requires his departure' (at 2022).

First, it seems that with its reference to deep public revulsion the UK Government carries the logic of the security system to the utmost and departs rather drastically from the logic of the criminal law. However, on second thoughts, is this really nothing but a reinvigoration of an ancient idea? This idea considers punishment as a healing or appeasement of the community from certain type of evils that will ravage it until wrongs and immoralities are rectified. To borrow a word from Sophocles, the presence of a stained individual creates *miasmas* in the community.[2] This has nothing to do with assessing the individual's future conduct; his mere presence is dangerous.

For the UK Government, threats to *ordre public* are not restricted to those posed by the probable future conduct of the European individual. This brings the security system closer again to criminal law that works on the basis of retribution. More important, however, is the subtle infusion of ancient elements that seem to be working underneath the UK Government's operation. Emotional tumults in the people, which may grow into riot and chaos, are also something that criminal laws have always had to screen away from view. Here lies also the systemic convergence that the UK Government's submission seems to suggest. When the security system is tasked with administering people's deep public revulsions, it in fact carries out something that the penal power is about as well: maintenance of order.

The UK Government's view in any event is that any future *actus* is not required, because expulsion is not a retributive punishment, but a proactive security measure. What unfolds at the same time, however, is the glint of an idea according to which, deep down, retributive punishment is a proactive security measure as well. A vision opened to some archaeological sediment where deep-structural hybridisation, if you will, has taken place. But can this sediment still have effects on today's legal life? Let us ask, once again, what we need to know about penal power? After all, it is not enough to know about the two great elements, *nulla poena sine lege* and *actus reus*. There is more to know. Perpetrators of crimes are punished, but why? Is it because they need to be rectified, or because of the general preventive effect, or because of the disorder created in society by deep public revulsion?

Ordre public and the rule of law

As discussed above, we were already moving away from the level of strategies and tactics, at which the field of legal practice is a field for confrontational situations. In that field, the law provides the grammar that not only constitutes the reality of singular battles but also confines and regulates the way in which actors must carry out their actions: production of justifications. As long as the field exists, every command will meet there a corresponding countermand; it is a field of obstinate insubordination, resistance and recalcitrance. At this point, however, we have entered another kind of struggle, a struggle for the existence of the legal field, where the juridical system must be defended against its permanent antagonist in the general field of power: order.

The frontier between law and order is perhaps a constantly moving one, but it nonetheless should keep the different forces on their own side of the barrier. With such peculiar sounding ideas as deep public revulsion, however, one can hear echoes, not perhaps of the original unity of the two, but at least of some undying conquests or inroads that order has made into law. It is very important to pay attention to these echoes, because they tell about the more 'silent thoughts' of law: law is silently thinking order. Therefore, the contest between law and order has to be taken at once as a tribulation internal to law, where the law fights not only order, but also itself. The next question is whether the Advocate General and the judges can regain and reliberate these conquests, and whether they manage to make the law think differently.

The Advocate General seems not to have rejected the view of the UK Government. He accepted that in certain circumstances a person's acts can cause deep public revulsion. As a general rule, the kind of conduct that would show 'a particular propensity' for dangerous antisocial behaviour is relevant and required for a use of *ordre public* measures (at 2022). Exceptionally, however, past conduct alone can constitute a sufficient *ordre public* ground for expulsion, even when 'not necessarily evincing any clear propensity' (at 2022). In that case, a security threat is not posed by the future action of an individual, but by the reaction of the crowd to his or her past action. It is really a matter of governing the national population, not foreigners. The Advocate General depicted the underlying morale as follows: 'I think that in such a case a Member State may exclude a national from its territory, just as a man may exclude from his house a guest, even a relative, who has behaved in an excessively offensive fashion' (at 2022).

Indirectly, the criminal law logic of retribution applies in the security system too, although it is now apprehended through the security risks caused by the reactions of the civic body that express the exigencies of collective sentiment. Seeing, with Durkheim, that the legal apparatus of criminal justice should govern this very same sentiment – by reinforcing and satiating the revivals of the *conscience collective* in its disapproving marvels at crime spectacles – one is reminded that judiciary institutions there have a specific security function (Durkheim 1997: I:II). They should control the collective surges of emotion caused by individual insults to common morality. The waxing and waning of popular discontent are a real political force, and the one area in which this force is even more powerfully present than in criminal policy is immigration policy and control.

The train of thought that the UK Government brought to light, and which was in principle accepted by the Advocate General, is not only about some peculiar and isolated amalgam of the criminal law system and the security system. It unfolds the concealment of certain elements of penal power, elements which by nature pertain to a system foreign to the criminal law, or at least its humanist-legalist ideology that considers criminal law to constitute liberty in that it checks arbitrary violence in the exercise of penal power. The archaeological finding in the *Bouchereau* case – let us call it the theory of *miasma* – suggests that deep down the legal system also secures the interests of *ordre public* and can even converge with it.

The Advocate General was not happy with this. He needed to tackle the issue of *ordre public* legally, but found neither Community law nor English law very helpful. Common law judges, for example, would describe this concept as an 'unruly horse' (at 2025). Therefore, the Advocate General turned to the juris-dictions of the six founding Member States of the Community. In his exposition of the Continental use of *ordre public*, the Advocate General relied on an article by a French professor of labour law, Gérard Lyon-Caen.[3] On the basis of that article, brought up in the proceedings by Mr Bouchereau, the Advocate General could elaborate an illuminating exposition of the problem of *ordre public* in the overall systematics of the law. Professor Lyon-Caen had separated three different legal branches in which *ordre public* is used and, respectively, three different operations that can be carried out with it.

The first of these branches of law is private international law. In this area, invocation of *ordre public* serves, typically, to negate or invalidate some private law arrangement (eg contract, marriage/divorce, distribution of an inheritance) that has been or should be carried out according to a foreign legal system. Even if foreign law would normally be applicable according to the domestic rules for resolving conflicts of laws, a particular arrangement made on the basis of foreign law is not valid if something in it runs counter to the *ordre public* of the domestic legal system. A typical example would perhaps be some racist or gender bias in it. Here the notion of *ordre public*, the Advocate General observes, is clearly not one 'of Government but of the law, developed by the Courts' (at 2025). Thus, *ordre public* is likened to the elementary values enshrined in the foundations of a legal system, values that simply may not be compromised.[4]

The second area is that of public law, where the concept of *ordre public* operates to justify exceptions to the norms of domestic law. Exceptions are then necessitated by some overriding demands of general interest that constitute situations in which *ordre public* measures, restraining or waiving normal liberties, must be taken *au nom d'exigences supérieures* (at 2025). As an example of this, one might think that limiting the right of medical personnel to take strike action is justified by urgent exigency if a strike would lead to large scale mortal danger in the situation. Unlike the *ordre public* of private international law, this *ordre public* is a notion of government, not of law. Common to the operation of these notions, however, is that they both 'make an exception to whatever legal rule would normally apply' (at 2025).

The third branch that makes use of the concept of *ordre public* is the control of immigrants ('*police des étrangers*'). In the legal organisation of this area the concept of *ordre public* has a position that is profoundly different from either of the two previous areas: 'Reliance on "l'ordre public" is there no longer the exception but the very foundation of the law. It is seen as justifying the exercise by the executive of a virtually unlimited discretion" (at 2025).

Whereas at the two earlier points *ordre public* is used for justifying exceptions and derogations from the law, be it foreign or national law, in immigration law *ordre public* is the pervasive rationale of the entire system. In other words, *ordre public* is the law of the security system. This rationale embraces the use of such notions as 'public good', 'general interest' and 'social harm' in all situations, from start to finish. This has no connection whatsoever with something such as the exceptional and superior necessity that has no laws (*necessitas legem non habet*), as in public law. Nor is it the case that *ordre public* would reflect the fundamental norms and principles of the juridical system, as in private international law. In immigration law, which nonetheless is a branch of law, *ordre public* is the *suprema lex*.

For Professor Lyon-Caen the use of *ordre public* in immigration law had appeared so different from its use elsewhere in the legal system that he had preferred, in his article, to define it as '*un ordre public "special"*'. This special use of the concept of *ordre public* also marks the special ground of immigration law as such. The operation of *ordre public* in immigration law and policy is not that this concept can be made special use of in this branch of law. Instead, the operation of *ordre public* is fundamental; it constitutes the law. So there is an island in the legal system that is not constituted by the law in the normal way, but by something alien to it.

Constituted by order, the law of the *metoikos* (those who change dwelling) is an ancient conquest of the security system in the field of law (at 2025).

The foundational operation of *ordre public* in the special context of immigration law is crucial for grasping the situation of new-born Europeans. The special concept of *ordre public*, Professor Lyon-Caen had concluded, is something the EEC Treaty 'must be taken to have abolished'. The Advocate General agrees fully. Unlike in the *ordre public* that underlies immigration law, the *ordre public* in the Treaty 'is to afford a ground for making an exception to the general principle of non-discrimination'. Hence, the normal use by the standard of public law applies, not the special and fundamental use (at 2025).

The Advocate General was satisfied by this movement of foundations under the European individual: from the sphere of legal speciality to the sphere of legal normality. Beyond that, however, 'the authors of the Treaty appear to have left the concept of "*ordre public*" to be defined and developed by Community secondary legislation and by decisions of this Court' (at 2025). At this point one might have expected the Advocate General to proceed accordingly. It appears, however, that he stopped dramatically short of this. The failure was the result of a wrong choice between the two ultimate principles of justification, namely the rule of law.

The Advocate General first reverted to *van Duyn*, according to which 'Member States continue to be in principle free to determine [*ordre public*] in the light of their national needs' (at 2025). However, the exercise of that freedom is 'subject to control by the institutions of the Community' (at 2026). In this order of things, the Advocate General saw that the ECJ, as a Community institution, would need to find some rule in Community law that would cover the special problem of drugs and limit the freedom of Member States in that area. In his own words, one must enquire 'whether any specific provision of Community law limits, either expressly or by necessary implication, the discretion exercisable by a member State' in a case where someone has illegally had drugs in his possession (at 2026).

Considering the overall objective (movement of European individuals from the speciality of immigration law to the normality of public law), the strategy of the rule of law failed: the Advocate General did not find any provisions in Community law that would facilitate control of the power that Member States exercise with respect to drugs. Therefore, in Mr Bouchereau's case *ordre public* 'is not to be interpreted as excluding, as a potential ground for limiting the rights [. . .], the fact of his having been found repeatedly in unlawful possession of harmful drugs' (at 2028).

Ordre public and general good

Apparently, the conclusion of the Advocate General did not satisfy the judges, who therefore chose a completely different approach. They started by making two corrections, the first of which was to straighten things up after all the tactical and strategic turns that had taken place in the proceedings. Next came the final turn, the judges' own strategy, which was to operate with the principle of the general good instead of the rule of law. The public good needed to be subtly appropriated by the juridical system: from a counter-legal principle the judges developed a legal standard, a measure for controlling the exercise of power.

The first correction concerned the implications of the personal conduct requirement. The whole problem of connections between the criminal law and security administration (and thereby between law and order) came up in the case because of a provision in Community law saying: 'Previous criminal convictions shall not in themselves constitute grounds' for the taking of *ordre public* measures (Directive 64/221, Article 3.2). According to the judges, this provision decrees 'the national authorities to carry out a specific appraisal from the point of view of the interests inherent in protecting' *ordre public*. The security administration's appraisal of threats and dangers in the context of maintenance of order 'does not necessarily coincide with the appraisals which formed the basis of the criminal conviction' (at 2012).

One must look into the 'circumstances which gave rise to that conviction' and assess whether these circumstances 'are evidence of personal conduct constituting a present threat to' *ordre public*. Looking at the facts from the point of view of *ordre public* does not always mean looking for evidence of 'a propensity to act in the same way in the future'. Future propensity would be the standard implication of the personal conduct requirement, but there may nonetheless be circumstances, the judges admit, in which 'it is possible that past conduct alone may constitute' a threat to *ordre public* (at 2012–2013).

However, the fact that the security system may have to apply this kind of quasi-retributive logic, say, in fear of retaliation by the nationals of the Member State, does not make it juridical. Nor does the law itself carry out any administration of order in the interests of security merely because it gives legal frames to that administration. This is something the law has to do with respect to any exercise of public power, not because of the common tasks of the practice of law and that power, but precisely because this is the way the law subjects the exercise of power to legal control. Finally, what emerges from the criminal justice system neither justifies nor bars expulsion of perpetrators of crimes, because the appraisals are separate and independent.

Hence, the first correction that the judges want to make is that the two systems, justice and security, must be kept rigorously apart. The appropriate apprehension is that there are two different assessment perspectives to the same material misconduct, two appraisals that have different points of view: *ordre public* and law. These points of view must not converge as schemata of practical reason and action, despite the fact that they may coincide in any facts put forward before the two systems.

The second correction of the judges came in the form of an answer to the question that 'seeks to obtain a definition of the interpretation to be given to the concept of *ordre public*' (at 2013) In effect, this answer rebuts the idea that the law itself, or any part of it, could be founded by an element dramatically foreign to the basic task of the law, which is control of power, not of individuals. More specifically, the judges had to correct the Advocate General's reading of the

Court's ruling in *van Duyn*. For the judges, this case laid down Community law vis-à-vis the *ordre public* reservation in a way exactly opposite to that of the Advocate General.

For the Advocate General, the import of *van Duyn* was principally that (1) the Member States are free to determine the content of the concept, although (2) they are under the control of Community institutions. The judges recalled that this was not the order in which these points were put by the Court in *van Duyn*. First, there is the fundamental freedom of EC nationals, and only second comes the area of discretion for Member State authorities. Thus, the starting point is not the freedom of Member States, but the freedom of individuals. Powers are restricted from the start, which means that the latitudes of the room for manoeuvre will have to be strictly limited by law (at 2013–14).

Differentiating the main rule from its exceptions could have remained mere juristic hair-splitting. This was what happened to the Advocate General's otherwise very good reading of Lyon-Caen's article: Mr Bouchereau was moved to the sphere of legal normality only in theory; no material effects followed. Insofar as to prevent the security system from making inroads into law, or to reconquer what has been lost, the law itself must counteract by confining its antagonist and circumscribe it by legal limitations. At this critical point the judges chose to strike directly at the cardinal justification used by the security system: the principle of public good.

This manoeuvre was done in the guise of the concept of *ordre public*. The judges were not exactly defining *ordre public* legally, but they gave it a legal measure. Looking at this measure very closely, it is clear that the principle of justification working in the background of the measure, the rectifying *norma* that squares things up with the system of security, is the principle of general good:

> [. . .] recourse by a national authority to the concept of *ordre public* presupposes, in any event, the existence, in addition to the perturbation of the social order which any infringement of the law involves, of a genuine and sufficiently serious threat to the requirements of *ordre public* affecting one of the fundamental interests of society. (at 2014)

A backward glimpse at previous case law helps to see how the principle of public good is changing in the background of *ordre public* and to establish where the threshold for its use lies after *Bouchereau*. In *van Duyn*, the rather modest idea of what was 'socially harmful' defined the scope of *ordre public*.[5] Social harm, as an expression of the principle of general good, does no more than justify the exercise of power. In *Rutili*, a 'genuine and sufficiently serious threat' and 'necessary in a democratic society' were added.[6] This was a radical shift in the evolution of the principle of the general good: it starts to function as a limitation on the exercise of power.

Finally, the case of *Bouchereau* inserted the further requirement that one of 'the fundamental interests of society' should be threatened.[7] Here, the threshold is set very high: the principle of general good is appropriated by the law by giving it the strictest possible form of legal proportionality testing. Seen as a whole, a metamorphosis runs from social harm to genuine and sufficiently serious threat posed to the fundamental interests of society that are necessary in a democratic society.

Moreover, what is stated in a subordinate clause is worthy of special note: *ordre public* does not apply to 'the perturbation of the social order which any infringement of the law involves'. Normal crimes are not enough, because normal crimes are simply normal in society. Criminality as such must be trivial and insignificant from the point of view of the security system, because it belongs to the daily life of any society and is handled by the criminal justice system. While giving some anxiety to the social order, any transgression of the law would not shake its fundamental interests. The threshold is set much higher for the defence of society to override the rule of law.

Conclusion: law in the general field of power

In the foregoing analysis, the counterpart of the legal field was the security system, which should be taken as one of the regimes belonging to the general field of power that surrounds the field of law, belongs to its environment. 'Environment' makes itself effective and perceptible within the field of law in numerous ways, but there it will have to adapt to the legal mode of action: provision of justifications. Analysis of the different ways in which justifications were produced took place at three different levels: those of tactics, strategies and conquests.

At the level of tactics, one saw how individual actors (Mr Bouchereau and the Metropolitan Police) may form tactical combinations between the principles of justification. The rather easy switching of positions was determined by the filters of their concrete objectives: principles of justification were a means of attaining certain ends. At the level of strategies, one saw actors (the Commission and the UK Government) representing somewhat more overarching interests. More convoluted ways of acting were contrived: principles of justification were used in ways that took into account the action of the other, which action both parties attempted to affect (juridification and purification).

At the level of conquests, one saw the different ways in which actors representing the legal system (the Advocate General and the judges) tried to defend their own base from intrusions. When defensive use by the Advocate General of the principle of the rule of law failed, the judges tried a counterattack through the principle of general good. Appropriation of the general good was a procedure used to deprive the opponent of its means of combat.

The case of *Bouchereau* and the 'military science of concepts' (Tuori 2007: ch VI) that I have applied to it, attest to what Foucault called tactical and strategic polyvalence. Polyvalence means that the same instruments can be used for entirely different purposes, which purposes may even contradict each other (Foucault 2003b: 76 and 190). At the level of legal battles, the principles of justification are polyvalent instruments. In the theory of legal practice, principles of justification will not merge into a consistent or coherent system in a way that would lay down the outcomes of practice if only the reasoning is correct. What defines the outcomes of practice is the use of those principles, not the principles themselves.

At this point, a central thesis can be presented. From the point of view of a theory of legal practice, more important than outcomes, as individual solutions to individual problems, are the effects that the law materialises in the general field of power as an *ateleological* practice. As an ateleological exercise, practice pertains to the Aristotelian notion of *energeia* (actuality), which designates 'all activities that do not pursue an end (*ateleis*) and leave no work behind (no *par' autas erga*), but exhaust their full meaning in the performance itself' (Arendt 1989: 206).

The full meaning of the principles of justification in the field of legal practice is justification as such. The fact that in the legal field one must perform justification and provide a discourse that justifies action is what differentiates legally filtered and controlled exercise of power from domination. In the general field of power, the practice of law distinguishes relations of power from relations of domination in that it provides a possibility of relative freedom: it provides a means of resistance against coercive measures, a possibility of flight from domination.

> For, if it is true that at the heart of power relations and as permanent condition of their existence there is an insubordination and a certain essential obstinacy on the part of the principles of freedom, then there is no relationship of power without the means of escape or possible flight. (Foucault 2000e: 346)

Insofar as 'the law' – in the sense of its principles of justification, and in the sense of its imperative requirement of justification – is a generalisable form of resistance, then one can say that 'the law' could have a constitutive role in the general field of power. If there were no means of resistance, the field of power would vanish and the field of domination and order would take its place. On these premises, the ongoing performance of justification forms not only the *energeia* of the practice of law, but also the *energeia* by which the general field of power is sustained. If that energy drains, the result would not be anarchy. On the contrary, the result would be a pervasive order.

The notion of order has so far been used in all too loose a manner. It has merely meant the opponent and antagonist of law, lacking any positive definition. As a matter of course, it has been present all the time in the problematisations of the concept of *ordre public*, but the difficulties that legal practice confronts in dealing with this 'unruly horse' suggests that there is something grievous behind it. In finding out what this is, the case of *Bouchereau* is especially precious: it provides a concrete point of reference to order as something that must remain subtextual in the practice of law.

This point of reference is the notion of *reason of state*. As in any research materials, the most intriguing thing is typically that which is not explicitly brought forth in the materials, something of which the material merely drops certain hints. If the material is textual, they are the things that are *not* discussed in the materials, things that remain subtextual because they are screened by the flow of speech.

Bouchereau is precious in that it makes this screening explicit: it states in clear terms what the practice of law cannot fathom.

The 'reason of state' was brought about by the British criminal court in its request for a preliminary ruling. One of its suggestions for the definition of the concept of *ordre public* was that it would include 'reasons of state, even where no breach of the public peace or order is threatened' (at 2001). This is why reason of state is mentioned in the case file in a couple of places, but always more or less in passing only. The Advocate General, however, notes especially that 'reason of state' 'is not an expression that belongs to English terminology' and that he did not 'know of any authority for its use in the context of Community law' either. Therefore, the Advocate General's advice was that 'it is an expression of such indefinite import that it is best eschewed'. The judges paid heed to this rather prudent advice and made no remarks at all on 'reason of state' (at 2023).

For an analyst who wants to take issue with the nature of order, this nearly invisible exclusion of the notion of 'reason of state' in *Bouchereau* is a breakthrough. Its steadfast expulsion from the surface level of legal discourse makes 'reason of state' all the more effective for the purposes of making sense of such kind of order that would take over if the practice of law could no longer fulfil its function of controlling the exercise of power. The next chapter will tackle the issue of 'reason of state' more thoroughly; let us at this point define it only negatively: juridical justifications do not belong to the doctrine of reason of state, which is why it engenders the absolute opposite of law, power that is pure of juridical reason.

Notes

1   *Rutili* 1231, emphasis added. 'Presence' as an alternative to conduct seems to have come from the Advocate General's opinion in the earlier case of *Bonsignore*: deportations may be ordered if the personal conduct of the individual 'constituted or was likely to constitute in the future such a threat to national *ordre public* that the *presence* of the individual concerned in the territory of the host country could no longer be tolerated' (*Bonsignore* 311, emphasis added). As an alternative to conduct, mere presence as a permitted ground is *contra legem*: Article 3 of Directive 221/64 demands explicitly that measures 'shall be based *exclusively* on personal conduct' (emphasis added).

2   In *Oedipus the King*, Thebes was cursed by *miasma* (it was defiled and polluted) because of the presence of Oedipus, who had committed patricide without knowing it. The *miasma* could be driven out only by rectifying the crime.

3   'La reserve d'ordre public en matière de liberté d'établissement et de libre circulation' (1966) Revue Trimestrielle de Droit Européen 693.

4   Similar to the *ordre public* of private international law is the *ordre public* of international procedural law. Under the latter, a judgment by a foreign court normally recognised by domestic law (and by the so-called Lugano Convention of 16 September 1988) will not be enforced if the procedure applied in the foreign court had not met the requirements fundamental to domestic procedural law.

5   *Van Duyn* 1351, 1352.

6   *Rutili* 1231, 1232.

7   *Bouchereau* 2014, 2015.

Chapter 8

Law and order

This chapter brings into the foreground the historical phenomenon of 'reason of state' to go somewhat deeper into the antagonism between law and order, which antagonism seems to be lying in the subtextual background of the cases analysed in this book – and perhaps more enduringly, in the background of European political history. As political doctrine and discourse, reason of state had a rather limited lifespan that coincided with the Renaissance. However, looking into the peculiarities of this bygone episode, a suggestion arises that certain elements of reason of state have remained effective, submerging state practices of maintenance of order. In any event, reason of state is an episode in the European history of political thought that aptly illuminates the nature of the antagonism between law and order.

A good example of reason of state is the Italian writer Giovanni Botero (1544–1617). His 1589 book on *The Reason of State* (*Della ragion di Stato*) addresses certain 'maxims of prudence' to princes, which we may take as an introduction to reason of state. The first three of Botero's maxims are the following:

> Take energetic measures at the first sign of trouble, because disorder grows and gathers strength with time. [. . .] Do not allow discussion of projects which involve any change or innovation within the state, for negotiation or discussion help such subjects to gain credit and favour however strange and pernicious they may be. [. . .] Do not neglect small disorders; for all troubles are small in their beginnings, but in the course of time they increase and lead to ruin, like barely perceptible winds which gradually become storms and fearful tempests. (Botero 1956: 41)

Botero's definition of the reason (*ragion*, 'principle') of state reads as follows: 'State is a stable rule over a people and Reason of State is the knowledge of the means by which such a dominion may be founded, preserved and extended' (Botero 1956: 3). Thus, reason of state is the constitution of a field of knowledge pertaining to the art of governing. One should note straightaway that this knowledge is not knowledge of legal laws and techniques – quite the contrary: legal knowledge is a 'considerable harm' for the knowledge on reason of state:

Laws are infinite in number, but this would not be of great importance were it not that subtle minds have discovered so many contradictions (or at least apparent contradictions), so many differing and even contrary interpretations, in short so many ways of obscuring the truth and casting doubt on what is certain [. . .]. (Botero 1956: 29)

Getting under way in the 16th century and reaching its pinnacle in the 17th century, the legacy of reason of state for posterity was a great controversy. For some, it stood for unforeseen candour in speaking about the realities of political life, but for many others it showed nothing but a bizarre lack of decency. In the following, this controversy will be introduced first, although very generally and briefly. Next, Carl Schmitt's views will be discussed, for whom law and order appear to be more or less the same thing. This makes him a perfect contrast to Foucault, in whose view the antagonism between law and order is permanent. Foucault's views on reason of state that will be discussed at the end of this chapter are instrumental for understanding this antagonism.

Machiavelli?

Niccolò Machiavelli (1468–1527) did not invent a word for reason of state, but the commonplace view is that he invented the thing.[1] Because reason of state 'seemed to him self-evident, it filled him completely', assumed Friedrich Meinecke, the major modern historian of reason of state, for whom Machiavelli's 'thought is nothing else but a continual process of thinking about *raison d'état*' (Meinecke 1988: 29). One possible way to enter the controversy on reason of state is the problem of the disunited appearance of Machiavelli's two main works, *The Prince* (1513) and *Discourses* (1513–1517). As is well known, these books seem to favour two entirely different forms of government. *The Prince* instructs unscrupulous one-man rule, whereas *Discourses* presents Machiavelli as a devout apologist for republican rule. Only a devil, people thought, changes sides or contradicts himself so dramatically.

However, there should be no doubt that Machiavelli's writing all along has a subtextual level at which his performance sometimes supports but sometimes works against what he says explicitly at the level of the text. For Rousseau, Machiavelli's virtuosity lies exactly in this type of literary engagement. 'He professed to teach kings; but it was the people he really taught', said Rousseau. Far from holding with the cause of princes, Machiavelli gave the people a lesson on the cruelty and treachery of princes. In other words, Machiavelli's *Prince* was irony, a clever political satire, whereas *Discourses* was Machiavelli's honest book. This way, according to Rousseau, Machiavelli's '*Prince* is the book of Republicans' no less than *Discourses*. Until Rousseau, Machiavelli had 'been studied only by superficial and corrupt readers', says the French philosopher confidently (Rousseau 1955: 59).

However, these other readers existed even after Rousseau; one of them was the hardly superficial Hegel. In his view, Machiavelli's idea of a state 'has for so long failed to get a hearing owing to the foolish vociferousness of what is termed "freedom"' (Hegel 1964: 220). Should Hegel have been superficial and corrupt for Rousseau, then here the compliment is returned. In Rousseau's person, Machiavelli was 'misunderstood from the start by the blind who took his work as nothing but [. . .] a golden mirror for an ambitious oppressor' (ibid).

Rousseau and his like are to be blamed for 'the experience of French libertarian madness' that makes one not see the truth: 'freedom is possible only when a people is united into a state by legal bonds' (ibid). Machiavelli wished to see a powerful state, said Hegel approvingly, and he was sincere in writing *The Prince*. The more sinister tones of this book Hegel understands against the Italian political situation at the time: 'When life is on the brink of decay it can be reorganized only by a procedure involving the maximum of force' (Hegel 1964: 221).

This controversy between Rousseau and Hegel sufficiently illuminates the multilevel nature of Machiavelli's work, but also the whole controversy around reason of state. It certainly cannot be taken at face value, and its legacy is not only a portrayal of a powerful state, but much more challenging political writing that cannot be comprehended by ordinary means. Political writing of reason of state, like that of Machiavelli, is not a straightforward description of what exists in the world of power, but an intervention to that word.

One point of crucial difference between the two books of Machiavelli should be noted. This difference concerns the law. In that relation, a summary of *The Prince* as a whole appears in one sentence: a capable prince 'holds to what is right when he can but knows how to do wrong when he must' (Machiavelli 1989a: 66). In turn, *Discourses* takes a different stance towards laws:

> Yet it is not good that in a republic anything should ever happen that has to be dealt with extralegally. The extralegal action may turn out well at the moment, yet the example has a bad effect, because it establishes a custom of breaking laws for good purposes; later, with this example, they are broken for bad purposes. Therefore a republic will never be perfect if with her laws she has not provided for everything, and furnished a means for dealing with every unexpected event, and laid down a method for using it. (Machiavelli 1989b: 268–269)

As for the ruler who legislates, there is nothing 'that sets a worse example in a republic than to make a law and not keep it, and so much the more when it is not kept by him who has made it' (Machiavelli 1989b: 288). How then to explain this special mystery of Machiavelli, the difference in his views of law in the two books? Louis Althusser has presented an interpretation of Machiavelli that mediates between Rousseau and Hegel, but it also addresses the problem of laws in Machiavelli.

Althusser's view is that *The Prince* and *Discourses* present a utopian plan for constitution of a stable state. This plan has two moments, the first of which is begetting. The state must be established by a single man, who must be absolutely pitiless and will use all and any means available; no questions of abuse of powers can arise at this point. *The Prince* stands for that moment, and it forms the first step in Machiavelli's plan. The second moment is one of guaranteeing the endurance of the state: 'the settlement of laws' that is also 'the end of the absolute power of a single individual'. Despite the absolute necessity of a prince who steps into a void, as it were, he can never guarantee the continuity and historical existence of the state. This existence will have to take root in laws. *Discourses* stands for this second moment in the plan. Therefore, the two books are two moments in a single plan, which presents their 'non-difference, their profound unity'. Therefore, Althusser argues that 'Machiavelli does not have two faces; [. . .] on the contrary, he has only one position' (Althusser 2000: 64–66).

For Foucault, Machiavelli was not one of the genuine thinkers of reason of state, despite his persistent centrality in the debates that go on around it (Foucault 2000d: 243). From Foucault's point of view, the view of laws presented in *Discourses* would absolutely separate Machiavelli from reason of state, because for Foucault reason of state 'by its nature does not have to abide by the laws' (Foucault 2007a: 262).

Reason of state is defined by its extra-legal and anti-juridical nature, so that juridical reason will always stand as an objection and limitation to reason of state; by nature, these two reasons must remain extrinsic to each other (see Foucault 2008: 8–10). In reason of state, Foucault was searching for a constitution of the art of governing that is cut off from law: 'reason of state is not an art of government according to divine, natural, or human laws. It doesn't have to respect the general order of the world. It's government in accordance with the state's strength' (Foucault 2000d: 317).

Schmitt: might and right

In his *Crisis of Parliamentary Democracy*, Carl Schmitt presented an interpretation according to which the controversy provoked by the reason of state is merely an episode in the evolution of the perennial problem: 'an example of the old struggle between might and right: The Machiavellian use of power is combated with moral and legal ethos' (Schmitt 1988: 37).

The struggle between might and right is indeed old; one may say that it goes back all the way to Thrasymachus: 'I say that justice is nothing other than the advantage of the stronger' (Plato, *Republic*: 338c). For Schmitt, this tradition of struggle goes even beyond that, down to Pindar, whose poem on *Nomos basileus* is all-important to Schmitt.[2] This poem can be found in Plato's *Gorgias*:

> Law, the king of all,
> Of mortals and the immortal gods
> Brings on and renders just what is most violent

With towering hand. I take as proof of this
The deeds of Heracles.
(Plato, *Gorgias*: 484b)

Elsewhere, Plato presents the view that Pindar justifies the use of extreme force, which he in fact 'turned into a law of nature' (Plato, *Laws*: 715a). According to Plato, Pindar says that 'the stronger should rule and the weaker should obey', which is a claim that again prevails 'by decree of nature' for Pindar. Plato's rejoinder was: 'In spite of you, my clever Pindar, what I'd called the "decree of nature" is in fact the rule of law that governs willing subjects, without being imposed by force' (Plato, *Laws*: 690b–c). This way Plato succinctly establishes what Schmitt would call the *normativist approach*.

One way in which Schmitt positioned himself in the old struggle between might and right can be found, for example, in his book *On the Three Types of Juristic Thought*. In that context, the struggle is between concrete order and rational principle. On the side of the rational principle stands the normativist approach, which Schmitt depicted as follows:

> In all ages, it has been demanded that law and not men should rule. Thus, the normativist explains one of the most beautiful and oldest coinages of human legal thought, the coinage of Pindar on *Nomos basileus*, 'Nomos as King', normativistically: only law, not the necessities of the momentary, continually changing situation, nor ever the arbitrariness of men, should be allowed to 'rule' or 'command'. [. . .] In the influential two-thousand-year stoic tradition it had further effectiveness through the definition of Chrysipp, that law is king, overseer, ruler, and master over morality and immorality, right and wrong. Likewise, the often-repeated antithesis of *ratio* and *voluntas*, *veritas* and *auctoritas*, supports the normativist demand for the rule of law [*einer Herrschaft von Gesetzes*] as opposed to the rule of men.[3]

For Schmitt, this normativist misunderstanding of Pindar neatly encapsulates the type of legal thinking that cannot see the inevitable impotency of abstract norms. Against this, Schmitt presented what he called the concrete-order type of legal thinking (*den konkreten Ordnungstypus*), that conceives Pindar's identification of the law as king the other way around: the king as law. Pindar's poem implies that *Nomos* is above all order. An order-guaranteeing king, *basileus* as *pouvoir neutre*, dwells in the body of laws – or rather, this king is an embodiment of law as order.[4]

> Concepts such as king, master, overseer or governor, as well as judge and court, shift us immediately into concrete institutional orders that are no longer mere rules. *Recht* as master, the *Nomos basileus*, cannot be merely an arbitrary positive norm, rule or legal stipulation; *Nomos*, which a legitimate king is supposed to embody, must have in itself certain of the highest, unalterable, but also concrete qualities of an order. [. . .] One can speak of a true *Nomos*

as true king only if *Nomos* means precisely the concept of *Recht* encompassing a concrete order and *Gemeinschaft*. (Schmitt 2004a: 50–51)

On the one hand, Schmitt's view was that in the concept of legal order (*Rechtsordnung*) both terms – law and order – mutually and inseparably define each other. On the other hand, insofar as the notion of king needs to be used it is really the legal-conceptual representation of order (*eine rechtsbegriffliche Ordnungsvorstellung*). 'Just as *Nomos* is king', said Schmitt, 'so is king *Nomos*' (Schmitt 2004a: 51). The essential point of Schmitt is that law and order not only belong together but constitute a unity.

Schmitt's view was that the political theory of reason of state is really an account of state secrets, the so called *arcane rei publicae*. This is a body of practical knowledge that is needed for the calculations and plots contrived in closed-door cabinets. It informs a style of governing which 'treats the state and politics only as techniques for the assertion of power and its expansion' (Schmitt 1988: 37).

Schmitt's view seems to have been that the reaction against reason of state produced a situation where the normativist approach got the upper hand and concrete-order thinking became the underdog. In other words, from repulsion for reason of state emerged the cornerstones of the political theory of liberal and constitutional democracies as antidotes to reason of state: openness and public discussion in parliaments, division of state powers between separated and mutually controlling authorities and, finally, a concept of law (legislation) that stands for 'a general rational principle' rather than 'a concrete decree, an order' (Schmitt 1988: 43). Foucault makes a similar point in his *Birth of Biopolitics*:

> [Modern] discussions of law, their liveliness and what's more the development of all the problems and theories of what could be called public law, the re-appearance of the themes of natural law, original law, the contract, and so forth [. . .], are all in a way the other side and consequence, and the reaction against, this new way of governing on the basis of *raison d'État*. (Foucault 2008: 9)

Apart from that, Foucault disagreed entirely with Schmitt: law and order do not belong together and cannot constitute a unity. To recapitulate, this is where we left him in Chapter 6: 'Law, by definition, is always referred to a juridical system, and order is referred to an administrative system, to a state's specific order [. . .] It's impossible to reconcile law and order because when you try to do so it is only in the form of an integration of law into the state's order' (Foucault 2000c: 417). The juridical reason and the reason of state are like 'lemon and milk' for Foucault (2000e: 438), or like 'oil and water', according to Meinecke (1988: 345).

Knowledge of the state

It is clear that reason of state stands for order for Foucault, but what else did he understand by this Renaissance doctrine? In the Middle Ages, said Foucault, one had believed 'that all the kingdoms on the earth would one day be unified in one last empire just before Christ's return to earth'. With reason of state, that sort of end point and goal vanishes altogether. History no longer indubitably approaches anything of the kind and each state is conceived as 'a set of forces and strengths that could be increased or weakened according to the politics followed by the governments'. This politics, the new art of governing, will have 'to deal with an irreducible multiplicity of states struggling and competing in a limited history' (Foucault 2000c: 408–409).

Reason of state establishes a relationship between politics and a new type of knowledge that will be knowledge of 'things rather than knowledge of the law'; that is, of 'the things that comprise the very reality of the state' (Foucault 2007a: 274). Politics is no longer related to the traditional, political, moral or legal ideas of the just and the good: 'government, therefore, entails more than just implementing general principles of reason, wisdom, and prudence'. Instead of those principles, 'a certain specific knowledge is necessary: concrete, precise, and measured knowledge as to the state's strength', which is systematic and objective information about the condition of the state (Foucault 2000c: 408).

> The state is something that exists per se. It is a kind of natural object, even if the jurists try to know how it can be constituted in a legitimate way. The state is by itself an order of things, and political knowledge separates it from juridical reflections. Political knowledge deals not with the rights of people or with human or divine laws but with the nature of the state which has to be governed. (Foucault 2000c: 408)

Reason of state 'has always existed, if by this we understand the mechanism by which states function' (Foucault 2007a: 241). However, this is not what Foucault understood by reason of state. In the 16th and 17th centuries the state's reason remade itself as 'a relationship of the state to itself' (Foucault 2007a: 277). Reason of state was a reflective event that laid the foundation for a body of knowledge about pre-existing practices, and then reinserted the knowledge into the field of these practices. At this moment, the state 'became an object of knowledge and analysis' that formed 'part of a reflected and concerted strategy' (Foucault 2007a: 247).

> 'With their telescopes', says Chemnitz:[5] 'modern mathematicians have discovered new stars in the firmament and spots on the sun. With their telescopes, the new *politiques* have discovered what the Ancients did not know or which they carefully hid from us'. (Foucault 2007a: 241)

While states, as well as all of their necessary institutions (taxation, armies, the judiciary), had existed long before, it was nonetheless only now that awareness of the state – as a distinct entity with its own principle and special order of things – grew into such measures that one can speak of knowledge of the state. The state appeared as a new thing 'on the horizon of reflected practice', as new stars may appear, not in the firmament as such, but on maps reproducing it (Foucault 2007a: 276).

Giovanni Antonio Palazzo[6] explained that the word reason (*ragion*) nonetheless carries not only a reflective but also an ontological meaning. It is really an *essence*: 'the entire essence of a thing' (Foucault 2007a: 256). More exactly, reason as an essence is 'the necessary bond between the different elements that constitute a thing' (Foucault 2007a: 256). When one speaks of the reason of state in this way, it means not merely the *reason why* a collective establishes an external agent to govern their communities, or only *the way in which* state authorities tend to 'reason'. It is more like an idea – an *eidos* – that is independent of empirical reality. It is the principle, logic and structure that constitute a thing.

Without reason of state there would be no state, as without gravity there would be no cosmos. However, whereas planets will continue on their orbits as ever before, regardless of what humans know about them, it is clear that this is not the case with social and political systems. Insertion of knowledge into these systems will change the course of events. This is because, in the words of Palazzo, reason is not only the essence of a thing, but also *power*, a certain power 'that allows the will to adjust itself to what it knows, that is to say, to adjust itself to the very essence of things' (Foucault 2007a: 256).

Hence, 'reason' refers to both essence and power, but it does even more than that, something that can perhaps be called a transcendental synthesis: the state not only has an essence and a power, but its *essence is power*. This is the new foundation for knowledge of the state, which forms a new starting point and principle of politics as statecraft: 'The state is organized only by reference to itself: it seeks its own good and has no external purpose, that is to say, it must lead to nothing but itself' (Foucault 2007a: 290). In other words, a state is an end in itself.

Let us say that the commonplace understanding of power is that it is the capacity of someone to have one's plans implemented without anyone being able to obstruct or prevent them. Power is about attaining set goals and ends. Therefore, power is on the side of the means: it is convenient to wield power but its value is instrumental, whereas ultimate goals and ends lie elsewhere. By contrast, the reason of state makes power the final, ultimate and only goal. Reason of state is 'government in accordance with the state's strength. It's government whose aim is to increase this strength' (Foucault 2000d: 317). It is good to be powerful, not because of some other more supreme good, but because the good, its definition by reason of state, is to be powerful.

Firm domination over people

In medieval kingdoms, individuals and social processes could be controlled and regulated only haphazardly. Feudal kings had no organisation for constant watch and peace-keeping in the streets of cities, towns and villages. It was simply impossible for them to know what was going on around every corner. Moreover, they did not even think it appropriate to bother with the petty affairs of ordinary people.

As long as taxes could be collected and soldiers recruited from the realm, every-thing was fine. For a medieval king, it was not important to watch over whatever his subjects were busy with. What mattered was to stage the king's own action so that his subjects could watch what he did through his spectacular manifestations of power. 'Everything [sovereigns and kings] do can be, and deserves to be, spoken of and must be remembered in perpetuity, which means that the slightest deed or action of a king can and must be turned into dazzling action and exploit' (Foucault 2003b: 67).

In Foucault's view, even Machiavelli's mind was still moving in this old world: 'Machiavelli's problem is whether the Prince should be just or unjust. Should he appear to be just or unjust? How should he appear to be fearsome? How should he hide his weakness? What is at stake in Machiavellian calculation is basically always Prince's epithets' (Foucault 2007a: 272).

Politics by reason of state relates to individuals in a completely different way: people do not watch the undertakings of the royal house, the royal house watches the people. In a certain way, 'governments don't have to worry about individuals', as the state's purpose is no longer the good or honest life of humans (Foucault 2000c: 409). States no longer had their final cause in individuals, but 'the state is its own finality' (Foucault 2000c: 409). Thus, while political society used to be an instrument to be used for the good of individuals, now, on the contrary, the individual has become an instrument, or material, of the state. The state's intrinsic value is supreme to the instrumental value of individuals.

> From the state's own point of view, the individual exists insofar as what he does is able to introduce even a minimal change in the strength of the state, either in a positive or in a negative direction. It is only insofar as an individual is able to introduce this change that the state has to do with him. And sometimes what he has to do for the state is to live, to work, to produce, to consume; and sometimes what he has to do is die. (Foucault 2000c: 409)

The good of individuals, or the good of the people, is not the goal. However, in another way, by reason of state 'one must think about the people and have them constantly in mind' (Foucault 2007a: 271–72). 'The state is a firm domination over people' as Botero said, and reason of state should constitute 'knowledge of the appropriate means for founding, preserving, and expanding such a domination' (Foucault 2007a: 238). The goal of governing according to the reason of state is not the good of a people, but domination over people. Clearly, while this may most of the time resemble governing by general good – just as it may most of the time respect the law – this is a mere dissimulation: reason of state is not pursuit of the common good. Power is not exercised for the sake of *salus populi*; power is exercised for the sake of power. And power, finally, is domination over people.

Domination completes our former equation: the essence of state is power, and power is domination over people.

People, in turn, are an inexhaustible source of all kinds of disturbances. As later history of revolutions would prove, internal strife was as great a threat to states as hostilities by external powers. This is why rulers needed a way to read the signs of developing popular discontent and sedition before these exploded into dangerous riots and revolts. 'Of Seditions and Troubles' (1625) by Francis Bacon instructed ways in which the signs of revolt were to be sniffed out: from rumours circulating among the people; from unexpectedly malign responses by the public to governmental action; and from suspiciously tardy or overly spontaneous behaviour of functionaries (see Foucault 2007a: 267–72).

One clear sign of mushrooming sedition was 'when the person who receives an order, instead of receiving it and executing it, begins to interpret it and insert his own discourse, as it were, between the injunction he receives and the obedience that should normally follow' (Foucault 2007a: 268). In the words of Bacon: 'disputing, excusing, cavilling upon mandates and directions, is a kind of shaking off the yoke, and assay of disobedience' (Bacon 1858: 98). Now, is this not exactly what the practice of law does: shakes off the yoke by cavils and excuses, insertions of discourses and interpretations? The field of law, it seems to me, should be seen as a possibility of this type of resistance. From the subject's point of view, it is an unwavering station of resilience inserted between injunction and obedience. But from the point of view of reason of state, the field of legal practice is really a place for growing sedition.

To have sedition dwindle before it grows into a tempest, governors must take preventive measures. As a remedy for sedition, people need to be well fed, of course, but equally important is to know, at every turn, 'what is going on in the minds of the governed' (Foucault 2007a: 272). Hence, the two main elements that the governors must get to know in reality and learn to manipulate are economy and opinion. Poverty and discontent are the two main causes of sedition, riot and revolt. When poverty and discontent are managed, people remain more easily under firm domination (see Foucault 2007a: 268).

Poverty can be managed by economic policies, but discontent is trickier. One possible remedy is to spread hope in the glimmering future: 'artificial nourishment and entertaining of hopes, and carrying men from hopes to hopes, is one of the best antidotes against the poison of discontentments' (Bacon 1858: 104). Sometimes hope is not sufficient to appease discontentment, which makes the situation difficult for the prince. On the one hand, the prince must maintain his authority and stay away from juridical and moral discussions and debates. On the other hand, some outlet for discontents should be provided, to prevent inflammation: 'To give moderate liberty for griefs and discontentments to evaporate [. . .] is a safe way; for he that turneth the humours back, and maketh the wound bleed inwards, endangereth malign ulcers and pernicious imposthumations' (Bacon 1858: 104).

Discontentment that has become suppurative must be lanced, otherwise it will lead to serious disturbances and tumult that may ruin state order. For that matter, Bacon and his prince could very well have turned back to Machiavelli again. His insight was that the juridical institution of public prosecutor can be used for the management of people's discontentment and anger. According to Machiavelli, there is 'no more useful or necessary authority than the power to bring before the people, or before some magistrate or council, charges against citizens' (Machiavelli 1989b: 211). The effect of this institution:

> [. . .] is that it provides an outlet for the discharge of those partisan hatreds that develop in cities in various ways against various citizens. When these hatreds do not have an outlet for discharging themselves lawfully, they take unlawful ways that make the whole republic fall. (Machiavelli 1989b: 211)

Where does this leave us in the end? After all the efforts to show the anti-juridical nature of reason of state, how it stands in opposition to legal thought and practice, what is finally tracked down, once again, is the ancient theory of *miasma* – or the modern (Durkheimian) theory of collective resentment – where the judicial system reappears as a helpful device of reason of state. Penal power is used for discharging popular anger, that is, for the purposes of security administration. Despite the heterogeneity and incommensurability of juridical reason and reason of state, intersections and connections form between the disparate practices of law and order.

Everyone knows that the law is an instrument of power. Indeed, the law must be involved in the exercise of power, because this is the condition and purpose of its existence. In short, the law is a system of power. However, this does not mean that it is always on the side of those regimes of practices that exercise domination. Law's connections and intersections with other forms of power do not necessarily contaminate juridical reason. Rather, this opens up for it an entry point to social existence, to the general field of power, where it must struggle for survival. From this point of view, it is not at all deplorable that prosecutors and other lawyers are involved in practices of reason of state, insofar as lawyers enter the game as lawyers. As lawyers, their function is to insert an element of juridical reason to the exercise of power.

To conclude, it should be pointed out finally that reason of state does not have people as enemies of the state. Knowledge of the state was founded on the idea that the state's essence is power, which is firm domination over people who may be more or less resilient and recalcitrant. However, people are not inserted into this equation as adversaries of the state. On the contrary, people make the greatest force of the state, upon which its strength ultimately depends. People are the state's quintessential resources, and reason of state is not merely some cold and cruel manner of governing, but also careful husbandry of these resources. This way, reason of state paved the way for a later development of what Foucault called 'the biopolitics of the population' (Foucault 1998b: 139). This and other off-spring of reason of state will be dealt with in the next chapter.

Before concluding, I find it relevant to make one last point regarding Schmitt. His *Leviathan in the State Theory of Thomas Hobbes* illustrates the relationship between the state and people in terms of a biblical battle of two enormous monsters: 'one of the monsters, the leviathan "state", continuously holds down the other monster, the behemoth "revolutionary people"' (Schmitt 2008: 21). In this picture, 'the state is, accordingly, the oppressor of irrepressible chaos inherent in man' for Hobbes – the man who is often regarded as a great forefather of juridical reason (Schmitt 2008: 22).

By way of contrast, Bacon, who appears as one of the forefathers of reason of state, likened people to the mythological Briareus, the 100-handed giant divinity. For Bacon the story of Briareus was 'an emblem, no doubt, to show how safe it is for monarchs to make sure of the good-will of common people' (Bacon 1858: 103). According to the legend, Briareus was loyal to Zeus in the most critical situation, where the father of the gods was in the hands of conspirators and nearly met the fate of his own father, Cronus:

> That day the Olympians tried to chain [Zeus] down,
> Hera, Poseidon lord of the sea, and Pallas Athena –
> you [Thetis] rushed to Zeus, dear Goddess, broke those chains,
> quickly ordered the hundred-hander to steep Olympus,
> that monster whom the immortals call Briareus
> but every mortal calls the Sea-god's son, Aegaeon,
> though he's stronger than his father. Down he sat,
> flanking Cronus' son, gargantuan in the glory of it all,
> and the blessed gods were struck with terror then,
> they stopped shackling Zeus.
> (*Iliad*: 1.470–1.483)

Notes

1 The word was first used by Machiavelli's contemporary and Florentine compatriot Francesco Guicciardini (1483–1540) in his *Dialogue on the Government of Florence* (*Dialogo del reggimento di Firenze*, 1523–1527). Murdering or imprisoning the vanquished Pisans, Florence's 'inveterate enemies', was recommended because this conformed to the *ragione e uso degli stato* ('the reason and practice of states') (Guicciardini 1994: 157–59). See also Meinecke (1988: 46 fn 2) and Viroli (1992: 194). According to Meinecke, however, the first use that properly corresponded to the idea of reason of state was made by the archbishop and humanist Giovanni della Casa in the mid-16th century (Meinecke 1988: 47).

2 For Schmitt's discussion of Pindar in context, see Schmitt (2003: 72 ff).

3 I have slightly changed the English translation (Schmitt 2004a: 49) of the first half of this quote. Schmitt's German original reads as follows: '*Zu allen Zeiten hat man verlangt, daß das Gesetz und nicht die Menschen herrschen sollen. So deutet der Normativist eine der schönsten und ältesten Prägungen menschlichen Rechtsdenkens überhaupt, das Wort Pindars vom Nomos basileus, vom "Nomos als König", normativistisch: Nur das Gesetz, nicht das Bedürfnis der jeweiligen, sich fortwährend verändernden Situation oder gar die Willkür von Menschen darf "herrschen oder befehlen"*' (Schmitt 1993: 12).

4 'In establishing the state order as a unity of power and peace', says Böckenförde interpreting Schmitt, 'one needs a policy of order and agreement on an encompassing scale. Such a policy, however, cannot be conducted by political forces that are tied to particular (though legally permissible) antagonistic interests'. This is the problem of 'a *pouvoir neutre* – whatever its actual constitutional location – for the maintenance and

capability of action of any state order' (Böckenförde 1998: 48–49). Another question is what Chantal Mouffe calls Schmitt's false dilemma: 'The unity of the state must, for him, be a concrete unity, already given and therefore stable', a fact of homogeneity of the people. At the same time, however, 'the existence of such a unity is itself a contingent fact which requires a political construction' (Mouffe 1998: 171–72).

5   Bogislaw Philipp Chemnitz is the author of *Dissertatio de ratione status in Imperio nostro Romano-Germanico* (1640), intended for the negotiators of the treaty of Westphalia (Foucault 2007a: 240 and endnote 24).

6   The author of Discorso del governo e della ragion vera di Stato (1604).

Part III

Knowledge

Chapter 9

Knowledge of society

The governor must know what it is to be one of his subjects in order to rule over them. The most famous example of this theme appears in the third book of Aristotle's *Politics*, concerning the conditions of possibility of genuinely political power, governing of free people. Aristotle says that this is possible by employing the republican system of regulated exchange of roles: each citizen must govern and be governed in his turn. The point is that one will learn how to govern only by way of being first subjected to government.

Another famous instance of this necessary exchange of perspectives at the foundation of the knowledge on governing is Machiavelli's dedication of his *Prince* to Lorenzo Medici: 'in order to discern clearly the people's nature, the observer must be a prince, and to discern clearly [the nature] of princes, he must be one of the populace' (Machiavelli 1989a: 10–11).

With Foucault, this ancient theme changes rather dramatically. It turns into the theme of knowledge-power, where neither knowledge nor power is any longer conceived as being possessed by anyone. On the contrary, everyone is possessed by knowledge-power. The following exposition has two objectives. The first is to show how Foucault developed the theme of knowledge-power throughout his work up until the 1980s. This involves, first, an overview of the variety of ways in which this theme appears in Foucault's work; next, taking up his investigation into prison as a concrete example of the functioning of knowledge-power; and, finally, discussing the analytical idea that forms the heart of knowledge-power.

The second objective is to consider the law in relation to knowledge-power. How does knowledge-power work in the field of legal practice, and how would legal practice work against knowledge-power? This latter question brings us to the ancient legal technique of *epieikeia* – equity.

Knowledge-power

The theme of knowledge-power is 'the way in which knowledge circulates and functions, its relations to power' (Foucault 2000e: 331). At one point, Foucault defined his project of exploring mechanisms of power as 'a political history of knowledge', where knowledge, not excluding its so-called universal or transcendental conditions, is conceived as 'the historical and circumstantial result of conditions outside the domain of knowledge' (Foucault 2000a: 13). At that point, the domain of knowledge still referred to science and academic institutions, whereas its outside was the wide domain of political struggles:

> If we truly wish to know knowledge, to know what it is, to apprehend it at its root, in its manufacture, we must look not to philosophers but to politicians – we need to understand what the relations of struggle and power are. One can understand what knowledge consists of only by examining these relations of power and struggle, the manner in which things and men hate one another, fight one another, and try to dominate one another, to exercise power relations over one another. (Foucault 2000a: 12)

The human being as an object of empirical knowledge had been at the centre of Foucault's interests in the 1960s. In his works of that time, power was hovering in the background rather than studied in its own right. However, what later became a pervasive tenet for Foucault, 'knowledges' (*connaissances*) that are overtly neutral and objective but would covertly impose norms and exert power on societies, appears in a lucid form already in 1963 in his book on medical knowledge, *The Birth of the Clinic*: 'In the ordering of human existence [medicine] assumes a normative posture, which authorizes it not only to distribute advice as to healthy life, but also to dictate the standards for physical and moral relations of the individual and the society in which he lives' (Foucault 1989: 40). More generally, human science is not a detached description of objects, but has the 'positive role that it implicitly occupies as a norm' (Foucault 1989: 41). Description adds in a concealed element of prescription.

Confining itself 'to describing the transformations themselves' of the epistemological space owing to which new forms of human sciences emerge, *The Order of Things* left aside the problem of the causes of these transformations (Foucault 1994a: xiii). *Archaeology of Knowledge*, too, was about the relations between knowledge and the epistemic conditions of its formation, but at the end of the book Foucault pointed out that this is not the only possible context to question the conditions of existence of knowledge; one may also consider them 'in a different set of relations' (Foucault 1994b: 195).

As a 'different set of relations' that would conjoin knowledge with power, Foucault's later historical projections on practices of power can be seen as tackling the problem of exactly those causes and conditions of knowledge that emerge outside the domain of science: 'We could call this the genealogy of knowledge, the indispensable historical other side to the archaeology of knowledge' (Foucault 2006: 239).

Moving from scientific systems of knowledge ('archaeology') to the historical analysis of mechanisms of power ('genealogy') in the 1970s, immersing himself entirely in problems of power, Foucault no longer seems to study problems of knowledge in their own right. However, in the same way as the problem of power had hovered in the background of knowledge, the problem of knowledge would continue hovering in the background of power. A few succinct glances into some of Foucault's genealogical theses show that there is continuity.

Power precedes knowledge. At the end of *Discipline and Punish*, Foucault discussed the possibility that the panoptic society (being a society that develops and uses techniques of minute observation for the purposes of domination and producing docility) 'gave rise in part to the sciences of man'. Those sciences were possible 'because they have been conveyed by a specific and new modality of power: a certain policy of the body, a certain way of rendering a group of men docile and useful'. In Foucault's view, the 'analytical investments' in the 'immense examination' of human individuals in networks of incarceration were constitutive of human sciences: 'Knowable man (soul, individuality, consciousness, conduct, whatever it is called) is the object-effect of this analytical investment, of this domination-observation' (Foucault 1991: 305).

Power takes the form of knowledge where it imposes systematic order on society. In many places, Foucault was fascinated by the system developed for controlling the plague as an emblem of modern power (Foucault 2006: 4–6; 2003a: 43–48; 1991: 195–99; 2007a: 9–10). Plague control applied a system of quarantine to those touched by the disease. In a city contaminated with plague, its victims were placed in quarantine in their own homes and subjected to a daily accounting of their condition and to the strictest possible surveillance. This system stood for a 'utopia of the perfectly governed city' (Foucault 1991: 198).

> But you can see that there was another dream of the plague: a political dream in which the plague is rather the marvellous moment when political power is exercised to the full. The plague is the moment when the spatial partitioning and sub-divisioning (*quadrillage*) of a population is taken to its extreme point, where dangerous communications, disorderly communities, and forbidden contacts can no longer appear. (Foucault 2003a: 47)

Knowledge takes the form of power in its determinations of what is useful and what is detrimental to society. On the basis of these determinations, societies may be purified from parasitic elements that do not contribute to common prosperity. In *'Society Must Be Defended'*, Foucault maintained that with the rise of the bourgeoisie: 'we see the appearance of a State racism: a racism that society will direct against itself, against its own elements and its own products' (Foucault 2003b: 61). State racism is hygiene that the state exercises over its own population, because the society 'is threatened by a certain number of heterogeneous elements which are not essential to it' – idle people such as aristocrats and useless rabble without decent employment (Foucault 2003b: 81). When the bourgeoisie took over the state machinery for good, it could install itself as 'the agent of the universal' (Foucault 2003b: 237), whereby knowledge of the bourgeois life-form was imposed on humans living in the state as the only possible form of humanity.

Working together with knowledge, power becomes impersonal. Knowledge-power does not need the state or any other agent to mastermind its strategies.

According to Foucault's Rio lectures of 1973, society itself has established a 'web of microscopic, capillary political power [. . .] at the level of man's very existence', which enabled individuals to be attached 'to the production apparatus' of the industrial society. Maintaining the workforce and making people 'into agents of production, into workers', certain mechanisms of 'infrapower' (*sous-pouvoir*) formed the historical precondition of the capitalist system that extracts 'hyperprofit' (*sur-profit*) from human labour. This, again, 'gave rise to a series of knowledges [. . .] that proliferated in these institutions of infrapower, causing the so-called human sciences, and man as an object of science, to appear' (Foucault 2000a: 87).

Power generates entirely new domains of knowledge. For example, the emergence of reason of state as the new principle of governing created a 'reflective prism' into which society as 'population' may later enter as a new domain of knowledge (Foucault, 2007a: 276–77). In this respect, Foucault used for the first time in '*Society Must Be Defended*' his notion of 'biopolitics' to designate state polices on population: births, morbidity and public health, and 'what might broadly be called endemics or, in other words, the form, nature, extension, duration and intensity of the illnesses prevalent in a population' (Foucault 2003b: 243). In *The Will to Knowledge* Foucault again referred to the biopolitics of the population as the most modern modality of power (Foucault 1998b: 139). Finally, in *Security, Territory, Population*, Foucault defined population as 'a multiplicity of individuals who are and fundamentally and essentially exist only biologically bound to the materiality within which they live' (Foucault 2007a: 21). Biopolitics, care of the health and vitality of the whole population, is the last function on our list that knowledge-power has taken.

It is clear, for one thing, that in Foucault's mind knowledge generates power, and for another that power generates knowledge too. Knowledge-power relations are mutual feedback relations. Foucault's archaeological phase in the 1960s dealt with human sciences and the genealogical phase in the 1970s explored mechanisms of power, but one perceives that these phases are intertwined. Where one part ends and another begins is not as important a question as the question of the nature of the whole, the broader trajectory, in which knowledge and power are interdependent parts. Before discussing what forms the heart of that whole, let us yet explore one concrete example of the functioning of knowledge-power: the prison.

Prison as an apparatus of security

At the end of *Discipline and Punish*, Foucault came to ask why prisons still exist, despite the fact that they had failed in their social policy objective of reducing the crime rate as well as in their philanthropic project of rehabilitating individual offenders. 'Instead of releasing corrected individuals, then, the prison was setting loose a swarm of dangerous delinquents throughout the population' (Foucault 1991: 266). In fact, prison became a workshop for the production of an entirely novel type of human existence, a stray delinquent, who will be permanently incapable of living in any society.

A prison-made delinquent would always return to prison and become an entirely institutionalised, 'pathologized subject' (Foucault 1991: 277). However, the production of pathological delinquents and their unending circulation between the prison and the world outside it, made it possible for the security apparatuses to make novel use of them, to insert them into the work of maintaining order, in which 'the penal system operates as an anti-seditious system' (Foucault 1986a: 16).

Steady production and circulation of delinquents intensifies their two principal uses, one of which was 'as informers and *agents provocateurs*' working for the system of policing order (Foucault 1991: 280). Entirely dependent on prisons, they would function much more efficiently and unfailingly as helpers of the police. With their assistance, the police could collect knowledge of such deep regions of society's underworld where the long arm of the law had never reached. With this new and more penetrating gaze, the police could tighten their grip on mushrooming disorders at their very root.

> Delinquency, with the secret agents that it procures, but also with the generalized policing that it authorizes, constitutes a means of perpetual surveillance of the population: an apparatus that makes it possible to supervise, through the delinquents themselves, the whole social field. Delinquency functions as a political observatory. (Foucault 1991: 281)

The second, no less important, use of delinquents was that of 'moralising' the working class. This entails fanning hatred between workers and all sorts of mischief-makers who undermine social order. In effect, this was an application of the *divide et impera* tactic on the governance of dominated groups, the generation of antagonism and discord between antisocial elements and honest workers. Having produced a class of desperate outcasts, the prison would have them injected into society to show workers – the agitated proletariat – what devastating monsters those who do not submit to the demands of order really are.

This more or less subliminal generation of repulsion for insubordination would make workers more reliable and law-abiding citizens. Moreover, they would start to assimilate with bourgeois culture and values to distinguish themselves from delinquents. In other words, the tactic of the circulation of delinquents was 'to maintain the hostility of the poorer classes to delinquents' (Foucault 1991: 285); it was pacification of society through maintenance of conflict. Hence, 'the role of the penal system: to make the proletariat see the non-proletarianised people as marginal, dangerous, a menace to society as a whole, the dregs of the population, trash, a "mob"' (Foucault 1986a: 15).

That crime serves a social function – notably in the fabrication and reproduction of collective consciousness *à la* Durkheim – is certainly an old theme. However, with Foucault's autopsy of the penal system, organised punishment is not conceived as an appendage of some more genuinely moral reaction of the public to criminal offences. Instead, the penal system and penal power make it possible for police authorities to go down to the dark underworld of society and carry out their work from within that nether milieu. Moreover, their work is not to fight against the freaks and villains who inhabit that *milieu*, but with them proactively to intensify a tendency towards orderly behaviour among the worker-citizens. Delinquents are used in the maintenance of the basal order of society through the nausea they as abject humans would engender in people who are better off.

A couple of years after the publication of *Discipline and Punish*, Foucault introduced a new notion: 'the apparatus (*dispostif*) of security' (Foucault 2007a: 6). This novel form of power applies a technology radically different from the juridical and disciplinary forms of power. Likening this technology to the vaccination programmes – where the disease itself is injected into the body to create resistance – of public health campaigns against epidemics (Foucault 2007a: 10), Foucault defines the guiding idea of the security apparatus as the use of elements of *society's own reality* in its own governance.

> The mechanism of security works on the basis of this reality, by trying to use it as a support and make it function, make its components function in relation to each other. In other words, [. . .] the essential function of security [. . .] is to respond to a reality in such a way that this response cancels out the reality to which it responds – nullifies it, or limits, checks, or regulates it. (Foucault 2007a: 47)

Foucault's concept of the apparatus of security is usually understood in the context of economic liberalism and governing of societies through market mechanisms and competition, where his analyses were moving at the time. However, his earlier exposition of the social use of the antisocial elements (for the purposes of creating repulsion for insubordination in the population) foreshadows the idea of the apparatus of security. We may think that the delinquency produced in prison is injected into the social body like a vaccine, intensifying, as it were, its own defence mechanisms rather than trying to weed out delinquency in the repressive ways of disciplinary and juridical power.

Another defining feature of the apparatus of security is its design of social spaces and structures of governing so that *circulation* – traffic of things, people and money – would not be blocked but rather enhanced (Foucault 2007a: 17–20). The genuine site for the development of this idea, too, is surely economic governance. Nevertheless, at this point we may also see the analysis of the penal system foreshadowing instruments of security: confined in prison, delinquents are useless; but if they are put into circulation, they become useful.

Finally, the example of the penal system demonstrates at a more general level how knowledge-power functions. Certain practices of power not only employ but entirely depend on knowledge. A good example of this is the ways in which the social control powers exercised through the penal system depend on the 'political observatory' established by prison through its tentacles into society. All of this knowledge concerns not the juridico-political system of public government, but its underside. This knowledge of society is not knowledge of its legal rules or its highly esteemed political principles such as democracy. Knowledge-power is not the production and use of public knowledge, but the most undemocratic knowledge circulating in those practices of power that work best in secret.

Jurisdiction and veridiction

Now let us return to the question of how to grasp the heart of the broader trajectory covering Foucault's works on knowledge-power. One of the conceptualisations of this by Foucault himself was his notions of *veridiction* and *jurisdiction*. Taken by itself, veridiction as truth-locution is the plain observation and accounting of what exists externally to the observer. In turn, jurisdiction as legal locution is the equally plain intervention into society, the imposition of norms that depends on the authority of the speaker to tell others – or oneself – what the law is. Analytical separation of these two echoes Hume insisting on the incommensurability of 'is' and 'ought'.

Let us say that knowledge of society at the birth of sociology (perhaps coinciding with the figure of Auguste Comte) confronted the law (or the juridical concept of political society) and thus created the problem of the nature of norms. Drawing on Georges Canguilhem, the problem was whether norms are *external* or *immanent* to society. The law as an externally imposed social order conceives norms as constituting an artificial organisation that is always fundamentally arbitrary. External norms require that they are especially concerned by those who would live under them, or at least by those who are tasked with their administration.

The requirement of concern implies for Canguilhem that external norms are rules that will first have to be *represented*, then *learned*, then *remembered* and, after all this, *applied*. At the birth of sociology, the social order that is sustained this way was contrasted with the idea of an organism, where no such activities of sustenance are necessary. In an organism, 'the order of life is made of a set of rules lived without problems', that is, without concern and consciousness. Norms that are immanent will act 'without being represented', and 'neither deliberation nor calculation' is required on the part of anyone or anything regulated by immanent norms (Canguilhem 1991: 250).

Hence, a norm can be either 'the effect of a choice and a decision external to the object' or 'intrinsic to the object' – the latter norm works well 'in the absence of an act of awareness', whereas the former can never do so (Canguilhem 1991: 238). Legally conceived norms are external norms, and they will always require acts of awareness – representation and reflection. Because of their necessary mediation by consciousness, there will always have to be a certain 'divergence', 'distance' and 'delay between the rule and regulation' (Canguilhem 1991: 238). The practice of law takes place in this space of divergence, distance and delay, which it will have to create for itself between the rule and regulation. In other words, the practice of law is a game of representations and reflections, which will necessarily break down the social norms that are 'lived without problems' and without divergence, distance and delay between rule and regulation.

However, the whole distinction between immanent and external norms – and thus between veridiction and jurisdiction – is highly problematic. Immanent norms may very well exist, but knowledge of these will not remain neutral and innocent. Knowledge of society is regulation of society at the same time. Especially for Foucault, the regulation of society that employs immanent norms may be anonymous and impersonal, but it is nonetheless carried out in regimes of practices that exert power on individuals. These regimes of practices, where knowledge of society circulates and relates to power, are the site for what both Canguilhem and Foucault called 'normalisation'. Normalisation is regulation of society without its subjects' awareness of the concealed power of knowledge, without representations and reflections of norms hidden in what is presented as fact.

Here we come to the heart of knowledge-power: constitutive of the relationships of knowledge-power are intersections between jurisdiction as legal locution and veridiction as truth-locution. With that, one also understands the way in which Foucault's archaeological researches on systems of scientific knowledge and genealogical researches on mechanisms of power relate to each other. In an interview in 1978, Foucault explained his entire project in the following way:

> It is a question of analysing a 'regime of practices' – practices being understood here as places where what is said and what is done, rules imposed and reasons given, the planned and the taken-for-granted meet and interconnect.
>
> To analyse 'regimes of practices' means to analyse programs of conduct that have both prescriptive effects regarding what is to be done (effects of 'jurisdiction') and codifying effects regarding what is to be known (effects of 'veridiction'). (Foucault 2000h: 225)

In his lectures the following year (*The Birth of Biopolitics*), Foucault applied the notions of veridiction and jurisdiction to his analysis of the market-system vis-à-vis political power. The market, for Foucault, was one of the instances of 'intersections between jurisdiction and veridiction' (Foucault 2008: 34) in that it did indeed establish norms of action and effects of jurisdiction, on the basis of what was to be known about market-mechanisms. From the point of view of Foucault's researches on the whole, intersections between jurisdiction and veridiction belong to what he depicted as the *coupled history of truth and law* that defines his work:

> You can see that all these cases – whether it is the market, the confessional, the psychiatric institution, or the prison – involve taking up a history of truth under different angles, or rather, taking up a history of truth that is coupled, from the start, with a history of law. [. . .] I would propose undertaking a history of truth coupled with a history of law. (Foucault 2008: 35)

Epieikeia and the right to difference

In Foucault's history of truth and law, one of the theses is that juridical institutions, and therewith the juridical model of power, have been conquered, taken over by practices working through different logics and models. The common denominator of these practices appears to be that they all operate through veridiction, a certain type of knowledge that has 'effects of jurisdiction'. In other words, an element of jurisdiction hides in veridiction. I would like to conclude by posing a question to this 'coupled history', not from the side of the truth, but from the side of the law. Insofar as the practice of law is plain jurisdiction, might there be an original veridictional element hiding in this practice in a similar way as the jurisdictional element hides in knowledge-power practices?

To address that problem, let us elaborate a little on Aristotle's two forms of judicial justice: justice as fairness to the facts, *epieikeia*, and justice through laws, *kata nomoi* (*Nicomachean Ethics*: V.10 and *Rhetoric*: I.13). In other words: equity and legality. Judicial justice is different from political justice; it is not about which laws are good and which are bad, and how to distinguish them, but it concerns the practice of law, application of general legislation to individual cases.

Accordingly, the legal mechanism of *epieikeia* and legality is not based on the distinction between justice and law, but on the distinction between law and facts. This latter distinction, in turn, works out in an institutionalised division of labour between legislators, who enact general laws; judges, who apply general laws to individual cases; and litigants, who present the facts of individual cases before the judges (*Rhetoric*: I.1). For Aristotle, the problem of *epieikeia*, as a distinct form of justice appearing in legal practice, is the following: 'The source of the difficulty is that equity [*epieikés*], though just, is not legal justice [*dikaion kata nomos*], but a rectification of legal justice [*nomímou dikaíou*]' (*Nicomachean Ethics*: 1137b.3).

The point about rectification is 'the essential nature of the equitable: it is a rectification of law where law is defective because of its generality' (*Nicomachean Ethics*: 1137b). Remarkably, this depicts the fact that the legal system can look upon itself critically: the injustices to be considered are not those wrongs that the subjects summoned before the court may have committed, but wrongs that the legal system (the practice of law) itself might commit by too rigid, imprudent and indiscrete an application of general legislation.

Judges facing a situation calling for equitable justice should decide the case 'as the lawgiver would himself decide if he were present on the occasion, and would have enacted if he had been cognizant of the case in question' (*Nicomachean Ethics*: 1137b). In *Rhetoric*, Aristotle stipulates further that to be equitable is 'to look, not to the law but to the legislator; not to the letter of the law but to the intention of the legislator; not to the action itself, but to the moral purpose; not to the part, but to the whole' (*Rhetoric*: 1374b). It is notable that here, too, justice as *epieikeia* connects with justice *kata nomoi*, by its construct of a legislator that is not the real legislator, but only a device of interpretation.

Despite the fact that at the moment of the judge's decision to invoke *epieikeia* there is a departure from legislation, *after the decision* a new law (judge-made law) has been established. Previous 'decisions are useful to those who are arguing about similar cases', Aristotle says in *Rhetoric* (1376a), but a stricter requirement of consistency of practice and equal treatment finds support in Aristotle's elaborations of justice as equality. In his *Politics* (1280a), Aristotle stipulates the following: 'For instance, it is thought that justice is equality [*ison*], and so it is, though not for everybody but only for those who are equals; and it is thought that inequality [*anison*] is just, for so indeed it is, though not for everybody, but for those who are unequal'.

The context of this statement is political justice – the right distribution of honours and riches that requires an assessment of the merits of individuals. *Mutatis mutandis*, however, the same precept – according to which *equals should be treated equally, but unequals unequally* – underlies the requirement of consistency in the practice of law. A new state of legality will emerge from any application of *epieikeia* in that it constitutes a model (precedent) for future cases.

Epieikeia connects to legality in all these ways, but it is still something that one uses for the purposes of departing from legality. To achieve this, the strategy of *epieikeia* plays two registers, both of which are external to legality as justice *kata nomos*. The first register by which *epieikeia* is activated is that of facts, the special circumstances of the case. Aristotle illustrated the basic function of *epieikeia*, adaptation of the law to facts faced in a case, by likening it to the technique of measuring stone-blocks of indefinite shapes by construction engineers.

> For what is itself indefinite can only be measured by an indefinite standard, like the leaden rule used by Lesbian builders; just as that rule is not rigid but can be bent to the shape of the stone, so a special ordinance is made to fit the circumstances of the case. (*Nicomachean Ethics*: 1137b)

The other register played by the strategy of *epieikeia* is that of so-called *unwritten laws* that are customs and *general laws* that are 'those based on nature' (*Rhetoric*: 1373b). Thus Aristotle's *epieikeia* has at its disposal not only the register of facts, but also the register of supra-statutory law and extra-legal justice: 'equity is justice that goes beyond the written law' (*Rhetoric*: 1374a). In the philosophy of law, this sort of reference to justice that goes beyond positively enacted legislation has always triggered the problem of the relationship between the law and morality. At that point, morality means supreme normative standards, which do not depend on legality. However, *epieikeia* is not first and foremost about universal, rational or godly justice that serves as a measure for the legitimacy of legal laws. But what then is *epieikeia* about?

This is the point at which the question of *epieikeia* brings us to the problem of veridiction hidden in the practice of law that is supposed to be plain jurisdiction. *Epieikeia* is not set in motion by an intervention of universal morality in legal affairs, but by the singularity of some extraordinary circumstances that occur in time and place. In the first place, *epieikeia* requires sensitivity to concrete facts – that transpire to be in some significant way different from those more or less unquestioned presumptions that have formed the basis of legislation.

To consider what these presumptions are, here are some examples from today's law. Certain tacit views one has of family life underlie the complex of laws that regulate marriage, the upbringing of children, inheritance, and so on. However, a child may be living, not with his or her mother and father, but with a mother and her female partner. Received knowledge on the driving forces of the market clearly underlies the branch of commercial law (company law, competition law, consumer law, and so on). However, companies exist that do not aim at profiting their owners, but have set themselves some entirely non-economic objectives.

To make sense of labour law, one thinks of the sorts of power relations that normally belong to a workplace. However, paid work can be done in an entirely different social setting. Understanding the legal protection against ethnic agitation comes out of our historical experience of nationalism and persecution of minorities. Yet someone who has slandered an ethnic group that forms the majority of the population may find himself accused of the offence of ethnic agitation. Finally, the legal stance taken towards the practice of prostitution in each country builds on the culturally arbitrary views on normal sexuality.

Judges constantly find themselves facing situations unanticipated by legislators. Things develop in directions that depart from what the legislators had in mind – or in the back of their mind – when enacting laws. What causes troubles in individual cases, and thus also creates the need for *epieikeia*, are not the deviations from legal norms as such; rather, it is deviations from the *normality* that had formed the basis of legislation that create the need to adapt by way of practising *epieikeia*. Normality in the background of laws is not necessarily something that legislators had been aware of. On the contrary, normality was the world in which they lived without troubles – the world of *immanent norms*, in the language of Canguilhem. Legislators certainly wanted to change the world by implementing their policies through laws, but a greater part of that world certainly remains untouched; this part they meant neither to change nor not to change. This type of normality is always already hidden in all laws.

The veridictional regulation that silently forms the basis of the work of legislators remains outside their intentionality, but not outside all discourse in legal practice. With its focus on the exceptional circumstances of individual cases, *epieikeia* can be conceived as exactly the mechanism for bringing into discourse the normality presumptions underlying legislation. *Epieikeia* is not so much a counter-measure against legality, but against normalisation at work in the silent, unthought-of veridictional element, indeed knowledge, hidden in what can be called the *law's unawareness*.

Through its reflection on the particularity of individual circumstances, *epieikeia* also brings into consciousness veridictional regulation or prejudice that works best in silence – and breaks it down at once. Practice of *epieikeia* takes immanent norms of society away from their unthought-of spheres, and brings them into the sphere of external norms and legal discourse. In that sphere, norms are artificial and arbitrary; they require attention – representing, learning, remembering and applying. Furthermore, *epieikeia* creates a space of delay and distance between the norm and regulation – a space of mediation and discourse – that breaks down the immediate nature of normalisation. Nevertheless, what is to be learned is that veridictional normality remains at work in the immensely vast sphere of law's unawareness, and this is one of the types of knowledge that circulate in practices of power.

It is perhaps somewhat strange to speak about knowledge that circulates in practices, insisting anyway that awareness is somehow absent. What kind of knowledge operates without awareness? This strange knowledge was nonetheless the subject matter of Foucault's philosophical exercises with history, of his explorations of ever new forms of knowledge-power. For him, the objective of these exercises and explorations was to 'free thought from what it silently thinks, and so enable it to think differently' (Foucault 1992: 9). One may perhaps say that the practice of *epieikeia* does something similar in the field of law.

Translating all of this into the juridical language of rights, one may also say that corresponding to the fundamental right to equal treatment entailed by the principle of legality, *epieikeia*, in its turn, entails the *right to difference* that is just as fundamental. The right to difference seems to underlie the very usual business of law, that of invoking fairness to the facts in order to trump overly strict and indiscriminate application of legality. This is what lawyers do in their field every day, but assertion of the legal right to difference has a function in the broader field of social power as well. There this genuinely legal mechanism generates a counterforce against the force of normalisation. Its employment is a form of what Foucault designated as *anti-authority struggles* provoked by normalising exclusion of difference. Finally, what are these struggles?

> They are struggles that question the status of the individual. On the one hand, they assert the right to be different and underline everything that makes individuals truly individual. On the other hand, they attack everything that separates the individual, breaks his links with others, splits up community life, forces the individual back on himself, and ties him to his own identity in a constraining way. (Foucault 2000e: 330)

Chapter 10

Adoui and Cornuaille: legality and equity

My objective in the following analysis of the case of *Adoui and Cornuaille* is to make perceptible the basic mechanism internal to the practice of law that deals with the dilemma of jurisdiction and veridiction: power through laws, power thorough knowledge and the way they connect. The legal mechanism in question belongs to the elementary structures of the field as fortification against the storming of all kinds of forces that play by the register of knowledge and truth. What makes it magnificent is its perfect permeability or, as Niklas Luhmann would describe it: cognitive openness (Luhmann 1988). All kinds of veridictional communications can freely enter the field, but when they are inside, the law will strand and engulf them on its own ground.

The mechanism of equity and legality by which legal practice confronts veridictional power was explained in the previous chapter through Aristotle. Let us quickly recapitulate. In the basic design, questions of fact will have to be distinguished from questions of law, and then general legislation from individual decisions. This is the set-up for the dilemma between justice *kata nomos* and justice as *epieikeia*, between legality and equity. Equity connects with legality in three ways: it corrects deficiencies in legislation, it uses the methodical construct of the legislator for the purposes of interpretation and, finally, every decision based on equity creates new legality for the future. At the time of the decision, however, practice of equity disconnects from strict legalism by drawing on two extra-legal registers: facts, on the one hand; and unwritten law and justice, on the other hand.

Further complexity had already been generated in this structure by Aristotle in his observation that sometimes the foresight on the part of the legislator also covers the possibility that particular circumstances may arise in which their legislation would not be applicable. That is to say, legislators may sometimes intentionally insert an element of *epieikeia* to the *nomoi*. The normal case is that the possibility of such circumstances simply 'escaped their notice', but it may also happen that legislators are very well aware that they are 'unable to define [the law] for all cases'. Then the legislator would employ 'a universal statement, which is not applicable to all, but only to most, cases' (*Rhetoric*: 1374a).

Now, in a sense, our little natural laboratory of legal theory presents in the structure of its legal norms the modern version of precisely that complexity;

namely, the complexity of legislation that incorporates mechanisms of equity. The laboratory has two instances of this. Recall that the law of the Treaty (justice established *kata nomoi*) is first of all that 'Freedom of movement for workers shall be secured within the Community', which includes the right to move freely and to stay in the territory of Member States for the purposes of employment (Article 48).

The first mechanism of *epieikeia* is inserted into that structure by way of the *ordre public* reservation: the provision of rights is 'subject to limitations justified on grounds of *ordre public*' (Article 48(3)). This means that the treaty-makers took into account the possibility that special circumstances may arise in which the general rule would not be feasible. The second mechanism of *epieikeia* is, as a matter of fact, inserted inside the first mechanism. This second mechanism is the personal conduct requirement provided in Article 3(1) of Directive 64/221: *ordre public* measures 'shall be based exclusively on the personal conduct of the individual concerned'. The meaning of this is that one must always look at the special circumstances of each case.

With *ordre public* and personal conduct, two openings appear in the legal texture. Both open up the way for insertion of argumentation from the particular circumstances of the case at hand. As will be seen, this means more precisely: the particular circumstances of the Member State in question, on the one hand, and the particular circumstances of the person in question, on the other hand. What this will make visible in *Adoui and Cornuaille* is the variety of ways in which juridical employment of legality and equity embraces and integrates veridictional discourse within its structures. The objective of the following analysis is to put forward as an object the shifts and transformations that the different participants' tactical conjoining of the elements of equity and legality effect, or purport to effect, on the issue.

While this analytical device constructed on the basis of Aristotle seems to be affording something like a universal structure of the legal field, it should be noted that within that structure the practice of law, where the device is not a schema of analysis but a scheme of action, makes the framework into a moving thing. When the legal struggle (or in Aristotle's terms, the rhetoric) begins, the analyst must be prepared for an endless process of reconceptualisation. Legality and equity will appear quite different in the action of the participants, whose question is: 'what use should be made of them when exhorting or dissuading, accusing or defending':

> For it is evident that, if the written law is counter to our case, we must have recourse to the general law and equity, as more in accordance with justice; and we must argue that, when the dicast takes an oath to decide to the best of his judgement, he means that he will not abide rigorously by the written laws; that equity is ever constant and never changes, even as the general law, which is based on nature, whereas the written laws often vary. (*Rhetoric*: 1375a)

If legality would not support one's objectives, 'it is necessary to see whether the law is contradictory to another approved law or to itself'. Furthermore, if 'the meaning of the law is equivocal, we must turn it about, and see in which way it is to be interpreted so as to suit the application of justice or expediency, and have recourse to that'. Finally, if 'the conditions which led to enactment of the law are now obsolete, while the law itself remains, one must endeavour to make this clear and to combat the law by this argument'. All of these are tactics of justice as *epieikeia* for getting round the type of justice that is established *kata nomoi* (*Rhetoric*: 1375b).

> But if the written law favours our case, we must say that the oath of the dicast 'to decide to the best of his judgement' does not justify him in deciding contrary to the law, but is only intended to relieve him from the charge of perjury, if he is ignorant of the meaning of the law; that no one chooses that which is good absolutely, but that which is good for himself; that there is no difference between not using the laws and their not being enacted; that in the other arts there is no advantage in trying to be wiser than the physician, for an error on his part does not do so much harm as the habit of disobeying the authority; that to seek to be wiser than the laws is just what is forbidden in the most approved laws. (*Rhetoric*: 1375b)

So there is a legal mechanism working on an axis that connects two concepts: *legality* and *equity*. These two concepts constitute the practical device functioning in the legal field, where it is used all the time by legal actors. Yet these concepts also constitute a device that can be used in analysis of legal practice to find out how the legal practice confronts veridictional practices and normalisation that comes with them. Let us call them the basic concepts of justice in the practice of law.

Facts of *Adoui and Cornuaille*

Ms Rezguia Adoui, 'a young person in good health' (at 1648), was a French national who had moved to the city of Liège in Belgium. In June 1980, she applied for a residence permit in Belgium. In October, the Belgian Minister of Justice decided to refuse the permit: '[. . .] on the grounds that her personal conduct made her residence undesirable for reasons of *ordre public* and that she worked in a bar which was suspect from the point of view of morals and in which waitresses displayed themselves in the window and were able to be alone with their clients' (at 1668).

Later, in proceedings before the ECJ, the Belgian Government stated that Ms Adoui had been 'on view in a window on a public thoroughfare' (at 1685). Ms Adoui herself denied 'engaging in prostitution' (at 1680). Ms Adoui left the country, but came back one month later, in November 1980, and informed the local authorities about her return. In reaction to that, the authorities ordered her on 27 November to leave Belgium within four days. On 1 December, Ms Adoui applied to the *Commission Consultative des Étrangers* for an opinion, but the

Minister of Justice considered that action to be out of time, and reiterated the order to leave. Ms Adoui refused to comply, regarding the action of the authorities as unlawful. She summoned the City of Liège and the Belgian State before the *Tribunal de Premier Instance* at Liège.

Ms Cornuaille, also a French national, had been staying in Belgium since June 1978 and had at that time applied for a residence permit. She never received an answer to her application, but remained in Belgium with 'a certificate of registration' having been renewed for her several times. Meanwhile, however, the *Office des Étrangers* had received a 'report on morality' drawn up by a policeman that described 'her as a waitress of questionable moral character who "in scant dress displays herself to clients"' (at 1669). Among other things, the report on Ms Cornuaille's morality had claimed that she had contracted a venereal disease, but this turned out not to be true (at 1683).

The *Office des Étrangers* requested an opinion on Ms Cornuaille from the *Commission Consultative des Étrangers* that stated on 25 April 1979 that Ms Cornuaille's 'presence in Belgium is detrimental to the requirements of *ordre public*'. Ms Cornuaille, who also denied engaging in prostitution, protested on several grounds and lodged a complaint with the *Procureur du Roi*, the public prosecutor, against those who had reported on her morality and thereby had, according to her, committed 'false written statements, defamation, injurious statements and calumnies'. While these criminal proceedings were still pending, the *Commission Consultative* reconsidered the case, did not change its opinion and recommended Ms Cornuaille's expulsion in September 1980. Ms Cornuaille summoned the Belgian State before the *Tribunal de Premier Instance* at Liège (at 1669).

According to Ms Adoui and Ms Cornuaille, the 'Belgian authorities make no secret of the fact that they are systematically expelling all French waitresses, perhaps because they may be "the logistic support" for the French underworld' (at 1680). They also said that 'they wished to perform work other than that of waitresses and that the file of the case proves that they have sought other employment', but explained their situation to be such that the Belgian authorities' practice purposefully makes their success in this impossible. This is because the only document given to them is in fact the 'order to leave' that expires after a given date and is renewed monthly until the residence permit case is finally decided. They claimed that the Belgian authorities prolong the procedure (ie, rather than handling the case, they just keep renewing the order to leave) with an intention to 'discourage the alien'. With a mere 'order to leave' it is impossible for them 'to find new employment, except in particular environments such as those of bars' (at 1680, 1682).

Belgium, in turn, explained that connections with the 'international underworld' were not the reason for expulsion in the cases at hand, but working 'in a bar which was suspect from the point of view of morals'. Beyond that, however, Belgium stated that 'prostitution in certain circumstances promotes criminal activities, in particular by the money which it raises for those who exploit prostitution'. All in all, the point is that prostitution 'intrinsically jeopardizes *ordre public*' if it is carried on 'in a provocative manner' (at 1685).

'Incitement to debauchery', as well as procuring and brothels, were prohibited under Belgian law but not prostitution as such, while the local Police Order of the City of Liège made the 'act of displaying oneself in a window punishable'. Belgian law will be further discussed below. It should be pointed out, however, that in addition to prostitution pure and simple, it was the practice of being in view 'in a window on a public thoroughfare' (at 1685; comparable to the offence of 'incitement to debauchery') that seems to have been the crucial determination of what in this case was considered to pose a threat to *ordre public*.

The president of the *Tribunal de Premier Instance* at Liège stayed the proceedings in both cases and requested a preliminary ruling from the ECJ. As the Advocate General disapprovingly notes, the Liège court 'saw fit to adopt practically the whole of the detailed questionnaire submitted to it by the counsel of the plaintiffs' and transmitted it '*in toto*' to the ECJ (at 1715). From the point of view of research, however, it is only interesting to see how different the case file becomes when one of the filters, namely that of the referring national court, is removed and more of the original discourse channels in.

Out of the 29 questions presented by the tribunal, only the discussions on the first one-third of the file will be analysed here. These discussions revolved once again around the concepts of *ordre public* and personal conduct. 'Would the Court kindly give a definition of the concept of *ordre public*' (at 1671), the Liège Tribunal begins its requests. In other words, in what circumstances are Member States allowed to derogate from the rights of free movement? The Liège Tribunal spelled out its dilemma with the notion of *ordre public* as follows: 'On numerous occasions the Court has stated that the concept of *ordre public* could fall within the discretion of the Member States subject to the limitations of Community law. Would the Court specify those limitations?' (at 1671).

The same basic legal structure reappears once again and by now we are certainly familiar with it. It does no harm, however, to recapitulate it quickly. First, Community law (TEC Article 48) confers rights on European individuals, which considerably restricts the powers of the Member States. Member States are no longer free to decide who can enter their territory. Secondly, Community rights are subject to limitations justified on grounds of *ordre public*. This gives some of the powers back to the Member States: in circumstances where the *ordre public* of a country is under threat, they can still decide to restrict the free movement of a European individual. Thirdly, use of *ordre public* is subject to limitations of Community law.

These limitations restrict the powers of Member States to derogate from free movement. Authorities must move within a certain leeway, a margin of appreciation, rather than decide freely. On the one hand, limitations were provided in Directive 221/64. There was, most significantly, the personal conduct require-ment: measures derogating from free movement 'shall be based exclusively on the personal conduct of the individual concerned' (Article 3(1)). On the other hand, the semantic field of the notion of *ordre public* had been elaborated in the case law of the ECJ. The kernel of this semantic field, as it stood by the time of *Adoui and Cornuaille*, was delineated in the following way: a genuine and sufficiently serious threat to fundamental interests of society must be present to such degree that the measure of expulsion is necessary in a democratic society. Anything less is not a case of *ordre public*.

Despite the considerable narrowing down of the derogation powers of Member States, the Court had not abolished the basic doctrine about jurisdiction it had established in *van Duyn*. According to this doctrine, it was still up to each Member State to determine whether such a threat exists in a concrete situation. These situations vary from country to country and from one time to another: the same kind of conduct can be dangerous in one country or time, but not dangerous in another country or time. Community institutions may revise and supervise the measures taken, but Member States have the basic jurisdiction in matters of *ordre public*, albeit within the given limitations.

'How', the Liège court asked at this point, 'can the doctrine expounded in [*van Duyn*] be reconciled with the principle of non-discrimination contained in Article 7 of the Treaty' (at 1671)? Non-discrimination constitutes the main rule as for the whole Treaty. However, it applies 'without prejudice to any special provisions contained' in the Treaty. Article 48, with its permission of *ordre public* derogations from free movement, is such a special provision: it justifies discrimination. 'Subject to what precise conditions and limitations', the Liège Tribunal asked, 'may discrimination exist in the legislation and practice of a Member State between its own nationals and the nationals of other Member States' (at 1671)? Derogations from non-discrimination present a similar problem as derogations from the rights of free movement. What this problem adds, however, is a stronger concern for the requirement of equality before the law.

From fundamental state of legality to integrity of state interests

Ms Adoui and Ms Cornuaille were suggesting a radical revision of the concept of *ordre public*. Whereas the starting point of the legal life of this notion had been 'social harm', in the view of the plaintiffs *ordre public* 'permits the State and the municipalities to derogate from the observance of the rights of individuals when, if they did not do so, the existence or essence of the community governed by the rule of law would be threatened' (at 1678). Thus, for the plaintiffs, it is only protection of the rule of law itself that may justify derogations from it.

This suggestion deserves some reflection. Let us say that the prevailing state, after *Bouchereau*, was that *legality* (rule of law, non-discrimination) is the main rule, but it is recognised that *factual conditions* (threatened fundamental interests of society) may emerge in which derogations are allowed. On this basis, it seems that the plaintiffs' suggestion involves two steps. First, the argument implies that the state of legality (a community governed by the rule of law) is moved to the domain of factual conditions – the maintenance of which is one of the fundamental interests of society. Secondly, the argument is that safeguarding this interest should be the only permissible justification for derogations from legality. In effect, *ordre public* would mean a state of legality or, at any rate, the factual conditions for the possibility of a state of legality. Only concern for legality itself may justify exceptional derogations from it.

The plaintiffs' interpretation involves a somewhat drastic change. The ECJ should figure the identity and boundaries of the Community law system vis-à-vis Member State jurisdiction so that *ordre public* as a limit to legality is faced only in the necessary conditions of existence of legality. In other words, it means that *veridiction* (truth-locution, fundamental interests of society) is subjected to and looked at in the light of the requirements of *jurisdiction* (legal locution, legality). It is also a call to remove the derogation doctrine of *van Duyn* based on Member State exigencies, and to establish a new derogation doctrine on a peculiarly self-contained foundation of legality. Non-legality can be excused only in the name of legality.

From the perspective of economy of *power* in the European polity, it is clear that the *legal* system for its distribution would at this point close up and become fundamentally self-referential. Significant facts of *ordre public* would no longer represent extra-legal interests of Member States, but become interpreted as reducible to conditions of existence for the law (state of legality) in its factual environment. It is not surprising that all the Member States participating in the proceedings rejected the suggestion of the plaintiffs. They held on to the *van Duyn* doctrine on Member State jurisdiction. They flatly refused to talk about anything like a state of legality being the purpose of *ordre public* derogations.

Belgium submitted that the 'different treatment of nationals and aliens' – including those Europeans who are 'delinquent aliens' – 'is inevitable since a State can clearly not expel its own citizens'. In principle, it is equally clear that a Member State can expel non-nationals who are also Europeans. 'There is no contradiction', therefore, 'between the doctrine enunciated in *van Duyn* and the principle of non-discrimination' (at 1684, 1685).

In turn, the meaning of the concept of *ordre public* should not be fixed, Belgium submitted, but left open for evolution and adaptation: 'it should be able to evolve [and] adapt to the progress of each society'. Progress is a more important concern than legality. Legality of *ordre public* – the same or a more cohesive concept of it in all Member States – would require a 'definition which is too precise' to allow adaptation and evolution. For Belgium, it seems impossible 'to lay down the limits' for use of *ordre public* on the Community level, because each country has its own 'specific circumstances', that is, its own progress and therefore its own concept of *ordre public* (at 1684).

The French Government supported the position of Belgium: a Community definition of *ordre public* is not desirable. It took 'the view that for obvious reasons the national authorities of each Member State must be able to determine the content of the concept'. It resorted to Article 48, which allows each Member State 'to maintain in their legislation and practices exceptions applicable to Community citizens'. What it called 'differential treatment' on the basis of personal conduct is justified on grounds of *ordre public*, which is distinct from discrimination that is unjustifiable. Discrimination proper would mean measures 'based on reasons of a general preventive nature' – instead of on the personal conduct of the individual (at 1689).

For the French Government, Member States have been conferred 'general powers' to determine their own concept of *ordre public*, 'subject only to the rules laid down by the Court'. The Community institutions, in turn, carry out an '*ex posto facto* supervision exercised case by case on consideration of the particular facts' (at 1689).

The Italian Government supported the views of Belgium and France. The ECJ cannot prohibit discrimination against European individuals, because this 'would be tantamount to abolishing the reservation expressly laid down in Article 48(3) of the Treaty'. European individuals are not nationals, they are foreigners. 'It is a fact', said the Italian Government, 'that restrictions justified on grounds of *ordre public* may create for an alien a situation different from that in which nationals find themselves. As to the concept of *ordre public*, it must necessarily rely on fluid facts that may constitute 'a social danger'. 'This concept differs specifically from one country to another and changes as time passes'. Therefore, on the one hand, each country has its own *ordre public*; no legality exists at Community level (at 1692).

> On the other hand, the limitations [to use of the concept of *ordre public*] may be common to the Member States, but they are 'limitations', that is to say limits beyond which it is forbidden to go but which do not define the concept. (at 1692–93)

Interestingly, on the side of limitations (threats must be *genuine* and *serious*, interest must be *fundamental* and measures *necessary in a democratic society*, and so on) legality prevails at the Community level, but not with regard to the concept itself. What does it mean that limitations do not define the concept? Clearly, it means that Member States retain their powers. But what are these powers? What, in the end, defines the concept if Community law does not define it? As will be seen, for most Member States it is not national law either that does this. At this point, Italy suggests that 'social danger' defines the concept. Perhaps one should say that social danger *undefines* the concept: the idea is to leave *ordre public* unfixed and open to evolution, adaptation and progress. Beyond the problem of distribution of powers between different *jurisdictions*, would social danger after all be a matter of truth – *veridiction* – rather than law and legality at all?

The Dutch Government supported the views of the other Member States. As for the possibility of engendering legality by a generally applicable legal definition of the concept of *ordre public* at Community level, the Dutch Government submitted the following statement: 'It is not possible to give an all-embracing definition of the concept of *ordre public*, since it involves variable interests which the State or public executive bodies consider to be fundamental public interests which they must protect on their own initiative' (at 1697).

The United Kingdom stated plainly that: 'it is neither necessary nor even possible to give a definition of *ordre public* as such. The term may be interpreted only in the circumstances of each individual case' (at 1698). Instead of legality, one should hold on to the basis prudently delivered by the ECJ in its existing case law.

> That basis enables a careful balance to be made between the needs and aims of each Member State which seeks to protect its legitimate interests (and those of individuals) within its borders, on the one hand, and the needs of the Community and nationals of Member States within the Community, on the other. (at 1698)

In sum, the file shows that all the Member States vehemently protected their freedom in the sense of the widest possible margin of appreciation. In other words, they guarded the opening in the Community legal texture against its closure by more legal texture. They fought against further juridification of the practices of their immigration authorities.

From weighting and balancing to semiotic of dangers

From today's legal theoretical perspective, it seems probable that the case file presents the Commission's contribution in a somewhat distorted manner. We have become accustomed to distinguishing between two types of legal reasoning in this context. On the one hand is the application of rules whose scope of application cannot intersect. On the other hand is the weighing of legal principles whose scope of application overlap. From the perspective of this distinction, the case file appears to present the Commission's submissions as internally inconsistent. On the one hand, the principles approach is endorsed; on the other hand, it preserves a very strict rule approach.

According to the case file, the Commission first stated that there is no common definition of the concept of *ordre public*; nor did it want to proceed by way of giving a specific list of Community law limits to its use. Instead, the Commission drew on 'the legal foundations on which such limits are based'. In the case at hand this foundation consists of two 'fundamental principles of Community law': *non-discrimination* and *proportionality* (at 1699).

According to the Commission, one must 'strike a balance between the application of the principle of non-discrimination [. . .] and the power accorded to Member States to adopt *ordre public* measures' (at 1699). This is, in today's terminology, an application of the general principle of proportionality, which as a meta-principle covering the entire field of legal principles: colliding legal values and other legitimate interests must be weighed against each other. In the words of the Commission, 'a comparison [should be] made of the two interests involved, the protection of national *ordre public* on the one hand and the free movement of persons on the other' (at 1700).

Then appears what one would today term the special sense of the principle of proportionality: the Commission requires that it must be ascertained 'whether the measure [of expulsion] is really necessary in order to uphold *ordre public*' and whether 'the threat is sufficiently serious to justify the measure envisaged'. To recapitulate, in its special sense proportionality requires that the measure restricting individual rights is *necessary* for achieving a given end, and that the (collective) interest protected is *sufficiently serious* in comparison to the seriousness of the individual's loss of rights (at 1700).

An orientation to principles of legal reasoning envisaged by the Commission is easy for a lawyer in this day and age. The Commission seems to be well acquainted with the theoretical currents of the time in its elaborations. It presents a model of legal reasoning that is more sophisticated and elastic than the Member States' two-track model of rules, according to which non-discrimination simply does not apply because a special provision exists. Strangely, however, the judgment then goes on to assess the manner in which the Commission had endorsed the two-track model just as rigorously as the Member States: non-discrimination 'only applies subject to special provision laid down in the Treaty and the regulations and directives issued for its implementation'. Hence, non-discrimination does not 'operate' in matters of free movement, because for these matters special provisions are laid down, namely Article 48 and Directive 221/64 (at 1700).

This is very strange, but considering only the first part of the Commission's contribution, in any event it is an invitation to embrace all interests in the evaluative scales of law. The import of this, on the one hand, is that fundamental interests of society are not extra-legal *facts*, but *values* that are legally protected to a greater or lesser extent. In other words, any particular factual conditions that may vary from one Member State to another do not allow an exit from the domain of Community law assessment.

On the other hand, if legality is no longer a matter of rigorous observance of a single rule of law that either applies or does not apply, it will incorporate, at the level of comprehensive principles, all possible concerns that claim legal recognition. One consequence of this is that the state of legality does not obstruct progress. On the contrary, argumentation from principles can be seen as a mechanism of law's adaptation to the evolution of society.

Moreover, the orientation to principles undermines the significance of the distinction between veridiction and jurisdiction; they are no longer entirely disparate types of locution and intelligibility. In the framework of the general principle of proportionality, all factors collapse in the same category where everything is subject to evaluative comparison. In the framework of the special principle of proportionality, *veridiction* – the discourse on the technical expediency and necessity of certain individuated means with respect to certain individuated ends pursued – is assigned a function within the practice of law. In other words, veridiction (truth-locution) becomes an element of jurisdiction (legal locution).

For the Advocate General, doubts about unlawful discrimination ensuing from Member State jurisdiction in matters of *ordre public* are 'manifestly without substance', because free movement involves and recognises the 'special treatment of foreign nationals', even European individuals: 'Essentially, the fact must be borne in mind that *ordre public* allows derogations from the principle of non-discrimination as well as from that of equality of treatment: the Treaty is very clear in that respect' (at 1718).

As for the concept of *ordre public*, the Advocate General notes that 'Community law does not define or purport to give an independent definition'. In Community law, 'there are numerous expressions derived from the laws of the Member States, whose interpretation involves reference to the principles, rules and concepts peculiar to those States'. *Ordre public* is one of these expressions. 'It is pointless, therefore', the Advocate General submitted, 'to ask this Court, whose function is to interpret Community law, for a definition of *ordre public*' (at 1716).

Moreover, he notes that *ordre public* is a concept whose meaning not only varies from Member State to Member State, but has multiple uses even within one Member State: 'It is hardly necessary to point out that within the national legal systems themselves there are areas of uncertainty and inconsistency in that respect, particularly since the concept of *ordre public* is used in various contexts (for example, in administrative law, criminal law, conflict of laws and of jurisdiction, etc.)' (at 1716).

So, *ordre public* is not a Community law concept, but rather an opening, a hatchway, that gives vent to what may come up in Member States. True, Community law places limitations on the scope of *ordre public*. The Advocate General surveyed these limitations as they were expounded on in the previous case law (restrictive interpretation of derogations, genuine and sufficient threat, fundamental interests necessary in a democratic society) and concluded: 'Frankly, I do not believe that further development of these concepts is necessary or desirable'. For him, the *van Duyn* doctrine about Member State jurisdiction is unquestionably valid: 'Member States continue to be, in principle, free to determine' *ordre public* 'in the light of their national needs'. The Court had acknowledged this in *Rutili* and so it should also in the present case (at 1717).

At this point a pause is necessary. It seems that the Advocate General made no new contributions to the discourse on *ordre public*. His opinion appears as a mere reiteration of what is the established law: it suggests no change, no further specification, but mere conservation of what the Court has already achieved. However, for the present purposes, his contribution makes a crucial resettlement of the distinction perceptible – *a new way to place the distinction* – between fact and norm, between veridiction and jurisdiction. The problem is: what are national laws from the perspective of Community law thus conceived?

The simple idea would be that national laws are, depending on their subject matter, either subject to Community law (as mere implementation measures or otherwise subject to Community law revision), or not within the scope of Community law at all. Certain intermediary categories exist (such as the areas where the Community legislator has regulatory competence, but has not for the time being exercised its powers), nevertheless we can ignore these categories for present purposes. Let us say, accordingly, that issues such as movement of labour are Community issues, but issues such as *ordre public* are national issues. One must fit one's discourse and action into one of the frameworks, Community or national, but not both. Hence, it is *either/or*, not *both/and*.

Considerable complexity is added to this simple idea by the Advocate General in that there are 'expressions' in Community law that are 'derived from the laws of the Member States'. What is the effective meaning of that? The Advocate General explains: interpretation of these expressions 'involves reference to the principles, rules and concepts peculiar to' the Member States. So far so good: Member State law is the superior meaning-context for interpretation of Community law at this point – just as at other points Community law is the superior meaning-context for interpretation of Member State law. Hence, in all possible conflicts of jurisdictions, it is never *either/or*, but always *both/and*.

However, let us ask again: what are national laws from the perspective of Community law? As to the expression '*ordre public*', relying on the Advocate General, one might come to the conclusion that national laws *are* Community law as well. Member State 'principles, rules and concepts' define Community law on *ordre public*. However, Member State principles, rules and concepts vary, and therefore Community law on *ordre public* remains explicitly indeterminate. It is a kind of no-law. The effective meaning of this would be that Community law only acted in this case as a multiplier of the power of the Member States by constituting any of the outcomes of the exercise of that power as legitimate.

It seems to me that this is not the right way to see things. Community law on *ordre public* is not just a ceremonial affirmation of Member State laws. What here deserves the name of 'Community law' is law that sets external limiting standards on Member State law, power and practice.

On the one hand, if Member State law incorporates Community legislation, the latter will still function externally as a standard. On the other hand, Member State powers as such are in no need of constitution by the Community law. Therefore, Community law pertains only to limitations (as so many participants have asserted) and these limitations are extrinsic to Member State powers, practices and laws. Even if Community law recognises the power of the Belgian authorities to define prostitution as dangerous to its *ordre public*, Community law only does this with a view to limitations on this power. Prostitution ought to be something that poses a genuine and sufficient threat to the fundamental interests the protection of which is necessary in a democratic society.

Once again, what are the 'principles, rules and concepts' of Member State law from the perspective of Community law? In a certain way, it seems to me that they turn out to be *facts*. They are facts in the same way as enactments of legislation by the parliament are facts before their constitutional review or human rights review; or in the same way as insertions of clauses into a contract are facts before the law of obligations. These facts engender valid legal norms only if they pass the critical test of the law that either recognises or does not recognise them. Thus, within the domain of 'legal phenomena', if you like, a distinction can be made between *facts* that express an intention, but sometimes fail to create valid law and *norms* that regulate which ones fail and which ones succeed in this.

In legal theory, following H. L. A. Hart, we have become accustomed to designating the former as 'primary rules' and the latter as 'secondary rules'.[1] This usage, I think, is blind to the reality that it is only on condition that laws can be (and are) relegated to the realm of facts that legality may generate a meaning as justice. The point of view from which it is possible to reflect the legal system and law as a *fact* is crucial in modern law. The injustices to be considered are not those wrongs that the individuals before the court may have committed, but wrongs that the legal system (the practice of law) itself might commit. Without that point of view, the law seemingly staying completely on the side of norms would in fact be identified with the fact of power. In other words, the law would be binding merely because 'a law is a law' (Radbruch 2006: 1). The 'is' slips in the normative system, where it either devours the 'ought' or assigns it to the hobbyism of philosophers.

The judges' submission clearly states that the principle of non-discrimination is applicable in the case at hand, despite the special provision on *ordre public* in Article 48. Expulsions are measures that Member States cannot 'apply to their own nationals', but can adopt with respect to European individuals. Therefore, in the dimension of the *choice of measures* the judges acknowledge that 'difference of treatment [. . .] must be allowed'. However, this does not oust the principle of non-discrimination from all validity. Member State authorities have the power to expel European individuals on specific grounds, but the exercise of this power must not be based 'on assessments of certain conduct which would have the effect of applying an arbitrary distinction to the detriment of nationals of other Member States'. So there is a dimension of the *assessment of conduct* in which difference of treatment is not allowed (at 1707).

What is this division between the dimensions of *measures* taken and *conduct* assessed? In the case at hand it is simply this: while the specific measure of expulsion is not possible in the case of prostitutes who are nationals of a particular Member State, nonetheless many other measures are perfectly available to a Member State insofar it assesses prostitution as dangerous. On that basis, it was clear to the judges that if none of these other measures is taken against nationals who practise prostitution in that Member State, then 'that conduct may not be considered as being of a sufficiently serious nature'. Only if the Member State concerned has also taken 'repressive measures or other genuine and effective measures intended to combat such conduct' with respect to its own nationals is it reasonable to think that this Member State truly considers its *ordre public* to be endangered by this conduct (at 1708).

As for the relativity of the concept of *ordre public*, the judges could still maintain that: 'Community law does not impose upon the Member States a uniform scale of values as regards conduct which may be considered as contrary to *ordre public*' (at 1708). The *van Duyn* doctrine on Member State jurisdiction in matters of *ordre public* is certainly retained.

However, it is this self-same jurisdiction that knocks back and rebounds on Member States by abolishing their power to discriminate in matters of *ordre public*. The judges do not try to teach Member States what, as a matter of fact, is dangerous and what is not, but simply feeds them here what they themselves have cooked up elsewhere. Interestingly this negative feedback effect is in actual fact created by a peculiar method of *veridiction*. From the viewpoint of veridiction, judges provided a semiotics for finding out about what is *truly* regarded as dangerous in a Member State, that is, dangerous beyond the false pretence of its immigration authorities. One must simply examine the Member State's exercise of power over its nationals – that is, the presumptions and outcomes of its *jurisdiction*, its legal locution, in the domain of the law of national citizens.

The Advocate General and the judges relate with Member State practice – the exercise of power in matters of *ordre public* – in an utterly different manner. For the Advocate General, Member State principles, rules and concepts simply enter the normative organisation of Community law. The law of the Member States on *ordre public* becomes the law of the Community. A hermeneutical symbiosis exists between the two jurisdictions at the level of interpretation. For the judges, instead, there is not a hermeneutic relationship but a semiotic one. Member State practices do not enter the normative meaning-context of Community law; rather, they are signs to be interpreted in their own game. The Member State exercise of *jurisdiction* provides a legally filtered but, in a way, still *veridictional* vision of the social dangers in the country. That is an insight as to what the Member State truly fears.

It is surprising that the judges appear to be able to do two mutually incompatible things at one and the same time. On the one hand, this practice can completely open itself up towards the realm of facts, affirming the total cultural arbitrariness and social contingency of what can present dangers to society. As if disregarding all the Court's previous elaborations of evaluative criteria to define what can constitute danger by some limiting standards (eg genuine, sufficient, necessary in a democratic society), in this case these dangers end up being nothing more than matters of definition. What the Member States have stated within the framework of their jurisdiction constitutes the body of signs to be deciphered; there is nothing relevant beyond those. In other words, there is no definitive reality external to the discourse; reality is what is said to be so.

On the other hand, however, it seems to be part and parcel of this openness towards facts that the legal system nonetheless manages to close up in an absolutely watertight way. For their purposes of determining a rule (for their purposes of *jurisdiction*, legal locution) at the Community level, nothing in the domain of true reality (and sociological veridiction) was significant to the judges in their legal construction of social dangers.

Once again, what matters is what the different Member States had defined through their legal locution and exercise of jurisdiction. The result of this is not only a *'reversal of the mimetic relation'* (Hurri 2005: 22), where images *produce* the reality that they should mean only to describe. The result is also that legal practice writ large closes in upon itself, because the signs that are put forward before it (ie, before the practice of the ECJ) and that it looks upon are also legal (these are Member State laws). Thus, there is a mechanism by which the domain of law may become insulated from the realm of facts.

This is another way of once again affirming cultural arbitrariness and social contingency. However, looking at the normative effects of this affirmation, setting up practice in this manner leads not to affirmation of some perspectivist madness in a way that would moreover engender abuses of power. Quite to the contrary, it tightens up the web of legal justice binding on the exercise of power in a much more intricate way than it would do by specifying further the semantic field of the notion of *ordre public*. All this is a result of the peculiar logic of strategy – that is, 'the logic of connections between the heterogeneous' (Foucault 2008: 42) – prevailing in the legal field between the two types of discourse: *veridiction* and *jurisdiction*, truth-locution and legal locution.

The last observation to be made at this level, before moving to another, concerns the way in which equity and legality, justice as *epieikeia* and justice *kata nomos*, work together at this point. Recall the way in which Aristotle presented the problematic between the basic forms of justice. Because justice *kata nomos* is meant to be generally applicable, it may in certain circumstances produce overly indiscriminate results. Justice as *epieikeia* would enter at this point to correct the injustice ensuing from the indiscriminate application of *nomoi*. What *epieikeia* does is that it first inserts a discerning analysis of facts and then discrimination between cases. This is the way in which the relation between formal legality and equitable justice is understood in the legal world.

However, our case shows that in the practice of law the operations of the two forms of justice may also exchange functions. In our case, justice *kata nomoi* had in fact incorporated a system instructing discrimination, as it legitimised the different treatment of nationals and non-national individuals in Member States. At this point, *epieikeia* introduces a correction through comparisons, but the effect of this correction is not discrimination between cases but, on the contrary, abolition of the discrimination produced *kata nomos*.

From strict legality to socio-political hermeneutic

A fine distinction ensues from the foregoing. The ECJ would *not* assess the fact of prostitution as such (or the fact of someone's being on view in a window whilst scantily dressed`), *but* the fact of Member State practices with respect to prostitution. Community law is a body of norms against which Member State practices are assessed and these practices include Member State legislation. In the foregoing, the question of legality was posed at the level of Community law: what are the requirements it imposes on Member States with respect to their use of the *ordre public* derogation? Next, the question of legality is posed at the level of Member State law: should national authorities promulgate definitions of the types of conduct that threaten *ordre public* in their country – definitions publicly accessible to everyone, preferably in the national legislation of each country? These definitions could still vary from country to country; the idea is that within one country legal certainty should be guaranteed.

In its requests, the Liège Tribunal's question of legality on the level of national legislation consisted of three parts. To begin with, it asked whether in fact nothing less than *criminalisation* of conduct can show that a Member State truly considers the conduct in question as sufficiently serious a threat: 'Is it conceivable that "personal conduct constituting a genuine and sufficiently serious threat affecting one of the fundamental issues of society" [*Bouchereau*] may not be criminally punishable in the Member State [. . .]?' (at 1672).

In this connection, the Liège Tribunal asked whether Article 7 ('no punishment without law') of the European Convention on Human Rights should apply to the case by analogy. This comes up because, in view of the request, 'a measure expelling a person from the territory of a State often has repercussions which are sometimes much more serious than a criminal penalty'.[2] Anticipating the result that this analogy turns out to be not feasible, the tribunal asked critically: 'Alternatively, what other solution would the Court suggest in order to avoid an arbitrary decision on the matter by national administrations?' (at 1672).

Generally speaking, avoidance of the arbitrary exercise of power – that is, upholding the normative expectations of individuals – is the function of legality. Legality fulfils this function irrespective of the justness or unjustness of laws by other standards than this formal one. In criminal law especially, legality (*nulla poena sine lege*) has a particularly strong status. Since Beccaria and others, this principle has been regarded as one of the cornerstones of a decent society. However, it is clear from the previous case law of the ECJ that *ordre public* derogations are not connected to criminal law: criminal law offences are neither sufficient nor necessary elements in assessing conduct from the point of view of security.

The import of invoking criminal law and its principle of legality in the case at hand is that it brings out the principle of legality in a certain form, perhaps in the most cogent legal form. Certainly, the principle of legality applies to all exercise of public power, but not equally rigorously as it applies in the exercise of penal power. All in all, the Liège Tribunal's most important formulation of the question of legality to be targeted was the following:

Is it conceivable that one of the fundamental interests of society is involved if that interest is not at the very least embodied as such beforehand in a law, a regulation or a practice having the same effect of the State relying upon it, even if such conduct is not criminally punishable? (At 1672)

In other words, the question is whether Community law requires that Member State powers are subjected to legality through their *exercising their own jurisdiction in a way that would become binding on themselves* and abandoning free discretion (arbitrary action) in this manner.

Ms Adoui and Ms Cornuaille asserted that 'it is clear' from the latest case law of the Court (*Bouchereau*) that personal conduct pleaded by immigration authorities must be not only 'incorporated in legislation' but made 'criminally punishable' as well. Otherwise, the plaintiffs' argument implied, the requirement of a genuinely serious threat to the fundamental interests of society, whose protection is necessary in a democracy, would turn out to be empty talk. An interest which is not reflected in the criminal laws of the country, as prostitution was not in Belgium, cannot be fundamental to society, not to speak of interests that do not appear at all in the whole body of national laws (at 1679).

One must 'ensure that migrants seeking entry feel that there is certainty in law', the plaintiffs asserted. Producing this feeling involves not only that any misconduct lesser than crime cannot affect the rights of migrants but also that 'arbitrary actions by Member States prohibited by the Court in its case-law be avoided'. 'The door' must not 'be left open for expulsions for concealed reasons',[3] and the central means of closing that door of arbitrary actions is to require that reasons for expulsion are made public in the legislation of the Member State (at 1679).

This reasoning by the plaintiffs makes a point about the functioning of the legality of criminal law vis-à-vis state power. Accordingly, criminal law as a body of regulation is *directed primarily against the state*, namely against the state's arbitrary exercise of punitive power. Consequently, criminal law is there for the protection of the accused, namely those suspected of committing criminal offences. This perhaps militates against the lay understanding of the law of crime and punishment: is not criminal law the legal branch pertaining to the most coercive kind of power? Any modern lawyer would say that it is, and this is precisely the reason why this law sets the strictest possible limits on power. Hence, the plaintiffs invoked a well established professional understanding of legality: the rationality of criminal law. The classic criminal law principle of legality, being a principle fundamental and constitutive to the whole field of punitive power, works *against* that power.

Legality in criminal law *does not require* that any conduct specified in criminal law needs to be punished. Instead, it *does require* that any conduct whatsoever that is not specified as a crime (in laws that are promulgated and valid prior to the deeds themselves) must not be punished. There can be no sentence without law. By extending this idea beyond the field of criminal law, the rigorous principle of legality can be seen as the true constitution of liberty in modern societies: where there are no explicit prohibitions there can be no coercion. In criminal law, *malum in se* (wrong in itself) is not possible; only *malum prohibitum* (wrong because prohibited) is possible. This sort of legality, where the state confines its own power quite dramatically by making legislation a precondition for its exercise, is what the plaintiffs clearly had in mind when they argued that it should be ensured that migrants can 'feel that there is certainty in law' (at 1679).

It was not significant for the plaintiffs that the police orders of the city of Liège in fact did prohibit 'being on view in the window'. Only the national level is significant, they seemed to think, and the fact that many municipalities did not prohibit 'being on view' proves that it presents 'a small danger to *ordre public*' in Belgium. Moreover, 'where there is such a prohibition, as in Liège, offences are punished merely by minor penalties (*peines de police*)'. 'In any event', the plaintiffs maintained, 'prostitution is not prohibited in Belgium' (at 1680).

The Dutch Government was the only Member State that agreed with the plaintiffs in the proceedings in stating that, indeed, the 'interests which the national authorities consider must be protected should be embodied in legislative provisions'. These need not be criminal law provisions, but nonetheless provisions 'with which individuals are in a position to become acquainted', and with which the courts are then enabled to control use of the *ordre public* exception by the authorities. Such 'legal definition of interests', in the view of the Dutch Government, 'provides the first criterion for an assessment' of the dangerousness of conduct (at 1679).

The United Kingdom was content with one single sentence to comment on the problem of legality with respect to the concept of *ordre public*: 'There is no question of excluding certain factors from its scope merely because they do not constitute criminal offences'. Otherwise there was nothing to be added, apparently because it could disturb the 'careful balance' to be made between the needs of the Member States and the needs of the Community, as well as between the needs of the nationals of both respectively. Community law, as it stood after the previous case law, had offered 'a wholly satisfactory approach' (at 1698).

The remaining three Member States took the challenge of *Adoui and Cornuaille* more seriously. Each of them brought different strategies of legality to bear on their submissions. Common to them was that all of them, each in its own way, tried to undermine the efforts of the plaintiffs to impose a strict requirement of legality on exercise of the power to expel European individuals. Let us have a closer look at this variety of legality strategies.

Belgium admits, to start with, that questions of legality 'raise an interesting point in jurisprudence'. However, these questions 'are of no relevance to this case' because, in fact, 'the act of displaying oneself in a window' was legally punishable in Liège. There existed a regulation to that effect in the form of a police order, 'adopted by the municipal council of the City of Liège'. Hence, the argument from arbitrary action does not apply on that count. It is not necessary that the concept of *ordre public* as such is 'specifically defined in any legal provision'; the conduct in question was 'criminally punishable and justifies expulsion from the territory'. Hence, legality is an academic question as far as this case is concerned (at 1684).

According to these lines, Belgium's intention was to dismiss the relevance of the question of legality in *Adoui and Cornuaille*. On a closer look, however, Belgium as a matter of fact endorsed and put into practice an understanding of legality that builds on a rationality that is completely different from the rationality of the *nullum crimen, nulla poena sine lege* inbuilt into criminal law. This different version of legality is no less generally accepted by professional lawyers of the West than is the concept of legality in criminal law. What we have there is legality as something that has the second-order power to constitute and distribute the primary or direct exercise of power. This legality-concept becomes clear in the following explanation of Belgium as to its organisation of the legality of exercise of power in matters of 'morality and the public peace':

> The Belgian Law of 21 August 1948, repealing the national rules on prostitution, provides that supplementary provisions may be adopted by the municipal councils if their purpose is to ensure morality and the public peace. (at 1648)

The legal act that had liberated prostitution in Belgium at the national level was also an enabling act at the local level. It gave the local authorities a mandate to continue prohibiting prostitution. The idea behind this structure is not restriction of power and protection of freedom, but rather the redistribution of power, moving it from one level to another. Thus conceived, legality means, not the legal constitution of liberty in the sense of classic criminal law, but the diversified constitution of the exercise of power in different places of the political structure of society. Its function is not to entrench the subject's rights of liberty – the right to autonomy – but rather to reorganise the right of the public authorities to rule over their subjects, who without doubt remain heteronomous subjects. Legality means not the constitution of self-rule of an individual, but precisely the opposite – the subjection of the individual to the rule of others.

Speaking in terms of the law as a system of nomination and pronouncement of those entitled to rule over others, the Belgian Law of 1948 is a case in point of the general legal structure of relegation of powers. Powers are moved from central and distant authorities to authorities operating in the proximity of subjects. In the Community context, the notion of subsidiarity was later coined to designate the idea and to support it normatively. In Belgium, what at first seems to have been liberation on the national level had in fact meant authorisation on the local level – at least this is where Belgium built its legality argument in the *Adoui and Cornuaille* proceedings.

Belgium's concept and organisation of legality relative to governing prostitution (ie, morality and the public peace) reveals a structure more specifically similar to the Community law structure. Namely, the Belgian legislative solution resembles the division of powers between the Community and the Member States in Article 48 of the EC Treaty. There, too, we have liberation (of movement) on the one side, but on the other side (as to matters involving *ordre public*) Member States retain their powers. In this mechanism, the Community notion of *ordre public* is an element comparable to Belgian matters of 'morality and the public peace'. *Ordre public* designates something in the competence of Member States; morality and the public peace, in turn, designate something in the competence of municipal councils.

In matters involving *ordre public*, morality and public peace, there is a perceptible continuity in the delegation of powers. The function of legality, for Belgium, seems only to be that of guaranteeing the formal legitimacy of delegated powers. As a matter of fact, this delegation can be seen as running down all the way from the Community level to that of municipal councils. In Belgium's view, legality in any event was guaranteed, only in a form different from that which was intended by the plaintiffs.

The French Government reiterated the doctrine that had been developing in the previous cases, notably in *Bouchereau* that had established that there are two appraisals that have different points of view: that of *ordre public* and that of criminal law. A measure of expulsion must be based neither on provisions in criminal law nor on criminal convictions. Instead, it must be based on personal conduct and its possible dangerousness as such. This same conduct may or may not lead to criminal convictions, but it is immaterial to the examination of the threats posed by this conduct to *ordre public* whether there are convictions or criminal law provisions or not (at 1690).

As soon becomes clear, the French Government argues and explains that acts that count as crimes are not a *sufficient* ground for expulsion of non-national Europeans. In principle, this rule should have benefited the European individual, in that it compels Member States to investigate the dangerous nature of conduct instead of merely automatically expelling every criminal law offender. Yet another agenda is hidden in the argument. The practical import, if not intent, of the French Government's submission is to undermine the requirement of legality in general, to the detriment of the individual. The subtle ruse of France builds on the *irrelevance* of criminal law. In fact, France assimilates *legality in general* with the criminal law type of *special legality* in the same way as the plaintiffs had done. Only now, the intent is to establish that because criminal law is irrelevant, legality (in general!) must be irrelevant as well.

The French tactic is not only to liberate Member States from the requirement of legality, but also to make insidious inroads for the immigration authority into the inner 'nature' of the European individual through that individual's conduct. How does this happen? For the French Government, criminal law is not suitable for control of immigrants because of its *externality* with regard to the 'nature' of human conduct: 'A criminally punishable offence merely establishes and penalizes the conduct but cannot affect its nature', whereas an 'expulsion order based on a threat to *ordre public* [. . .] requires a definition of the nature of the conduct' (at 1690).

This rather cryptic notion of the externality of law in relation to the 'nature' of the conduct of an individual deserves a pause for reflection. Recall, first, the Italian

Government's submission with respect to the relation of legal limitations with the concept of *ordre public*. The Italian immigration authorities *use* the concept of *ordre public*, whereas the law ('specific rules of Community law' and 'general principles of law that safeguard fundamental rights that safeguard democratic society') is supposed merely to limit this use. More exactly, this is what the Italian Government said about the legal limits: '[. . .] but they are "limitations", that is to say limits beyond which it is forbidden to go but which do not define the concept' (at 1692).

Laws cannot define the concept of *ordre public*, that is, they cannot define an immigration authority's activity that uses the concept. This activity, the use itself, defines the concept. What becomes perceptible is a clear parallel. The relationship of *public law* with the *controlling power exercised by the immigration authority* is conceived as external. No intrusions to nature. Comparable to this is the relationship of *criminal law* with *individual conduct*; that relation too is conceived as external. In both spheres of activity (control and crime) the law does not penetrate into the 'nature'. Instead, the law works by way of setting boundaries not to be transgressed, leaving the goals pursued within those frames and the means put in use otherwise untouched.

If the law works only externally, both with respect to immigration control and with respect to the conduct of the individual, the question emerges whether there is then an intrinsic mutual relationship between the latter two. Are control and conduct – unlike law and control or law and conduct – located in the same order of things, or do they indeed make up one single thread? Is immigration control thus correctly considered to operate somehow *internally* to the conduct of the individual? Does this control work, unlike law, within the interior 'nature' of immigrant human beings?

These problems I will have to postpone until the next chapter for further elaboration in a different way. For the moment, it suffices to note that the French Government's reiteration of the distinction between dangerous personal conduct and punishable criminal conduct was in fact somewhat beside the point. According to the agenda of the Liège Tribunal's request, the task was *not* to argue about the *sufficiency* of the existence of criminal conduct as a ground for carrying out expulsions. Instead, the task was to argue whether or not it was *necessary* that the interest of society being under threat should have been, if not protected by criminal laws, 'at the very least embodied as such beforehand in a law, a regulation or a practice [. . .] of the State relying upon it'. The task was, moreover, to tell what then would be the way 'to avoid an arbitrary decision on the matter by national administrations', if even the most rudimentary legality could not be called for (legality now in the sense of some publicly pronounced statement on society's interests not to be endangered by foreigners) (at 1672).

In spite of – or in the guise of – its somewhat misplaced or one-sided recasting of the problem of legality, the French Government was able to generate an answer to the question of legality overall on the basis of its distinction between criminal and dangerous conduct: 'A measure expelling a person from the territory cannot be assimilated to a criminal penalty, since it is an administrative decision. For that reason it seems unnecessary that the acts which are the reason for the measure should constitute an offence laid down by law' (at 1690).

This conclusion does not merely concern legality in the form of criminal law. It appears from the file that the French Government indeed also suggested that 'an affirmative answer should be given' (at 1690) to the more general question of whether it is 'conceivable that one of the fundamental interests of society is involved', despite its absence from the body of the State's laws and established practices, that is, despite the absence of legality in the sense of legal certainty on what interests are fundamental (at 1672). To put it more plainly: states' crucial interests are not bound by legality. They are matters pertaining to another rationality, the rationality of the administrative state which reigns exclusively over the field of immigration control.[4] As for the avoidance of arbitrary action, the only remaining safeguard in the French Government's submission seems to have been '*ex posto facto* supervision exercised case by case on consideration of the particular facts' (at 1689) by the Community institutions.

The Italian Government seems to have endorsed the same basic viewpoint as to the question of legality on the level of national legislation as the French Government. On closer inspection, however, there was a remarkable difference. Unlike criminal law, the Italian Government began, immigration control that relies upon *ordre public* is preventive action; it looks to potential future threats, not threats that have already materialised. According to the Italian Government: 'Aggression [. . .] need not be criminally punishable' to constitute a threat to *ordre public*. So far everything in the Italian Government's submission is in line with the previous case law of the ECJ (at 1693).

Next, however, Italy came up with something with which one must be very careful. Namely, for the Italian Government criminal law is also after all about 'deterrence' and 'repression' of aggressors. Now it is a matter of 'choice of legislative policy' whether the state decides to use criminal law means or other means – and this choice it justifies by assessing which option is the most effective. Criminal law penalties are used where: '[. . .] such penalties are regarded as the most effective deterrent and, to a lesser degree, a means of repression' (at 1693).

Thus we have another concept of criminal law. It is a means of repression and deterrence that can, moreover, be replaced by some other instrument if that suits better for the purposes of repression and deterrence. This is markedly different from the view of the French Government, which wanted to distinguish rationalities. In the view expressed by Italy, the rationality of reason of state is imposed on the law, making the latter an instrument in the hands of governors.

This throws the ideas of the Italian Government on legality very far from the liberal criminal law ideology relied on by Ms Adoui and Ms Cornuaille, whose submission suggested that the classic principle of 'no sentence without law' is indeed the true constitution of liberty upon which Community law on free movement must be conceived. This criminal law principle they wished to see applied, by analogy, to expulsions of Europeans in order to avoid arbitrary action by the state.

Despite the distance between the liberal concept of the plaintiffs and the deterrence concept of the Italian Government, today's criminal law without doubt embodies them both. At this point, the *Adoui and Cornuaille* case is perfect material for observation of the ways in which the strategic polyvalence of the law comes about in the practice of law. Whereas the plaintiffs in *Adoui and Cornuaille* attempted to impose, by analogy, juridical reason on the field of immigration control, the Italian Government's movement was precisely the opposite: imposition of security reason on criminal law.

Juridical reason, for which practising lawyers can barely see significant competitors in the field of legal practice, as a matter of fact is involved in a constant struggle against other types of reason – even on its very own ground. This struggle is a struggle of objective structures and objective interests; it need never attract notice in the subjective consciousness of practising lawyers themselves. This subjective consciousness is determined to pay attention only to the rules, concepts and principles of law, within the confines of which we compare the facts brought to our desks with the abstract legal designations of circumstances in which legal norms are meant to apply. This pervasive abstractness, which external observers may sometimes consider short-sightedness and structurally engendered misrepresentation, forms part and parcel of the practice of law. It is based not only on the power of general concepts but also on a very basic imperative, according to which laws must apply *generally*. The name given to this, too, is legality.

As to deterrence and repression of prostitutes especially, the Italian Government's opinion was that 'from the socio-political point of view it may be inappropriate to adopt' measures against them, despite prostitution being 'from an abstract point of view' regarded 'as a dangerous phenomenon for society'. The socio-political point of view – taken by security administration – is not supposed to be *abstract* in the way the legal point of view always is. There is a 'concrete point of view', said the Italian Government, and from that viewpoint 'it is very difficult to regard' the individual exercise of prostitution as seriously dangerous, since 'prostitution is a widespread phenomenon tolerated in all Member States' (at 1694).

This concrete, socio-political point of view provided the Italian Government with the substructure necessary for what can be called a special hermeneutics of legal interpretation. How does one cull the fundamental interest of society from the body of laws of the country, if these interests are not explicitly stated there? 'It is not always by seeking a specific rule', the Italian Government explained, 'but by analysing the totality of the provisions existing in a particular country' that one can determine fundamental interests (at 1693). As a matter of fact so far this is perfectly in line with the general ideas of legal interpretation.

However, unlike in the general models of legal interpretation, in the Italian special model the horizon of meaning informing (and resulting from) the totality-analysis of law is not to be invoked by way of drawing on (and reproducing) something such as the prevailing principles of political morality inherent in the legal system. Rather, interpretation of the totality of legal provisions must be carried out 'in a specific period having regard to the safeguard of public welfare', the Italian Government stated (at 1693). While each period has its own peculiar flexible exegesis of exigencies, adhesion is nevertheless guaranteed by the constant demand to safeguard public welfare. This is the socio-political hermeneutic of legal interpretation – maybe one could call it *need-orientation* – proposed by the Italian Government, to meet the requirement of legality.

From reign of principles to consistency of practice

Before moving on, let me at this stage point out what Pierre Bourdieu once said about the way for actors to excel in social practices. The following is from one of the texts where he reflected retrospectively on the guiding ideas and motivations behind his past research and theorising on social practices. What he there calls 'modes of formalization' substitute for what, as regards the legal practice I would call strategies of legality:

> All these modes of formalizing which [. . .] are also ways of getting round the rules of the game, and are thus double games, are a matter for virtuosi. In order to make sure you are on the right side of the authorities, you have to have a rule, adversaries and game at your fingertips. If one had to propose a transcultural definition of excellence, I would say that it's the fact of being able to play the game up to the limits, even to the point of transgression, while managing to stay within the rules of the game. (Bourdieu 1990: 78)

The modes of formalising, or the strategies of legality, by which the different parties have so far argued their case on legality, are clearly also elements of precisely this sort of double game. The participants have had to stay within the rules of the game (within legality), while at the same time they have tried their best to get round the rules of the game (ie, to get round legality). Another way to put it is that they all had to proceed by way of providing redefinitions of the meaning of legality, because they had realised that legality as such (the sheer fact that a game has its rules) cannot possibly be done away with.

According to Bourdieu, this strategic redefinition of rules is not peculiar to the practice of law, but in fact it is a characteristic of all social practice, indeed with 'transcultural' universality. To my mind, however, there still is something strange in the practice of law, being a game about changing its own rules. (All rules, including even such fundamentals as legality, are subjected to contestation that makes them change.) Why, then, is the game of law so strange among other games? This question will have to be returned to in the end.

The Commission, as we have seen, had conceded that Community law incorporates no definite rules determining the concept of *ordre public*. Therefore, the Commission had preferred 'to describe the legal foundations' that delineate the scope of this concept (at 1699). In effect, application of Community law must differentiate between rules and principles. For application of the latter, the Commission had argued for an endorsement of the model of weighing the different values and the different interests against each other, which also involves the operation of expediency-testing of the measures with regard to their objectives. Equitable justice in this rather pervasive form was, for the Commission, what Community law requires from the exercise of adjudication and administration alike. Turning to the question of the possible necessity of legality (explicit rules) at the level of national legislation, the Commission presented a rather unique tactic of legality.

For the Commission this was in fact not a question of a *possible necessity* but, on the contrary, a question of the *necessary impossibility* of national legislation. With regard to *ordre public*, the power that 'was left to the Member States' was that 'of attributing a specific content to the concept of *ordre public* by the application thereof', but: 'not of defining in the abstract' that concept. The prohibition of 'defining in the abstract' means, in effect, that Member States *must not legislate*. While it was true, according to the Commission, that the Community legislature had 'endeavoured not to give a common definition of *ordre public*', that form of jurisdiction was not left to the Member States either (at 1699).

The basis on which the Commission could present this argumentation seems to have been the personal conduct requirement provided in Article 3 of Directive 64/221: 'Measures taken on grounds of *ordre public* or of public security shall be based exclusively on the personal conduct of the individual concerned'. Therefore, any intervention by general legislation is excluded because this would prejudice the requirement to examine the particulars of the conduct of an individual, and the requirement to 'base exclusively' the measures of expulsion on these particulars. As a consequence of this, 'the Court's intervention' (meaning the intervention of the ECJ) as regards the practice of the Member States' authorities is limited: 'it may not be called upon to criticize a case of specific application'. However, this is *not* to say that the space is empty of any intervention by the judicial authorities: 'It is in fact the responsibility of the national courts to ascertain whether individual decisions conform to the provisions of Community law' (at 1699).

The above statement is worth a pause. The opinion of the Commission seems to be not only that the requirement of legality is not there, but moreover that in fact there is a requirement of *not-legality*. To put this in terms of the Aristotelian dilemma: the Commission's tactic of legality is to exclude justice *kata nomoi* and to demand unlimited equitable justice, justice as *epieikeia*. There seems to be a special strategic sense in this. For the Commission and from the point of view of protecting Community interests, national courts were more reliable than national legislators. National legislators were regarded by the Commission as opponents of itself as Community legislator.

Clearly the Commission believed that national courts could be persuaded to ally with it. In the eyes of the Commission, the best possible perlocutionary effect[5] of *Adoui and Cornuaille* would have been that national courts – also in a sense opponents of national legislators – would endorse in their reasoning apparatuses a model of weighting and balancing that incorporates the fundamental principles of Community law. That would be a better place to slot Community law in national law: not in its rules, but in its culture.

Be that as it may, the Commission saw that review of national authorities by national courts is guided directly by Community law. No national legislation may intervene. For the Commission, the way to relate with the aperture (or lacuna) created by *ordre public* in the web of legality is this: open legal texture should be protected against national legislators, who might close it up to the detriment of the Community interest. It is interesting to point out that this tactic of legality is in fact comparable with the tactics of the Member States. In principle, the Commission followed the same pattern as the Member States: the concept of *ordre public* should be left open. But for the Member States the way in which the aperture is related is this: it should be guarded against intervention by Community law.

Thus, the intended effect of the openness of the *ordre public* aperture is entirely different in the tactic of the Commission, on the one hand, and that of the Member States, on the other hand. Nonetheless, both tactics do prefer exclusion of explicit legislation. It seems that for both the Commission and the Member States it was desirable that the matter be guided by something that underlies practice, prevails in practice somewhere, but not in the explicit rules of legislation. It prevails in legal culture, ideology, tacit knowledge and principles. So it seems that protecting the openness of the aperture against juridification *kata nomoi* (through laws) is demanded by both participants under the presumption that some more abstract, more fundamental, regimes should then reign without the constraints of positive enactments of legislation.

The Advocate General brought the discussion back to its normal track. National legislation is not *sufficient* for taking a measure of expulsion; this is the meaning of the personal conduct requirement in Article 3 of Directive 64/221. This provision bans abstract definitions only insofar as these instruct indiscriminate mandatory expulsion – say, in cases of criminal offences – without allowing for examination of the details of the case from the perspective of dangerousness. But neither is it *necessary* for taking a measure of expulsion that there is national law. This was established by *van Duyn*: 'grounds of *ordre public* may be relied upon with regard to antisocial activities with regard to which the authorities of a Member State have manifested their disapproval and adopted measures to prevent their being carried out'. However, this manifestation does not need to be performed by legislating on the matter. Thus, *van Duyn* had established that 'conduct may be declared contrary to *ordre public* even if it is not classifiable as an offence or as being in some other way unlawful' (at 1718–19).

What about the Liège Tribunal's request, which asked whether or not it was conceivable that the facts on the basis of which measures of expulsion are taken are not indicated in the body of Member State legislation? The conclusion of the Advocate general is the following: '[. . .] the principle of legal certainty may not be relied upon in order to demand a kind of legislative catalogue of instances of conduct contrary to *ordre public*' (at 1719).

However, what 'appears necessary' for the Advocate General was that the 'public interest' apprehended by a Member State 'should be referred to in some way, even if indirectly, in the domestic legal order'. Moreover, the *van Duyn* judgment had stipulated that 'authorities should have manifested their disapproval of certain activities, indicating that they regarded them as antisocial'. So, this sort of indication must be present somewhere in the domestic legal order, or at least it must be possible to extrapolate this indication from between the lines of national legislative texts. This is necessary, but it is also 'sufficient', said the Advocate General. For him, it seemed that 'Belgian legislation contains prohibitions' pertaining to prostitution 'from which it is easy to deduce that the legislature considered that to restrict that phenomenon was in the public interest' (at 1719–20).

For the judges, this deduction did not seem to be as easy as that. Despite the fact that Belgian law prohibited, among other things, 'living on immoral earnings' (at 1706), it was also 'a fact that prostitution as such is not prohibited by Belgian legislation'. Belgian prostitutes were free to practise their profession. What Belgian legislation prohibited, in the view of the judges, was only 'certain incidental activities, which are particularly harmful from the social point of view, such as the exploitation of prostitution by third parties and various forms of incitement to debauchery'. It appears that, for the judges, this did not meet the formal Community law criteria of equality of treatment. What alone would indicate a sufficiently serious threat was that prostitution – when practised by Belgian nationals – gives 'rise to repressive measures or other genuine and effective measures intended to combat such conduct' (at 1707–708).

As far as the normative result of the case is concerned, the above statement also formed the operative part of the judgment of the ECJ in *Adoui and Cornuaille*:

> A Member State may not [by virtue of the *ordre public* reservation] expel a national of another Member State from its territory or refuse him access to its territory by reason of conduct which, when attributable to the former State's own nationals, does not give rise to repressive measures or other genuine and effective measures intended to combat such conduct. (at 1712)

This simply implies that Member States need only be consistent in their practices, which is another way of imposing the requirement of legality on the exercise of power. Whatever they do, they may not contradict themselves. Concerning the requirement of legality in this form (that is, in the form of consistency of practice) as to the ECJ itself, it transpires that the ECJ at this point effectively abolished its former ruling in *van Duyn*. In the operative part of that ruling (on the practice of scientology in the United Kingdom) the ECJ had said that:

> Article 48 of the EEC Treaty and Article 3 (1) of Directive No 64/221 must be interpreted as meaning that a Member State, in imposing restrictions

justified on ground of *ordre public,* is entitled to take into account as a matter of personal conduct of the individual concerned, the fact that the individual is associated with some body or organization the activities of which the Member State considers socially harmful but which are not unlawful in that State, *despite the fact that no restriction is placed upon nationals of the said Member State who wish to take similar employment* with the same body of organization. (*van Duyn* 1352: emphasis added)

While its practice should be consistent, the legal game is still about changing the rules.[6]

From equals equally to unequals unequally

The previous discussion dealt with the problem of legality at two levels. At the first level, the question was: what is Community law on *ordre public* or should there be any Community law? At the second level, the question was: should Community law in any case require that in matters of *ordre public* each Member State establishes a law? 'A law', in the latter case, can be thought of either in the narrow sense of legislation that prevails generally over the Member State practices (considered as practices of application and execution of that legislation), or in the broader sense that includes the living law formed within those practices (considered as relatively independent administration of public affairs, carried out without a statutory basis as far as the substance of this activity is concerned and deliberated for example on the basis of expediency).

As to the sort of *legality* that comes about within practices, in the sense of legal equality of treatment and consistency, legality is indeed conceivable irrespective of any positive enactment of laws. Legality in the sense of generally applicable norms emerges in practice from the simple imperative of consistency. *Equals should be treated equally and unequals unequally*; this precept has the capacity to serve alone as a mechanism of check against arbitrary exercise of power, albeit it does not guarantee legal certainty from the perspective of subjects uninformed of the distinctions that guide practice. Legality in any event is inscribed in and self-generated by any jurisdiction; any discourse, action and power will not get away with it insofar as it stays legal. That a practice 'stays legal' does not mean that this practice will never be inconsistent, but that its inconsistencies may be pointed out as mistakes. In other words, it is meaningful to examine whether it transgresses consistency in its consecutive actions. Where this examination is not meaningful, the practice in question is not conceivable in legal terms and it claims no legal legitimacy. Legality in the sense of consistency and equal treatment defines any practice that claims legal legitimacy.

Against the requirement of legality, at both levels and in any form, most of the Member States drew upon equity. Their idea was that *ordre public* refers to a variety of contingent exigencies (dangers) upon which no definitive norms can be established in general terms. In other words, they argued for equitable justice as subjects of Community law. In their view the circumstances that need to be appreciated were indefinitely variable, not only with respect to different countries, but also within one country.

As to these circumstances, equity is the gateway for veridiction; in our cases, this means knowledge and discourse on what poses a threat to society. Generally speaking, equity is an expression of the second basic principle of justice – the requirement that proper attention is paid to the facts and circumstances of each individual case – observed in the practice of law and measuring any exercise of power.

Next, this Aristotelian dilemma between legality and equity (between justice *kata nomos* and justice as *epieikeia*) is not discussed from the perspective of the Member States and their contingent and circumstantial exigencies. Instead, the focus will be moved to individuals as subjects over whom Member State power under the *ordre public* derogation is exercised. This is the third level at which the *Adoui and Cornuaille* case brings the basic concepts of legal justice to the fore in the practice of law.

Individuals, too, have a potential claim for both kinds of justice: legality and equity. Up until now the individuals of our case, Ms Adoui and Ms Cornuaille, had insisted on the strictest possible legality, against which the Member States had presented their argument from the widest possible equity. In what follows, we will see the plaintiffs in turn arguing for equity, ie, for justice as a proper concern for the circumstantial exigencies that characterise their situation, in which expulsion would lead to extraordinary distress. Not surprisingly, some of the Member States, who had just called for concern and respect for the nebulous fortuity of their own circumstantialities, did not hesitate to rebut this kind of request for discriminate singularity by arguing for rigorous legality and equal treatment.

If equity and legality, as concepts of justice, are perennial and universal as structures of the practice of law, what constitutes the dilemma between them in the structures of our small legal-theoretical laboratory is the personal conduct requirement. Directive 64/221 required that measures taken by the Member State authorities 'shall be based exclusively on the personal conduct of the individual concerned' (Article 3(1)). This means, in the first place, that Member States may not expel individuals for any other reasons save that the person, as an individual, poses a threat to *ordre public*.[7] As discussed above, the Commission inferred, apparently on the basis of the personal conduct requirement, that Community law at this point prohibits Member States from legislating on (that is, from 'defining in the abstract'; at 1699) the concept of *ordre public*. This was because abstract definitions would undercut the requirement to examine each case individually.

Hence, the structures of our laboratory contain an element that seems somehow to eliminate legality altogether, at least the type of indiscriminate legality that turns against persons who would be harmless as individuals. This element seems to instruct scrupulous attention to the details of each individual case and a deliberation exclusively based on these particulars: *pure equity*. It goes without saying that pure equity is unworkable and impossible in the practice of law; it would simply mean arbitrary exercise of power yet again. At the very least, legal discourse and practice necessitates some broad substantive guidelines, for example, in the manner of the so-called *Kadijustitz* (Weber 1978: 795). In other words, a norm can never emerge from facts only.

What is now inserted into this structure is the question of whether, in addition to examination of the potential dangerousness of the personal conduct of an individual in the particular circumstances of the country, there should likewise be an examination of the specific life-circumstances of the individual. If the measure of expulsion is too devastating for the individual – if it would be too harsh for the individual to live somewhere else – should equitable justice then require extenuation or dropping of the measure? In other words, the principle of proportionality should be applied to create a balance between the dangers posed by the individual, on the one hand, and the consequences to that individual ensuing from expulsion, on the other hand. In its request for clarification of the implications of the Court's notion of 'sufficiently serious threat', the Liège Tribunal formulated the question in the following way:

> Does the Court mean that it is necessary to measure, on the one hand, the seriousness of the perturbation which is threatening the requirements of *ordre public* and, on the other hand the seriousness, which varies from case to case, of the expulsion order? (at 1672)

The Liège Tribunal went on to ask whether or not 'expulsion become so serious in certain cases that it may no longer be contemplated owing to the fact that it constitutes inhuman treatment'? As examples of personal life-circumstances that would amount to 'inhuman treatment', the request enumerated situations where the person to be expelled is a 'father or mother of a large family, spouse or parent of a national of the expelling State, a minor, a person who for reasons of age or health does not have a sufficient chance of becoming readjusted to life in another country, a person who was born and has lived for a considerable period in the territory of the expelling State, etc' (at 1672).

The problem of legality and equity at this level involved three separate questions. First, should equitable justice and proportionality be affirmed as binding Community law with respect to the circumstances of the individual? Or maybe the contrary should be affirmed: strict legality and equal treatment of all dangerous individuals irrespective of other factors pertaining to their individual life, needs and character.

Secondly, if it is considered that equitable justice requires that certain factors, such as those enumerated by the Liège Tribunal (father or mother of a large family etc) exclude the measure of expulsion, then should it mean that a general norm is thereby constituted for future cases in which these factors reoccur? Thirdly, how should one deal with the notion of 'inhuman treatment'? Can this notion be inserted, or rather not inserted into the unceasing interplay between legality and equity? In other words, the last question is whether some values are absolute for the practice of law.

From indiscriminate equality to prudence

The only Member State that rejected the equity argument completely was Belgium. At this point, it advocated legality just as strictly as the plaintiffs had done at the earlier point. Hence, all individuals deserve the same treatment; anything other would mean unjust discrimination:

> It is clear that no account should be taken of the difficulties caused by expulsion from Belgian territory, which vary from person to person. Whatever view is taken concerning the scope of *ordre public*, it is nevertheless clear that within the same society it must be applied to the same category of persons without discrimination. (at 1684)

Strangely, this plea for legality and formal equality by Belgium concerned only Ms Adoui. In Ms Cornuaille's case, Belgium was ready to concede that regard 'is of course had to [. . .] private or family interests'. In any event, the stricter attitude of Belgium towards Ms Adoui is highly interesting from the point of view of its earlier statement concerning the legality of *ordre public*. To resume at the point where the Community law definition of *ordre public* was discussed, Belgium had just stated that a 'definition which is too precise would be likely to fix the concept', which would be very bad because it would be a nuisance 'to the progress of each society'. Belgium requested that application of this concept must 'meet the specific circumstances of each of the Member States' (at 1684).

In Belgium's view, the specific circumstance of each individual – or at least: *the specific circumstances of each individual in the case of Ms Adoui* – must *not* be met, however, because this would jeopardise legality. Member States must be consistent in their exercise of power over individuals; Community law cannot possibly prescribe anything else. 'Regard is of course had' to *the specific circumstances of each individual in the case of Ms Cornuaille*, said Belgium, however. This is a strange discrimination between the two women: of course their life-circumstances were not identical, but why present the *general norm* differently in the two respective cases? Let us forget this mystery; for the purposes of constructing an ideal-type, let us stick to the views Belgium presented in the case of Ms Adoui. So, on this basis, Belgium stands for rigorous legality.

For the plaintiffs, proportionality is the legal principle to be used for the purposes of determining the matter. They suggested that this principle must now be elaborated further by introducing the notion of 'double proportionality'. Single proportionality would apparently mean only weighing the Community principle of free movement against the urgent needs of Member States. Double proportionality adds another axis, where a similar optimisation is required. On this other axis, two external causes of perturbations are compared: on the one hand, perturbations to *ordre public* caused by the individual and, on the other hand, perturbations to the personal circumstances of the individual caused by the measure of expulsion taken by the Member State: 'It is not sufficient to consider in itself the perturbation to *ordre public* but account must also be taken of the personal circumstances of the Community national' (at 1679).

Together, these two comparisons constitute what the plaintiffs call double proportionality. In the mechanism of double proportionality, the importance of legality obviously diminishes. At this point, too, it is interesting to note what was previously presented, this time by the plaintiffs. Speaking of the necessity of legislative provisions indicating publicly the interests fundamental to Member States, the plaintiffs had insisted that one must ensure 'that there is certainty in the law' with respect to *ordre public* grounds; otherwise 'the door would be left open for expulsions for concealed reasons' (at 1679). Moreover, the plaintiffs maintained that if Member States were allowed to expel European individuals for any other reason but protection of the state of legality itself, 'the existence or essence of the Community governed by the rule of law would be threatened' (at 1678).

The picture starts to take shape. On the one hand, Belgium rejects equity at this point by the same reasoning that had been the reasoning of the plaintiffs when they had rejected equity at the earlier point: arbitrary exercise of power is not legal. On the other hand, the plaintiffs advocated equity at this point in a similar way as Belgium had advocated for it at the earlier point. These submissions are perfectly well set on the parameters of the Aristotelian dilemma. Justice as *kata nomos* and justice as *epieikeia* can form different tactical combinations. In other words, they are strategically polyvalent elements in the practice of law.

The governments of the Netherlands and France presented a different view, but both nonetheless stayed within the Aristotelian parameters. Their argument was that it is up to the Member States to decide whether personal circumstances matter or not. Despite this basic agreement, the views of the two governments differ in one respect, which adds some interesting complexity to the structure.

For the Dutch Government, national *law* is decisive. Accordingly, whether national authorities 'should have regard to particular circumstances relating to the person in question', is for the Dutch Government 'in principle a matter governed by national law' (at 1698). This statement is in line with its earlier submission, according to which *ordre public* interests that Member States could invoke against European individuals 'should be embodied in legislative provisions' (at 1697). At that point, it had supported the plaintiffs' argument for legality at the national level. If an equity mechanism is inserted there, it is as binding a command on the authorities as any law would be. Community law: not relevant.

The French Government had not been willing to see the hands of national authorities bound by national law any more than by Community law. Expulsions are administrative decisions and it is 'unnecessary' that acts incurring expulsions 'should constitute offences laid down by law'. So there is no legality *kata nomoi* and the national authorities only *may* 'take account of any extenuating circumstances' of the individual. Does it mean that they may also ignore any such circumstances?

Turning its discourse into indicative mode at this point, the French Government started to describe administrative practices in France. There, the national authorities *usually* take 'account of humanitarian considerations, and in particular any family ties which the alien threatened with expulsion may plead' (at 1690).

What the contributions of the two governments add to the Aristotelian parameters and clarify in the structures of legal practice is that the legislator may explicitly establish *kata nomoi* (through laws) that there is *epieikeia*. (Generally speaking, this is of course a well known phenomenon, and adjustment provisions in laws have much inspired legal theory. We will discuss later another well known problem: could the legislator also define that with respect to certain vital things there is no possibility of *epieikeia*?)

However, it is equally conceivable that the legislator leaves it to the executive to decide whether *epieikeia* has a role to play or not. In the former case, it is evident that the element of equity can be inserted into the system of legality (as a body of legislation). In the latter case, it might be that legality (as consistency of practice) is inserted into the system of equity – that is, into the system that emerges from what the authorities *usually* take into account in their practice.

The rest of the participants saw the principle of proportionality, and thereby the requirement of equitable justice, as something pervasive without specifying differences between the levels of Community law and national law. The views of the United Kingdom we know already. For the United Kingdom, the whole thing is about a careful balance between different interests, needs and aims: those of Member States and of Member State nationals, on the one hand, and those of Community and European individuals, on the other hand. This balance is established by the previous case law of the Court that has offered 'a wholly satisfactory approach' (at 1698).

The views of the Commission on proportionality have already been discussed: legal reasoning in cases such as this must veer towards principles and interests, with the aim of establishing a fair balance between them. However, what the Commission added at this point was that the idea of balancing 'does not of course mean that expulsion, which thus constitutes a particularly serious penalty, may not, in a specific case, according to the circumstances, also have considerable personal repercussions for the person concerned' (at 1700). As to the legal nature of this balancing of interest, it is questionable whether the United Kingdom and the Commission had quite the same ideas in mind. However intriguing, we will have to pass on that issue here.

In the view of Italy, limitations on free movement 'must be reasonable and proportionate' (at 1693). The law that authorises expulsions – that is, Community law on *ordre public* derogations – must be interpreted restrictively and 'prudently' (at 1693); that is, in a manner that observes 'the principles guaranteeing the reasonable and proportionate nature of the measure adopted' (at 1693).

Along with Italy, the Advocate General advocated prudence in the practice of law and public power. State authorities should observe 'the criteria of reasonableness and proportionality' (at 1720). The factors that one must consider include not only those that present an individual as dangerous to society, but also their 'family situation' and 'any links which [the individual] may have established with the country' (at 1720). This implies that the principle of proportionality requires a comparison to be made between 'the seriousness of the perturbation' the individual has generated by his or her conduct, on the one hand, and the 'specific seriousness of the deportation measure' brought to bear on that individual: 'The matters of fact to which I have referred above must be verified in each individual case, insofar as they serve to establish whether each deportation or expulsion measure is compatible with the principle of proportionality' (at 1720–21).

In this statement, the Advocate General lays down in clear terms that what equity, equitable justice and proportionality refer to are matters of *fact* that need to be *verified*. In other words, they are matters of *veridiction*. Jurisdiction by *epieikeia* is that which corrects the faults of jurisdiction *kata nomos*; it reconstructs norms by recourse to another discourse, that on facts.

From singular justice to new general norm

In the discussion above, the legality-engendering mechanism of equal treatment, internal to and self-generated by any jurisdictional power even when no generally applicable legislation instructs its exercise, was treated at the level of Member State practices. Moreover, as a matter of course this question concerns the practice going on at that very moment: production of case law in the ECJ. Would the coming decision of the ECJ in *Adoui and Cornuaille* establish a norm that not only prescribes the necessity of weighing and balancing the circumstances of the individual and social dangers in general, but also defines more precisely what sort of personal life-circumstances might exclude the possibility of expulsion? The request of the Liège Tribunal had indeed included a list of examples of such circumstances:

> [. . .] father or mother of a large family, spouse or parent of a national of the expelling State, a minor, a person who for reasons of age or health does not have a sufficient chance of becoming readjusted to life in another country, a person who was born and has lived for a considerable period in the territory of the expelling State, etc. (at 1672)

Two of the Member States felt a need to react to the Liège Tribunal's request on this count. For Belgium, it seemed 'hardly conceivable to prohibit a Member State in general terms from adopting expulsion measures, in any circumstances, with regard to those categories' (at 1684–85). 'In no case', stated the French Government, 'can it be accepted that any particular type of circumstances may of themselves prevent the Member States from deciding to expel an alien whose personal conduct threatens *ordre public*' (at 1691).

The meaning of these submissions is that, even if in this case the Court established that certain particular circumstances of the individual excluded taking a measure of expulsion, in future cases the particular circumstances of a country may nonetheless again outweigh the needs of the individual. In other words, the case at hand must not create a judge-made norm excluding its future resettlement by equitable justice benefiting the state.

With this problematic, the case touches on the issue of *distinguishing* between existing precedents, on the one hand, and cases to be decided, on the other hand. Surely, the judgment in *Adoui and Cornuaille* would become *a precedent* for future practice, because all preliminary rulings of the ECJ are precedents. Belgium and the French Government wished to secure the possibility that *future* cases can be distinguished from *Adoui and Cornuaille*. However, *Adoui and Cornuaille* involved the problem of distinguishing in another way, that is, as a case to be distinguished from *earlier* cases. As we have seen, one of the core issues was whether the so-called *van Duyn* doctrine on Member State jurisdiction – and on the power to expel Europeans on the basis of certain activity even without legal action having been taken against nationals practising the same activity – applies in this case as well.

While all the Member States submitted that the *van Duyn* doctrine applies in this case too, the plaintiffs in their turn proposed that the present case must be distinguished from the case of Ms van Duyn. This was because 'the attitude of the United Kingdom' towards scientology, the core problem in *van Duyn*, was not the same as Belgium's attitude to prostitution. At the time of *van Duyn*, the plaintiffs explained, the legislation of the United Kingdom:

> [. . .] did not permit the punishment of the promoters of the sect complained of but an amendment to the law had already been planned which would allow the fundamental interests of the State to be relied upon. The situation is quite different when no-one has ever called into question the conduct in question. (at 1679)

As a matter of course, the operation of distinguishing is possible only on condition that the two cases are comparable in the first place. The idea of distinguishing is that, on the basis of this comparability, factual differences can be perceived and that, on the basis of factual differences, application of a different norm can be justified. Interestingly, however, what constitutes the *factual difference* in the distinguishing operation of the plaintiffs is the *difference of norms* in the two legal systems of Belgium and the UK. These norms constitute the facts that need to be compared. This is once again an instance showing that, from the perspective of Community law, Member State rules, concepts and principles are related as facts.

The Aristotelian dilemma between legal forms of justice incorporates the problematic of distinguishing between legal cases. In the beginning, the claim for distinguishing is one kind of *epieikeia*: difference in the circumstances of each case must be taken into account and unequals must be treated unequally. The plaintiffs tried to put the equity-mechanism of distinguishing into operation between the present case and the earlier case of *van Duyn*.

In the end, however, the result is not a loosening of the web of legality. On the contrary, an ever finer texture is woven in this web by the specifications made in the precedent. The effect of applying equity in the present will create an expanded legality in the future; this effect is no different from what it would have been if justice had been established *kata nomoi*. This effect was the concern of the French Government and Belgium. They wished to secure that equity as distinguishing would still operate between the circumstances of the present case and the circumstances of future cases. In other words, they wanted to make sure that the game can continue.

Absolute values

In spite of all this, is there a point at which the game will absolutely have to stop? Facing a certain absolute value X, would the practice of law simply have to admit that there will be absolutely nothing if not X. This value would simply not allow itself to be relativised in the weighting mechanisms normally used in legal discourse and practice. In the *Adoui and Cornuaille* case, the plaintiffs as a matter of fact did invoke this sort of dramatic idea in two different places. The first of these we have already discussed: the plaintiffs maintained that derogations from the rights of individuals are possible only if 'the existence or essence of the Community governed by the rule of law would be threatened' (at 1678). This was a clear reference to certain values without which there would be nothing; whatever these might be, they must be matters of life or death for any practice of jurisdiction or for any exercise of legally legitimate authority. The other place in which the plaintiffs suggested non-relativity is where they discussed the notion of 'inhuman treatment'.

It should be noted here that the Liège Tribunal's request (which was, in reality, penned by the plaintiffs' attorneys) had asked whether or not expulsions in certain cases constitute 'inhuman treatment' (at 1672). At this point, the plaintiffs stated that measures of expulsion 'would be dramatic for an entire community' of emigrants. In the view of the plaintiffs – and this is important legally – there are certain situations in which these measures:

> [. . .] would amount to cruel or inhuman treatment within the meaning of Article 3 of the European Convention of Human Rights, of Article 5 of the Universal Declaration on Human Rights and of Article 7 of the International Agreement [sic: *Covenant*] on Civil and Political Rights of the United Nations Organization. (at 1679)

It is worthwhile reproducing what these provisions say about inhuman treatment. According to Article 3 (Prohibition of Torture) of the European Convention: 'No one shall be subjected to torture or to inhuman or degrading treatment or punishment'. According to Article 5 of the Universal Declaration: 'No one shall be subjected to torture or to cruel, inhuman or degrading treatment or punishment'. Finally, according to Article 7 of the UN Covenant: 'No one shall be subjected to torture or to cruel, inhuman or degrading treatment or punishment. In particular, no one shall be subjected without his free consent to medical or scientific experimentation'. In international law, the rule against torture has been held – at least until the past decade – as an element of law indicating an absolute value. In other words, this is a *jus cogens* rule from which no state can derogate in any circumstances.

For Belgium, the question of inhuman treatment 'is merely of academic interest in this case'. With respect to Ms Adoui especially, Belgium stated furthermore that the issue 'does not directly concern the plaintiff in the main proceedings, a young person in good health who lives "by her charms" [. . .]' (at 1684). So, in Belgium's opinion, Ms Adoui could very well continue living by her charms in France, where she belonged. Nothing inhuman, cruel or degrading ensued from her expulsion.

Any talk about inhuman treatment in the present context, the Advocate General said, 'would be an abuse of language'. In the meaning of human rights law, this notion indicates such things as torture, he stated. Inhuman treatment of that sort, the Advocate General stipulated further, is an 'inexcusable disgrace' for authorities practising it. In the register of the Advocate General, the notion of inhuman treatment is to be reserved for entirely different matters. By using this notion in cases such as the present one, the Advocate General seemed to think, the practice of law would deprive itself of the language it needs for other, much more important occasions (at 1721).

This discussion of inhuman treatment is worthy of two comments, at least from the point of view of academic interest. The first concerns the different ways in which the plaintiffs applied their tactics of absolute values. In the first case, it was to set a very high standard for the circumstances amounting to threats to *ordre public*. The effect of that would have been that it becomes barely conceivable that any individual conduct could pose such a great threat as to endanger the sheer existence of a community governed by the rule of law.

Measured in this way by absolute values, any personal conduct whatsoever is most likely to fall within the range of normal life that goes on under the rule of law. Sometimes the conduct of individuals incurs punishment or other legal consequences, but this creates no trouble at all for the legal system. Before the practice of law, nearly anything fits into its mechanisms of imputation of sanctions, ascription of rights and duties and weighting of interests. Therefore, in this case the plaintiffs in fact suggest a line of thought quite similar to that of the Advocate General in the case of inhuman treatment. For the plaintiffs, we might think, the use of *ordre public* on minor occasions would deprive the law of language that is meant for much more important occasions, where the conditions of existence of the legal order are at risk. As a notion referring to an absolute value, the scope of its application must be narrowly interpreted.

In the second case, the plaintiffs employed the tactics of absolute values for the purposes of precisely the opposite analytical strategy. This time, breaking up families and other such things are considered as amounting to encroachments on an absolute value. 'Inhuman treatment', therefore, is not presented as something the applicability of which has the highest possible threshold or a standard that only some very rare and exceptional circumstances meet. This time, the tactic of absolute values was employed to borrow the exceptional normative power of those values. However, this requires that the scope of an absolute value, represented by the rule prohibiting inhuman treatment, is broadly interpreted.

The second comment is called for by the most urgent academic interests. It concerns the effect of absolute values on the Aristotelian dilemma. The picture drawn by the foregoing discussion of the structures of practice of law presents a field in which the 'static' element of legality (justice *kata nomoi* or as produced by practice) is in constant interplay with a 'dynamic' element of equity (justice as the always renewing demand for *epieikeia*). On the side of its effects on society, this presents an unceasing mechanism of vacillation between the two poles of stabilisation of society, on the one hand, and adaptation to changes in society, on the other hand.

Let us say, to begin with, that unlike in the field of criminal law, in the field of public international law pertaining to acts of states, *mala in se* (wrongs in themselves) are possible and independent from *mala prohibita* (wrongs because prohibited). However, it still seems that, generally speaking, absolute values are not part of the game of law. On the one hand, were it the case that absolute values are incorporated *kata nomoi* in legislation, then no possible argument from *epieikeia* can outweigh it.

On the other hand, however, these absolute values would in no way depend on legislation. Were it the case that an established positive norm allows – or perhaps even makes it mandatory, thus constituting 'statutory lawlessness' (*gesetzliches Unrecht*; Radbruch 2006) – in some given situation to encroach on an absolute value, that positive norm should be invalidated and rejected out of hand, that is, regardless of the level at which this positive norm occurs in the legal system.

The academic consequences of this necessary alienation of absolute values from the (otherwise so robust and comprehensive) weighting mechanisms of the practice of law are well known. The core question is whether absolute values really are legal values at all. If they stand for an idea of justice, can that form then be *legal* in a way comparable with the basic legal forms of justice, legality and equity? The most urgent concern is this: what would happen to these values if someone started to play the legal game with them – perhaps with an honest intent only to promote the type of justice that stands for these values – and inserted them into the eternal practice of correlations, rules and exceptions, and proportionality?

Unquestionably the practice of law can stomach anything, but what results is another matter. Because the legal field serves in the first place as a ground for strategic manoeuvring of all kinds of interests, it is clear that on this ground the absoluteness of values swiftly evaporates. In fact, this was precisely what has happened during the past decade with respect to the absolute value of the rule against torture: it was thrown into the playground of legal discourse and practice, where it was significantly diluted (see eg Waldron 2005).

However, according to Belgium, the appalling question of untouchables is indeed an academic problem, both with respect to the case at hand and with respect to the practice of law generally. The practice of law cannot be stormed by absolutes so as to present the acts of power in question as such inexcusable disgraces for the public authorities that the administration of justice would see it best to cease to cooperate with the administration of the state. The practice of law must go on arguing legally, either by invoking justice *kata nomos* or justice as *epieikeia*, either to condemn or to legitimise the exercise of power, but practise it must.

Private morality

The final problem of equity and legality is 'private morality'. If the above discussion about inhuman treatment brought us to the boundaries of the practice of law in the dimension of exercise of power, the question about private morality would touch these boundaries in the dimension of human interiority. The question is whether in that direction one has come to the limit beyond which veridictional control, as an examination of the individual's nature, should no longer have access. The way in which the Liège Tribunal presented this problematic in its request was as follows:

> To what extent are Member States entitled to take account of the private morality of the persons concerned as the ground for a refusal or withdrawal of residence permits if that morality is not of such a nature as to give rise in the host State to perturbations which are specifically and objectively ascertainable in public? (at 1673)

So a line is drawn between a person's internal or private life and that person's public life. On the latter notion, the request is further elaborated thus:

> Does not the adjective 'public' exclude any consideration of the private life, morality and convictions of the individuals concerned, if those matters should not normally find expression in external conduct capable of giving rise to perturbations which are specifically and objectively ascertainable in public? (at 1673)

According to the plaintiffs, a state cannot 'consider itself to be threatened' if there are no perturbations in public, that is, if the deplorable conduct of the individual stays in the realm of private life. Rather than public conduct, prostitution is a matter of 'an attitude of an individual', and even his or her 'convictions'. Should this attitude or conviction nonetheless result in public perturbation, the plaintiffs maintained that it should be the objectively ascertained perturbation, not the 'individuals' convictions themselves' that should be considered as grounds for expulsion (at 1680).

In fact, the plaintiffs asserted, the Treaty confers on migrant workers more than simply the right to work: they have 'a right to live in the host country like other workers of that country and to enjoy the same rights as those workers'. In the plaintiffs' view, the case involved 'respect for private life, freedom of conviction and freedom of expression'. Interestingly, the last point about 'expression' articulated the problem of posing in windows while scantily dressed to civil and political rights. In that context, a certain amount of perturbation to public life, generated intentionally by some brave individuals, is regarded as a value, indeed the core of citizenship that fuels a healthy democracy, rather than as something deplorable (at 1680).

In Belgium's view, first of all, public perturbation had existed since the plaintiffs had been 'on view in a window on a public thoroughfare'. The 'morality of the person' is not interfered with if it stays completely private, but insofar as it 'is reflected in his behaviour, which presupposes that certain specifically and objectively verifiable acts have taken place', expulsion may take place. For Belgium, it 'goes without saying that the activity of a prostitute intrinsically jeopardizes *ordre public* if she carries on that activity in a provocative manner, for example if she displays herself at the window of a bar in an indecent manner or if she solicits clients in the street in the vicinity of the bar'. Such 'disregard of [the] State's concept of *ordre public* and sound morals', said Belgium, is a legitimate ground for expulsion of an alien regardless of the fact that 'nationals commit the same offences' (at 1685).

For the Italian Government, 'private morality is a matter exclusively for each individual and no State intervention of any kind whatsoever is permissible'. Therefore, 'the morality of each individual is without importance with regard to *ordre public*'. Nonetheless, it is possible that such morality 'is characterized by outward behaviour which has the features of an unlawful act [. . .] or at least of a social danger'. In principle it did not seem possible for the Italian government 'to exclude the taking of the view that the behaviour of the person in question constitutes a social danger'. It warned, however, about abuses of power – in cases where prostitution is exercised in a 'discreet and reserved' manner – that may occur, 'having regard to the extreme difficulty of appraising sexual morality' (at 1694).

The Dutch Government did not endorse the view that invoking the *ordre public* derogation should have to involve 'public disturbances' at all, or even require that 'the conduct in question must manifest itself "in public"' (at 1697). 'In private life also', it said, 'interests which the State regards as public interests may be seriously jeopardized' (at 1697). The French Government, in turn, stated that 'in certain cases criminal conduct occurring in private life in certain circumstances constitutes a valid reason for an expulsion order', even though 'as a general rule' there would need to be public perturbation (at 1690).

The Commission did not regard it as possible to distinguish in any categorical way the private life of individuals from their public life. In its view, 'conduct forming part of a person's private life' can have (or may at least be 'regarded by a national authority as having') 'repercussions outside' that sphere of life. If there are repercussions, a state may consider it necessary to intervene. 'This is the case particularly in the field of morals', said the Commission. What is more, for the Commission purely private conduct, including sexual conduct, is one of those things typically viewed differently by different states and differently at different times. This being the case, private morality and sexuality is situated, not at all outside the problematic of *ordre public*, but as a matter of fact at its very centre. Thus defining something as residing on this or that side of the public/private divide can by no means have the effect of excluding anything from the scope of the *ordre public* derogation (at 1702).

The Advocate General also adopted the theory of repercussions. The 'private life of individuals is, as a matter of principle, not to be interfered with by the State authorities' (at 1721). However, 'the morality of individuals' can 'assume importance when it is reflected in their external conduct and thus has repercussions on the environment in which they live', the Advocate General stated (at 1721). This is the basis on which the existence of threats to *ordre public* must be assessed, which means, on the one hand, that protecting the sphere of private life and morality from state intervention does not exclude control of conduct whose origin, in one way or another, could be traced back to that sphere. On the other hand, 'private morality may be taken into account only in so far as it is reflected by conduct which constitutes a treat [sic; *threat*] to *ordre public*' (at 1731).

The judges did not consider it necessary to make any comments on the matter of private morality. This silence affirms the overall impression that the question of private morality seems to have been considered a minor issue in the proceedings. This is rather strange, because only here does the file touch the core of the problem from the point of view of the reality of danger. What, after all, is the nature of the danger that the individuals in question have posed to society? What is dangerous about prostitution?

There is the inconvenience and irritation of people who would like to pass by windows without seeing there what they perhaps regard as shameless obscenity, or symbolising the subjection and abuse of the female sex, or the like, which may engender deep public revulsion. The question is then whether fundamental interests, the protection of which is necessary in a democratic society, may be genuinely threatened by encroachments to the sentiments of chastity or to sexual equality. Whether they do or not, the judges thought, one must look into how the authorities of the Member State combat prostitution when conducted by nationals. No further discussion is necessary.

However, the question about the dangerousness of prostitution remains. What is the truth or reality of this danger beyond the representations of the state in its practices? More precisely, is it really the private morality, the interiority, of prostitutes that is involved, or is it rather the private morality and internal life of their potential customers? Maybe the point of concern is neither so much the private morality of immigrant prostitutes, nor public perturbation, but perturbation in the private interiority, the underworld, of the native inhabitants.

From the discipline of collective psychology and deep public revulsion, we have strayed to the equally dangerous area of individual human beings as subjects of sexual desire. The life of their mind should be formed by moral convictions, but beneath them are abhorrent forces rampaging in the excitable nether life of the human being. These are not perturbations in public, but riots run by forces that communicate at the level of one's body. The danger is that at some desperate moments these riots may destroy a person's moral convictions from within. Reading between the lines, the *Adoui and Cornuaille* file constantly hinted at this, albeit not at an explicit level of discourse.

Conclusion: system of representations and reflections

The uses of the basic concepts of justice in *Adoui and Cornuaille* attest to strategic polyvalence in the same way as the uses of the principles of justification did in *Bouchereau*. Equity and legality may be employed in different combinations and facilitate different tactical choices. Through different strategic filters, concepts of justice may be put into the service of entirely different objectives. The concept of legality turned out to be a protean spectre, whose meaning is just as changeable as any.

A variety of notions of legality – strict criminal law type of legality, formal legitimation of delegated powers, general applicability of legal concepts, legality as merely one policy choice among others, unambiguously determined limits to power, and so on – can all be thrown into the whirlpool of legal practice. There these notions will always confront, in different forms, the concept of equity. This concept is no less protean, because it is born from the experience of the variability natural to social life. When reality takes legality by surprise, the latter cannot but stand in awe. The unavoidable plurality, incessant change and pervasive unpredictability of circumstances, exigencies and needs is met by the concept of equity. Unlike plain legality, mechanisms such as proportionality-testing, weighting and balancing, orientation to principles, and other equity apparatuses have the capacity to adjust the law and make it fit into any situation.

However frenzied the mobility and rearrangement of concepts of justice that goes on in legal practice, below the surface there is a certain constancy and immobility, where the tread of law appears much firmer than it first seemed. Thus, the practice of law will not stop grinding up the social power of immanent norms of social physics, or what Foucault analysed as normalisation. This type of power needs no medium such as laws, because it works, not through reflections and representations, but directly within the social body.

My thesis is that social physics and normalisation can never penetrate and conquer the hard core of legal practice, because this practice always produces representations and reflections and works through these rather than directly. The Aristotelian mechanism of justice as *epieikeia* and *kata nomos* produces these representations and reflections through two contrasting transformations. First, it turns positive law into a kind of fact by making it stand for reality. Secondly, it turns facts into the midwifery of law by first representing them as something that calls for justice beyond positive law. This is a game of representation and reflection, which does not allow reality to govern itself directly. It constantly passes reality through the grinder of justice, legality and equity, upon which the reality is, as it were, forced to follow itself *dia mimeseos*, by way of imitation, but never directly.

In the foregoing analysis, we have seen a variety of ways in which an established law was made to stand for reality. To begin with, the fundamental state of legality invoked by the plaintiffs was the most dramatic staging of this substitution. The legal order as a whole was moved to the realm of facts, where it stood for social order in general. From another viewpoint, the same type of idea was put forward by the plaintiffs in their claim that the practice of law should be able to produce a feeling that there is certainty in law. Corresponding to the feeling of certainty, there was Belgium's legalistic invocation of indiscriminate expulsion of all dangerous individuals, irrespective of their personal circumstances. Both are examples of legality making the law substitute for the chaos of reality, thus guaranteeing justice as ontological security.

Furthermore, we saw how the mechanism of distinguishing – between the facts of the case at hand and the facts of a precedent – may indicate the laws of two different countries as facts to be compared with each other. Finally, the most illuminative finding was the semiotic that the judges developed for danger. In this system, national laws are not regarded as measures or norms for national reality. Instead, national laws stand for national reality as its exclusive representation.

All of these instances teach a lesson of the type of justice that legality brings forward. Legality expresses first and foremost the idea that the law should be able to look upon itself as a fact. Insofar as legality alone has the capacity to engender justice, this justice is always connected to law's existence as a substitute for reality. Legality alone has no other value as justice but its fact-likeness, certainty. This value, the value of ontological security, should not be underrated.

However, there is even more to it, because the law's ability to look upon itself as a fact is at once a necessary precondition for the other type of justice to emerge. In order to invoke extra-legal justice, the mechanism of *epieikeia* must be able to consider the system established *kata nomoi* as a social-structural element that in certain circumstances produces injustices. The foregoing analysis of *Adoui and Cornuaille* has shown a variety of instances also of this other transformation. Let us call it norm-creation through representation of facts.

Whereas the Member States did their best to present state interests as pertaining to inescapable necessities, the Commission transformed them into values and inserted them into the mechanism of weighting and balancing. The Commission's propagation for the reign of principles and equity went so far as to exclude totally the form of legality that would take place in the rules of national law. Against that, the concrete socio-political point of view of Italy was presented as a kind of counter-strategy, which nonetheless operated in the same way. The law must be interpreted in the light of concrete needs and people's welfare, whereby a standard of justice emerges from a scrutiny of the facts.

In another way, something factual has the capability to create laws in the requirement of consistency of practices, which gives rise to so-called living law. Insofar as considerations of fairness were effective in the one case, in the next case these must be equally effective: an element of legality has been inserted into the structure, because equals must be treated equally.

All instances of *epieikeia* follow the same procedure, which the Advocate General depicted acutely: matters of fact must be verified in each individual case, to establish whether a certain formally legal action is compatible with the principle of proportionality. In other words, *epieikeia* must play two registers, facts and extra-positive justice, in order to overcome legality. Any such employment of equitable justice will at once enact a more definite new norm for the future. All in all, the law can indeed arise, not from facts alone, but from a representation and reflection of facts in the mirror of justice.

Practice of equity and legality is the daily grind of justice carried out beside the stream of social life. It uses the energy of that life, but instead of going with the flow, it establishes a system of reflection and representation that generates justice as a power against the power of normalisation and social physics. 'We cannot make the river run backwards; but we do not therefore say that watermills "are not made, but grow"' (Mill 1962: 13). Equally, the practice of law cannot undo social physics and normalisation, but it does not follow from this that the law grows from and into these same forces. The power of law is rather generated against them, and insofar as it is also a force resisting normalisation and social physics, it develops this force by insertion of a system of reflections and representations.

This system is balanced by a play between three levels: *positive law* that is abstract and general, *facts* that are concrete and singular and *justice* that emerges from the friction between the first two levels. Unlike in the free play of normalisation that is nonetheless governed by social physics, in the legal play of representations and reflections there is also room for power and cultural arbitrariness. In fact, the genius of law is not only that it emphasises the pervasive voluntariness that it always projects into the exercise of power, but precisely that it makes use of this inherent relativism to check and control social power. As long as the law has capacity to carry out this task, normality will not be able to consummate into a dominating order.

In conclusion, *Adoui and Cornuaille* explored the problem of private sexual morality. This problem will open up a way to the final subtext of the present work, that of dangerous desires as the essential knowledge of the self. It is essential, because an individual will become a subject by becoming a subject of this knowledge. This means, at the same time, that the individual becomes subjected to his or her own self-knowledge.

Before entering the problem of self-knowledge on dangerous desires, let us once again ask why the plaintiffs really were so terribly dangerous in Belgian society. Does it not seem that they were dangerous because they said 'yes' to desire? The only crime here – there really was no other – was 'incitement to debauchery', which Ms Adoui and Ms Cornuaille had committed by being in view on a public thoroughfare. In the words of Georges Bataille, they 'lay themselves open to be desired' and 'put themselves forward as objects for the aggressive desire of men'. As 'prey', they exercised the most disastrous power, that of 'exciting desire in men' (Bataille 1986: 130–31).

Notes

1   Hart 1997: 194–99. In Community law the epithets 'primary' and 'secondary' are used precisely the other way around. Aristotle would have said that 'laws are distinct from the principles of the constitution' (*Politics* 1289a: 18–19).

2   1672. Article 7 of the European Convention on Human Rights provides, in addition to its general ban on punishments for acts that do not constitute criminal offences according to national laws, that states must not sentence individuals to *heavier penalties* for an offence than the penalty applicable at the time of the offence. Prostitution was not penalised in Belgium.

3   The concealed reason for which Belgium expels 'French waitresses' is, according to Ms Adoui and Ms Cornuaille, that it regards them as '"the logistic support" for the French underworld' (at 1680).

4   The mode of action of an administrative state would be 'the administrative degree that is determined only in accordance with circumstances, in reference to the concrete situation, and motivated entirely by considerations of factual-practical purposefulness' (Schmitt 2004: 5).

5   Kaarlo Tuori explains that *perlocutionary effects* are those that extend beyond the immediate action context, being modifications of the legal system on the level of legal culture. Someone whose objectives are at this level intends to change the structures of thinking and acting more broadly (Tuori 2007: 170).

6   In some sense, this change had happened already in the case of *Rutili*, which had stipulated that 'measures restricting the right of residence which are limited to part only of the national territory may not be imposed on nationals of other Member States, who are subject to the provisions of the Treaty in the cases and circumstances in which such measures may be applied to nationals of the State concerned' (*Rutili* at 1236–37, operative part). However, this rule was again changed in the later case of *Olazabal* (C–100/01), which stipulated that neither Article 48 (after amendment, Article 39) nor Community secondary legislation 'preclude a Member State from imposing, in relation to a migrant worker who is a national of another Member State, administrative police measures limiting that worker's right of residence to a part of the national territory' (*Olazabal* I–11017, operative part).

7   To take an example prevalent in Europe today, Roma people may not be deported en masse because their presence generally allegedly engenders perturbation. Rather, the dangerousness of each individual must be proved separately. In the present case this means that all 'French waitresses' may not be expelled en masse because this group would, according to the experience of the security authorities, generally function as logistic support for the French underworld. Instead, each one's connection with that underworld must be verified separately.

Chapter 11

Knowledge of the individual

In this chapter, the problem of desire will be revisited. As we saw in Chapter 3, economic liberalism works by saying 'yes' to desire, whereas juridical sovereignty works by saying 'no' to desire. As forms of humanity or subjectivities, it is typical for both *homo juridicus* and *homo œconomicus* that they require to be internalised by individuals who thus become *self-subjecting subjects* – subjects that submit willingly to laws without the use of force, or calculating subjects governed through their own interest. To use Foucault's words, in both of these cases an individual is made subject through being 'tied to his own identity by a conscience or self-knowledge' (Foucault 2000e: 331). So, in this chapter, knowledge of the individual will be self-knowledge – of desire.

Let us say that modern uses of desire are possible only after desire itself has been shaped into an element thorough which individuals may be governed. For Foucault, desire as an element of governability that operates from the inside of the individuals – an element to which the economic 'yes' and the juridical 'no' respond – was in fact a product of one thin but very long rhizome of history. 'Desire is an old notion', said Foucault, 'that first appeared and was employed in spiritual direction' (Foucault 2007a: 72). The practice of spiritual direction started to develop in the second half of the 16th century, alongside the much longer evolution of the Christian rituals of penance and confession (Foucault 2003a: 183). What would happen in a session of spiritual direction of conscience, Foucault explained rather succinctly during his interchange with the Lacanian psychoanalyst Jacques-Alain Miller:

> The Christian says, 'Listen, the trouble is that I can't pray at present, I have a feeling of spiritual dryness which has made me lose touch with God.' And the director says to him, 'Well, there is something happening in you which you don't know about. We will work together and find it out'. (Foucault 1986b: 216)

What I want to do in the end is to discuss Foucault's history of the ways in which the Christian church developed its technology for extracting hidden truths from individuals. This is, for Foucault, the history of a single institution, that of confession. He meant not the confession of faith, but the confession of sin that, in reality, turned out to be the confession of sexuality.

What I mean by 'confession' [*aveu*; avowal], even though I can well see that the term may be a little annoying, is all those procedures by which the subject is incited to produce a discourse of truth about his sexuality which is capable of having effects on the subject himself. (Foucault 1986b: 216)

Pastoral power, the power exercised by Christian shepherds and the Church, means power over the human soul, not over one's external actions, but over one's interiority. The technology developed by the Church for that purpose grew into a very distinct regime. At the origin of this regime was what the fathers of early Christian communities called *oikonomia psukhôn*, economy of the soul or, in Latin, *regimen animarum* – government, regimen and conduct of souls (Foucault 2007a: 192, 193). According to Foucault, the pastoral relationship is founded on a specific type of truth, the truth of the inside of each particular individual: '[The pastoral] form of power cannot be exercised without knowing the inside of people's minds, without exploring their souls, without making them reveal their innermost secrets. It implies a knowledge of the conscience and an ability to direct it' (Foucault 2000e: 333).

The question to be addressed to the 'history of the confession of sexuality' (Foucault 2003a: 170) is how pastoral technology came into being and what tactical turns by which its 'field of truth with objects of knowledge was constituted' were used (Foucault 2007a: 118)? As is well known, Foucault's general method was to move beyond single institutions and see how certain mechanisms of power were in the course of time distributed and communicated in a network connecting different institutions. His history of confession is the clearest possible example of an application of this method (genealogy). It is possible to observe how the Christian pastorate first receives techniques from a quite different institutional mechanism, that of law, and then modulates them for its own *regimen animarum*. Such observations require that one regards 'techniques with operative value in multiple processes', that is, techniques that have one kind of use somewhere, but other uses elsewhere (Foucault 2007a: 119, footnote).

In the seventh of his lectures at the Collège de France in 1974 (*Abnormal*), Foucault sketched a history of what he then called 'the discourse on sexuality'. That discourse is modern, but its history was formed and surveyed by Foucault in the practices of the Catholic Church, more exactly, in the evolution of the ritual of penance. What takes form gradually in that framework is the institution of confession. Within that institution emerged a very special type of power called spiritual direction, which, again, gave birth to desire as a notion and element fundamental to the modern art of governing.

The starting point is the early Christian communities in the first centuries after Christ. After this, Foucault's story goes through five shifts. Both the starting point and the ending point of the story are characterised by an absence of juridical forms. Through these shifts, juridical forms were first inserted into the Christian ritual of penitence, and when they had done their job in the cultivation process they were again distilled away. In the end and in the beginning this field is pure of law, but in the middle the juridical forms have clear functions that, in retrospect, can be seen as facilitating a tremendous transformation of human self-relation. The following presentation concentrates on three things in Foucault's genealogy: first, *the power of priests*; secondly, *the juridical forms*; and, thirdly, *the transformations of confession*.

From injection to rejection of legal forms

According to Foucault, in the beginning the Christian 'penance was a status', that an individual 'deliberately and voluntarily assumed'. The reason for which a Christian took on this status could be an act of sin, perhaps 'an enormous and disgraceful sin', but the reason might just as well be something else. (Perhaps the person in question simply felt immensely bad about everything.) Moreover, the individual who wishes to be a penitent does not necessarily have to tell the bishop, who would confer this status according to certain public rituals, what motivates the request. A public ceremony took place before the congregation, and then one was a penitent (Foucault 2003a: 171).

> After this ceremony, the penitent entered the order of penance that involved wearing a hair shirt and special clothes; scorning personal cleanliness; being solemnly expelled from the church, from the sacraments, or in any case from communion; undergoing rigorous fasts; suspending all sexual relations and being obliged to bury the dead. (Foucault 2003a: 171)

Bishops, or anyone else in the church, did not at this point have any power to remit the penitent of sins. Sin and salvation are matters between the individual and God; no-one else can get involved in this relationship. The penitent can only try self-help by repenting, and penance was a ritualised way offered in order to do that. 'The remission of sins', said Foucault, 'was possible only by virtue of the severity of the penalties the individual inflicted on himself, or allowed to be inflicted on him, by taking the status of a penitent' (Foucault 2003a: 172). All in all, what Foucault wanted to see in this original form of the ritual was the absence of three things: there was no obligation to confess sins; there was no power afforded to the church to remit sins; and, finally, there was no trace of any juridical forms in this practice.

The next phase, according to Foucault, occurred 'from about the sixth century'. At that point the first juridical form was adopted by the Christian church. It inserted into the practice a new model that Foucault called '"tariffed" penance' (Foucault 2003a: 172). Tariffed penance meant that there were tables that established a set of performances ('satisfactions') to be imputed on a corresponding set of sins.

This is, of course, the same thing that one finds in criminal law: there are defined circumstances to which the legal norm imputes defined sanctions. And it was indeed from criminal law, according to Foucault, that the church borrowed this basic element of legality: 'penance according to a tariff has an essentially lay, judicial, and penal model. Tariffed penance was established in terms of the Germanic penal model'; the penance 'was tariffed in the sense that for every type of sin there was a catalogue of obligatory penance, just as in the lay penal system, institutional reparation was granted to the victim for every crime and offence in order to wipe out the crime' (Foucault 2003a: 172).

Yet the church could still not wipe out the sin. The insertion of regularity by tariffs did not change the basic idea according to which the power to forgive remains with God. By performing the satisfactions correctly, the penitent could try self-help, but the final judgment was not in the hands of the church or its fathers. So there was no power, but at this point the mechanism of confession starts to take form: 'the statement of the transgression begins to play a necessary role' (Foucault 2003a: 172).

This role is purely technical, however. Without the statement, the priest could not look up from his table the appropriate satisfaction for the sinner. The statement would form the germ of confession, but it is not yet confession. Penance of this kind necessitates recounting and describing the sin by the sinner, because it 'allows the priest to fix the penalty'. Yet 'beyond this necessary implication, confession has no value and no effectiveness in itself'. The juridical form was made use of apparently because of the needs of the Church's administration: 'It is through this penance, whose origin is clearly judicial and secular, that the small kernel of confession – still very limited and with only utilitarian effectiveness – gradually begins to take shape' (Foucault 2003a: 173).

The next stage is that in which the Carolingian kingdoms were formed and imperial structures reinvigorated in Europe. In Foucault's story, that is a phase in which the autonomous social and political power of the Church generally speaking diminished, until it got the upper hand again in the second millennium. At any rate, Foucault explained, the Church lost its control of the ritual of penance: the practice of 'confession to the laity' emerges. Even before that, an idea had started to develop that the mere shame – being a painful thing – that the sinner incurs, not by sinning, but by telling about his sins to someone else might be sufficient satisfaction. So, confession as such could be not only an account of one's *culpa* but also and at once the *poena* that resolves the issue. Hence, from its juridically generated kernel, confession starts to gain value other than merely technical value.

> Thus, in the ninth, tenth, and eleventh centuries, confession to the laity becomes widespread. After all, if there is no priest on hand when one has committed a sin, one can quite simply express one's sins to someone (or several people) who happens to be available, and one becomes ashamed of oneself in telling him one's sins. (Foucault 2003a: 174)

Verbalisation, production of discourse, of one's misdeeds and the 'humiliation and blushes' (Foucault 2003a: 173) this induces would make good the damage done and provide the possibility of salvation. On the basis of verbalisation and blushes, God could be convinced of the genuineness of repentance and forgive the sinner without further penitential punishments. The important result of this is that 'the mechanism of the remission from sins' – a mechanism of salvation, in other words – 'closes around confession itself' (Foucault 2003a: 174). Therefore, during the time in which the power of priests was weak, the operational value of the mechanism of confession goes through a critical transformation.

The next development, 'from the twelfth century until the beginning of the Renaissance, is that the Church manages to restore ecclesiastical power over the mechanism of the confession that had, to a certain extent, deprived it of power in the operation of penance' (Foucault 2003a: 174). The Church took back exclusive power over the ritual of penance: from now on it was only properly ordained priests that could conduct it. But the Church took it back with the mechanism of confession that had developed in the meantime, and developed it further. A *regular* confession ('at least once a year for the laity') became obligatory in 1215. The requirement of *continuity* was established: 'one must express every sin committed since at least the previous confession'. Also, the confession must be *exhaustive*: 'One must express all one's sins, not only the serious ones, but also the less serious'; one must forget nothing because it is for the priest to judge what is serious and what is not (Foucault 2003a: 174).

So far, in doctrine at least, the power of the priest to remit or attenuate sins had been strongly contested. In the early Christian communities and in the Church of late antiquity, the final judgment on salvation was considered to be exclusively and entirely in the hands of God.[1] Now, however, it would become established by the Church that the priest would indeed have the so-called 'power of the keys', that is, the power to absolve individuals from sins or at any rate to attenuate the final punishment (Foucault 2003a: 176).

Later, in his *Security, Territory, Population* lectures Foucault would explain that at this point the institution of confession and rituals of penance became 'a system of modulated, provisional punishment' (Foucault 2007a: 203) that could guarantee the individual's afterlife and grant him salvation. What this means is that the 'Church was penetrated by a judicial model' (Foucault 2007a: 204): 'This is the introduction of an essentially and fundamentally secular model, namely the judicial model, into the usual pastoral practice. [Hence:] the existence of a permanent court before which every faithful individual had to regularly present him or herself' (Foucault 2007a: 203).

Furthermore, beside the introduction of this juridical form (the judicial model) the former juridical form (that of penal codes) was abandoned: 'the priest is no longer bound by the tariff of satisfactions but fixes the penalties himself according to the sin, the circumstances, and the person' (Foucault 2003a: 175). Therefore, one juridical element is inserted into the pastoral power-structure and the other juridical element deleted from it, the result of which is that the power of the priest over his subjects increases exponentially. This power revolves around the institution of confession, the type of *veridiction* that is worked out by way of facilitating extraction of the truth from the individual.

The historical conditions of possibility for the pastoral power-structure appear to be quite contingent in their formation. The first of these conditions was the insertion of a juridical form (legality) by way of codifying sins and satisfactions into tariffs. Later, however, this form became a useless handicap and was abandoned. The second condition, ensuing from the first, was the emergence of the institution of confession. Interestingly, at an earlier stage this institution (in its lay form) had deprived priests of their power. In the end, however, this very same institution – after its reinsertion into the pastoral structure, together with the juridical form of adjudication – became 'the element through which the pastor's power is exercised' (Foucault 2007a: 183).

Generation of empirical powers

With these developments, the historical condition of possibility – the ritual, the power-structure and the apparatus – was all set for the birth of desire 'as a question, posed in terms of truth' (Foucault 1986b: 213). This happened through two further shifts, the first of which took place in the 16th century. This was the revolutionary century of Luther and Copernicus: the Protestant reformation and empirical physical science. Both of these posed formidable threats to the Catholic Church. Politically, these developments would spark off, in the following century, the 30 Years' War. By the time this war ended in the Peace of Westphalia (1648), the medieval political system, where the power of Papal Rome had often towered over others, was abolished.

In Foucault's story, the 16th century was that of 'in-depth Christianization' set off by the Council of Trent (1545–1563). The Council of Trent, 'a gigantic cultural phenomenon' (Foucault 1986b: 219), took the task of counter-attacking the menacing hostilities that this century presented against it, notably by Protestantism. Hence, in-depth Christianisation was effected by a strategic function, that of 'responding to an urgent need' (Foucault 1986b: 195). The response of the Catholic Church is known as the Counter Reformation, which also involved reform of the practice of confession. In Foucault's view, the fathers in Trent did not so much concede to adapt their practices to the turn of the tide in Europe. On the contrary, in this period the 'Christian structures tighten their grip on individual existence' (Foucault 2003a: 177).

As for the ritual of penance and the practice of confession, this grip on individual existence required that the 'priest's empirical powers of the eye, the gaze, the ear, and hearing are developed in support of his sacramental power of the keys' (Foucault 2003a: 177) – the power that Protestants had not only revoked, but cursed by invigorating the old annoying doctrines of St Augustine on predestination. What needed to be facilitated was that 'all of an individual's life, thought and action must pass through the filter of confession' (ibid), not least perhaps in order to guard against the dispersion and mushrooming of Luther's ideas among the faithful. This called for new techniques and procedures to be applied in examining the contrition and conscience of individuals, as well as new qualifications and skills on the part of priests acting as father confessors.

To make the confession session as productive as possible, priests hearing confessions were first of all instructed to be as welcoming as possible to 'promote and encourage the right mood in the penitent' (Foucault 2003a: 180). The priest must show that he is 'available and open' (ibid). Secondly, when the session itself starts, the priest must give his penitents the impression that he is listening to them willingly. He must *rejoice for the contrition of the penitent*, because that can lead to the salvation of this one sheep of his, which is the greatest possible pleasure for all father confessors. Nothing in the appearance of the priest must show any repulsion or disenchantment that would not encourage the penitent to continue with their account.

More interesting than these two basic rules guiding father confessors is the third and more subtle rule that concerns the end result of the confession. That result must be consolation, but how would the father confessor produce this? The point is apparently that in the communication of his or her sins, the penitent would be able to transmit the burden of guilt to the father confessor, who would then participate in carrying it (or even relieving the penitent of the burden altogether).

In order to make this happen in the mind of the penitent, the father confessor must *show the pain that he feels* from receiving the burden of sins. Therefore, when the penitent communicates the pain of the sins lying heavily on her, the priest acting as a father confessor must communicate, in return, the pain that he feels from receiving this weight – a pain which, at another level, must nonetheless appear to be a pleasure to the priest. The end result of consolation arises from this reciprocal communication (or 'economy') of pains and pleasures: 'There is an economy of pain and pleasure: the pain of the penitent who does not like to confess his transgressions, his consolation in seeing that the confessor suffers pain in listening to his sins, but who also consoles himself for the pain he thus gives himself by securing through confession solace for the penitent's soul' (Foucault 2003a: 181).

The full responsibility of the shepherd for the wrongs committed by his sheep means, on the one hand, that the sheep can be relieved from responsibility and saved, but, on the other hand, it also means that the sheep relinquishes its independence as well. This is carried out by the verbal communication of sins, a verbalisation which 'is also way of renouncing self and no longer wishing to be the subject of the will' (Foucault 1993: 221).

Being a subject of the will would not really mean independence and self-mastery, of course, but that one is under the reign of Satan, the 'terrible serpent that this confession has forced out of its subterranean lair': 'Since under the reign of Satan the human being was attached to himself, verbalization as a movement toward God is a renunciation [of] Satan, and a renunciation [of] oneself. Verbalization is a self-sacrifice' (Foucault 1993, 220).

In addition to these rules, the Council of Trent placed certain rather high qualifications as to the skills and character of the priests acting as father confessors. The priest must not only be properly ordained and properly learned, but also well versed in the art of *regimen animarum*. Mastery of this art requires, moreover, that he is holy and prudent. 'What is to be understood by the priest's holiness',

Foucault explained by referring to confession manuals of the time, 'is that he must be "confirmed in the practice of virtue" precisely because of the "temptations" to which he will be exposed in ministering the penance' (Foucault 2003a: 178–79). Holiness would protect the father confessor from contagion of the sins that are communicated to him every day, against the heavy burden that he must carry in his heart all the time. Holiness is 'a kind of armour against the sin being passed on to him at the very moment of its utterance'. The forces that the father confessor fights against are terrible and he himself is constantly in the greatest possible danger of lapsing. 'The desire displayed by the penitent must not be turned into the confessor's desire; hence the principle of holiness' (Foucault 2003a: 179).

The requirement of *prudence* in the character of the priest is important as well. Referring again to the confession manuals, Foucault explained that: '[. . .] the confessor's prudence consists in this: "Observe all the circumstances, compare them with each other, discover what is hidden behind what appears, and foresee what might happen"' (Foucault 2003a: 180).

The empirical powers of priests were not strengthened and devised only by the above described theoretical architecture, by these rather abstract rules and qualifications guiding and facilitating the practice. The practice of confession also has a physical architecture, a *material apparatus* that was introduced to the Christian life-infrastructure in early 16th century. The confessional is still the principal workshop of Catholic priests today. The idea, practice and ritual of confession were

> [. . .] crystallised within an institution, or rather within a little object, a small piece of furniture with which you are quite familiar – the confessional: an open, anonymous, and public place within the church where the faithful can present themselves and will always find a priest available who will hear them, remaining close beside them, but from whom they are separated by a small curtain or screen. (Foucault 2003a: 181)

At this point, however, the practice of priests in confessionals was no longer equivalent to that of judges acting in criminal courts. While in the beginning the power of the keys was in need of support by development of empirical powers, this power would now start to function as a support to empirical powers – that is, to the more urgent and primary task of extracting the truth. The operation of the confession and penitence was no longer primarily punitive, but an 'operation of the examination, analysis, correction and guidance of the penitent' (Foucault 2003a: 180). This aspect of confession was called 'medicinal' after the Council of Trent, and it would soon devour the juridical aspect formerly inserted into the structures of the practice. This would be the final stage in the evolution that had begun by insertion of the juridical model of penal codes into tariffed penance.

> It is an evolution that inserts the juridical form of the law, of offence and penalty, which was originally the model for penance, within a field of practices that have the nature of correction, guidance and medicine. Finally, it is an evolution

that tends to replace, or at least to back up, the irregular confession of particular transgressions with an immense discursive journey that is the continual passage of life before a witness, the confessor [. . .]. (Foucault 2003b: 184)

Moral physiology of the flesh

Now let us turn to the final stage in the story, which presents two things at once: first, deletion of the last remnant of juridical forms from the discursive space of the confessional; secondly, and as if ensuing from the first, the birth of desire. With that birth, a new regime replaces the old one that had been formed and cultivated according to juridical models over 1000 years. Hence, what will come into being is 'the code of the carnal' that works in a very special field of knowledge: 'anatomy of the pleasures of the flesh' (Foucault 2003a: 186, 187). In other words, there must be 'a cartography of the sinful body' so that the Church may establish its 'moral physiology of the flesh' (Foucault 2003a: 187, 189).

All of these notions refer to a new interest, accompanied by rediscovery of an old object, in the body of an individual: the so-called flesh (*la chair, la volupté*).[2] The flesh is not the muscles and organs controlled by the individual, nor is it something in the order of the 'tonic forces' that 18th century medicine later saw vivifying the human organism. The flesh will become the Devil's acolyte, an agent that controls the individual. The flesh leads the individual secretly astray, that is, without his or her awareness of it. The flesh must be mortified to have the Devil exorcised, but in order to accomplish that, the Devil's subliminal existence in the voluptuous body must be realised. The flesh needs to be recognised as a great power that one can depose only with the help of the priest, by subjecting oneself unconditionally to the priest.

In Foucault's presentation, the change in the focus in the procedures of examining the conscience is best perceptible in the confessional interrogations pertaining to the Sixth Commandment (Do not commit adultery), that is, examinations concerning 'the sin of lust' (Foucault 2003a: 184). A lack of chastity is not just one variety among many sins, but the most important one, because through that the Church introduced a new idea about sin in general. It was 'an old theme that the body was at the origin of every sin', but at this point the Christian elites moved to think that, in fact and more precisely, 'there is concupiscence in every transgression' (Foucault 2003a: 192). The sin of lust is hidden behind what appears to be wholly other kind of wrongs; lust is the generative element of all sin.

The concept of sin moves from the basis of inter-relational wrongs to that of exclusive self-relation. Until this shift, the sin of lust had still been conceived juridically in that the reason why they were sins was because they constituted wrongs harming other people. Sexual offences (all kinds of sex outside the relationship of marriage) were looked at from the point of view of relationships between partners. Virginity, for example, was a precious thing for a young maiden, and her being deprived of that by someone who would not marry her afterwards was a real catastrophe. The rationale of the Sixth Commandment used to be connected to 'what could be called the relational aspect of sexuality' (Foucault 2003a: 185).

This relational or interpersonal rationale had still been informed by certain 'major transgressions at the level of relationships with someone else', but now the examination of conscience was moving away from the plane of such outward transgressions. For a long time scholars had distinguished between bad thoughts and wrongful acts, where bad intentions alone could also have been considered as transgressions. Yet that had concerned, according to Foucault, only 'the problem of the relations between intention and realization', a problem which can still be seen as confined by the juridical framework of human relations. What the priest now needs to reach is the 'primary and fundamental level of sin that constitutes the relationship to self and the sensuality of the body itself'. With the new focus on the penitent's self-relationship, the problem of the confessional discourse is no longer juridical and relational; 'it is the problem of desire and pleasure' (Foucault 2003a: 189).

The problem of desire was delicate and presented a need for further development of the techniques applied in a confessional. There was the danger, as already noted, that the father confessor must not be 'soiled' by sins, but in addition to this there was another worry. This was that the penitent 'must never learn through the confession more than he already knows'; in other words, the penitent's 'natural ignorance' must be preserved (Foucault 2003a: 185–86). Therefore, father confessors were instructed not to ask about specific acts, but about the penitent's thoughts:

> [The father confessor] must question the penitent on his 'thoughts' in order to avoid questioning him on his acts in case the latter have not been committed (thus avoiding the penitent being taught something he does not know). He must never name the kinds of sin (he must not name, for example, sodomy, sensuality (*la mollesse*), adultery, incest, et cetera). (Foucault 2003a: 186)

This kind of carefulness, according to the confession manuals of the time, would make it possible to 'draw from the penitent's mouth every kind of lust, without the risk of teaching him any'. From the point of view of the penitent, this kind of suggestive indirectness creates a discursive space where one must embark on a reflective probing on the life of one's mind that might very well have been entirely non-existent to the subject before. Thus, 'the movements, senses, pleasures, thoughts, and desires of the penitent's body' become by this new procedure of examining something 'whose intensity and nature is experienced by the penitent himself' (Foucault 2003a: 186).

While the penitent's own experience is meant to work as a filter or censor at one level, at another level it works in precisely the opposite way. At the first level, a 'rule of silence' and repression prevails in the confessional, but at another level censorship is 'governed by a positive mechanism' (Foucault 2003a: 169). The positive mechanism that is inserted into the discursive space of the confessional is a crucial historical instance in what Foucault later in his *Will to Knowledge* designated as the 'putting into discourse of sex', a 'putting' which should become perceptible from the general perspective of the discursive production of objects and domains of objects that transforms in connection to transformations of power:

> A first survey made from this viewpoint seems to indicate that since the end of the 16th century, the 'putting into discourse of sex', far from undergoing a process of restriction, on the contrary has been subjected to a mechanism of increasing incitement; [. . .]. (Foucault 1998b: 12)

The confessional becomes an apparatus whose mechanisms incite the subject's awareness of desire. While it is all the time about sins to be condemned, the procedure of finding out about them opens up for the individual a new vista of his or her own interiority. This is the body of desire, the sinful flesh. Despite the importance of the requirement that the penitent produces the discourse alone, it is nonetheless clear that the priest must lead the penitent's attention in the right direction.

This direction towards the body was assured by the new procedure that charts the whole sensual body of the penitent. Hence, the father confessor was instructed to ask about the thoughts and emotions that the penitent has experienced with respect to each of the senses. The confession would begin with the sense of touch ('Lust begins with contact with oneself'), then goes to the pleasures of sight ('Was your looking accompanied by sensual pressure?') and pleasures of the tongue ('Dirty words give pleasure to the body'), ears ('Have you experienced pleasure "hearing the voice singing and tunes"'?) and, finally, the whole external body ('Has dressing like this given you pleasure?', and so on) (Foucault 2003a: 187–88).

By this type of mapping the senses – 'cartography of the sinful body' (Foucault 2003a: 187) – the focus of examination concerning the sins of the flesh is moved entirely from the juridical sphere of interpersonal morality to the body of the subject. In Foucault's view: 'We are witnessing the flesh being pinned to the body. [. . .] Now the sin of the flesh dwells within the body itself' (Foucault 2003a: 188–89). This is where the story ends. Since the birth of desire in the confessional, its discursive space need no longer be structured by the juridical forms formerly guiding the practice. Instead, 'the whole process of examination focuses on this body of pleasure and desire that now constitutes the real partner of the operation and of the sacrament of penance. The reversal is total or, if you prefer, radical: We have gone from the law to the body itself' (Foucault 2003a: 191).

In the end, I would like to go a little further backwards, to the point at which pastoral institutions had not yet 'profoundly disrupted the structures of ancient society' (Foucault 2000d: 303). As against the Christian individual, the citizen of Greek city states is depicted by Foucault 'as a man of the law' (Foucault 2007a: 175). Whatever this ancient man may otherwise be, he at least had a completely different idea of self-knowledge. Plato, for instance, was ready to go so far as to maintain that no one but the ignorant does anything wrong or bad. In Plato's logic, wrong and bad must therefore always be done involuntarily (*Protagoras* 345e). Whereas Christian knowledge mortifies the will, for ancient man knowledge seems to have been a precondition of freedom of the will.

Plato himself surely knew about the type of desire that Christianity was interested in. Yet these 'desires seem to me to be lawless', he thought, 'awakened in sleep, when the rest of the soul – the rational, gentle, and ruling part – slumbers' (*Republic* 571b). Normally, man rules over himself and his desire. By this Plato means: 'Nothing very subtle. Just what the many mean: being self-controlled and master of oneself, ruling the pleasures and appetites within oneself' (*Gorgias* 491d–e).

Thanks to the Christian groundwork that awakened desire from ancient sleep and slumber, it could be turned from something that the individual should rule into a useful medium through which the individual can be governed. Then he is no longer master of himself, but subject to power through his self-knowledge and identity. By the time – our own time – at which desire 'makes its second appearance within techniques of power and government' (Foucault 2007a: 72), there is no need any more for the Devil who could dreadfully take possession of us. We ourselves are devils; this is what our thoughts silently think.

Notes

1   At most, it was conceivable at that time that Jesus – who was expected to return on earth in the near future – and the apostles could possess the miraculous power of forgiveness. St Augustine, for example, still insisted that anything one does, in the form of penance or good deeds, will not help because salvation is predestined. See Lea 1896: 108–14, 95.
2   For the old notion of the flesh, see St Augustine's *City of God*: Book XIV.

Chapter 12

Recapitulation, conclusion

What should remain, according to the classic rules of a good speech, is to conclude by 'summarizing everything at the end and reminding the audience of what they've heard' (Plato *Phaedrus*: 267d). A speech, however, is a unit of action which typically fails if along the way suddenly something crucial turns out that one did not know from before. The art of speech is 'charming and persuading the members of juries and assemblies and other sorts of crowds' (Plato *Euthydemus*: 290a). Speeches must be well prepared and presented in a determined fashion. In turn, research is rather like another art, the enchanter's art, that 'consists in charming vipers and scorpions and other wild things' (ibid). Unlike speeches addressed to juries and other crowds, research fails if along the way nothing emerges that one did not know from before; in other words, nothing has been learned. Learning is of two kinds: making new discoveries and understanding on the basis of what one already knows.[1]

Rather than merely inspecting legal and other material on the basis of what is already known, the aim of this work has been to add something to understanding. Drawing on Kant, I believe that something can be added to understanding by way of 'problematic' propositions. Problematic is an optional proposition, expressing 'a freed choice to admit the validity of such a proposition – a merely arbitrary reception of it into the understanding'. Even if problematic indications of directions turn out to be wrong, they nevertheless help in finding the right ones. That way they must 'be conditions of our knowledge of the truth'. The first moment of learning in the proper sense of the word is that in which we 'judge problematically' (Kant 1997: A68/B93–A75/B100).

The introductory chapter set out that reading Foucault's work on the genealogy of the modern subject provides a view on the mechanisms of power that are subtextual to law, which is at the same time a view of the general field of power. In turn, the general field of power should provide a view of the functioning of the law in that field, as one of its members. That functioning, finally, shows how the European individual was born as a problem. This plan will be revisited in the following conclusions.

Foucault's genealogy of the modern subject

The modern subject is what we can call a self-subjecting individual. This is someone in whose inner reality has been implanted a more permanent governability, a governability that works inside the agent. As Foucault put it, the self-subjecting subject 'is subject to his own identity by a conscience or self-knowledge' (Foucault 2000e: 331). Foucault's conviction was that the genealogy of this subject is inscribed in the history of practices of power, in which individuals are 'the bodies that are constituted as subjects by power-effects'. Power-effects constitute subjects in practices where 'power passes through individuals'. However, individuals are not passive objects only; 'individuals do not simply circulate' in the networks of those practices. Individuals are absorbed in the networks of power, but still they 'are in a position to both submit to and exercise this power'. Practices of power exist in individuals, and individuals exist in practices of power (Foucault 2003b: 29).

So there is a history of power practices, which is constantly passing through human individuals, endlessly transforming them from one form of individuality to another. Let me provide an extremely reductive reconstruction of Foucault's genealogy of the modern subject, the history of its constitution by power practices. By a flight of imagination, suppose that this history is not an evolving social structure or cultural phenomenon, but one of those insects (maybe a moth) whose life cycle consists of three stages or moments: crawling larva, encapsulated pupa and flying adult. Foucault's history of power-practices presents the same kind of miracle of total metamorphosis.

The emergence and development of the practice of confession was the first moment. Christian practice was able to produce something that is an absurdity. Fear and desire were connected, despite their definitions as opposites to each other as feelings. This connection produced, and still produces, what we are: individuals who fear our own desire. This amazing thing, therefore, has a logic that makes connections between disparate things, the logic of strategy.

Another absurdity was perceptible: the practice that made use of this logic was a concomitant use of negative and positive mechanisms: repression was interwoven into incitement. Desire is bad and therefore the penitent will understand the requirement to loathe it as one loathes the Devil. At the same time, the father confessor must unfold the penitent's sinful flesh before exorcising desire. Desire is manipulated into a fearful form of Devil's acolyte and inserted into individuals (pinned to their bodies) as the constitutive element of their governability.

The second moment happened when clergymen went to work in royal houses and deep Christianisation took place: old practices of the Christian church became an undercurrent. Secularisation in science and the breaking up of the old political universe became the surface current. The period of unbelievable political turbulence and war in Renaissance Italy produced reason of state as a theory of consolidated order, whereas the period of the state's perfect consolidation in absolutist France produced counter-history as a theory of unending political turbulence and war.

Together, this period meant the eyes of both power and subject turning to each other. Counter-history had subjects' eyes turned to power in a new and critical way. Reason of state had power's eye turned to subjects with unforeseen interest. This double casting of glances spawned the modern world, which soon saw a series of popular revolutions and finally Briareus the 100-handed crowning itself permanently. However, it also set out the process of developing mechanisms and practices preoccupied with all kinds of plans for making more of each individual and of the entire population.

The last moment is that of English radicalism and Rousseau, which saw the larva emerge from the pupa as something completely different. Juridical power as depicted by the social contract and economic governing through the market are the two major ways in which power now passes through individuals. Juridical power works by way of renunciation of one's natural desire: the will of the individual is disconnected from one's own desire but connected to the will of the sovereign. Juridical power works by a fundamental axiomatic between pre-social-contract rights that are relinquished, on the one hand, and positive rights that are afforded in exchange by the legal system, on the other hand.

In turn, economic governing retains the will of the individual in connection with natural desire, because this alone makes the individual work hard. The individual need only understand his or her best interest, which has to be exclusively egoist in order to steer the conduct of the individual from the inside. Whereas juridical power says 'no' to desire and supplants it by the collective will expressed in statute, economic governing says 'yes' to desire and works by placing incentives and prospects before the individual.

Taken together, one can see how these two wings connect in one torso that silently restores the larva's absurdities: repression of desire and incitement of desire, which work through a magnificent design where a negative mechanism is inscribed into a positive mechanism.[2] Best interest and political obligation are two disparate but connected agencies that constitute the current state of our civilisation, whose function was acutely depicted by Freud:

> Civilization, therefore, obtains mastery over the individual's dangerous desire for aggression by weakening and disarming it and by setting up an agency within him, to watch over it, like a garrison in a conquered city. (Freud 1962: 70–71)

Desire stands at the centre. As an object of Foucault's research, power is exercised ultimately neither by way of cultivating the moral consciousness as a self-legislating faculty, nor by generating a moral sense by appealing to benevolent feelings. Its ways of working may be discursive, but discourse is framed by things that are not discursive themselves: fears and desires. Ultimately, Foucault considers power as attaching to the irrational element in the individual, drives and cravings, pleasures and horrors, Eros and Phobos. In Plato's terms, governability of subjects is not instituted in the reasoning part of the soul (*to logistikon*) but passes through the appetitive, desiring part (*to epithumetikon*) (Plato *Republic*: 439d).

Legal practice in the general field of power

The main forces in the general field of power can be ascertained through a generalisation of three forces functioning side by side in the plurality of different practices of power: domination, normalisation and the law. Domination is a force functioning by the rationality of reason of state: the state's essence is power, power is firm domination over people and people are the state's resource by which the state's strength is measured.

Normalisation is a force that takes hold on people from the inside of society: it imposes society's own reality – its empirical verity – as a norm on people through silently working jurisdictional operations that exclude pathological individuals too far from the average of the population as a whole. The law and its force will be returned to shortly; at this point negative definition is sufficient: it is a counterforce to both domination and normalisation.

Three ways of using Foucault in legal theory can be indicated here to pave the way for outlining a theory of legal practice, although ultimately it departs from all of them. By somewhat harsh reduction, these ways are anchored in three theses concerning the law in the general field of power: the penetration thesis, the polyvalence thesis and the expulsion thesis.

The penetration thesis claims that legal institutions are taken over by mechanisms and modes of power that are in one way or another foreign to the institution itself. The most famous example of this is Foucault's conclusion in *Discipline and Punish*, discussing the connection created by panoptic rationality to the functioning of criminal justice. The prison turned out to be the black heart of the surveillance system of policing of order in society. Circulation of delinquents enable the police to infiltrate into society's nether regions and to keep an eye on every small movement at the interface between the working class and the more violent and excitable underworld. Earlier, in his *On Popular Justice* Foucault had presented a more radical view: the courts of law themselves operate 'as an anti-seditious system'. Their functions were to isolate hooligans from the working class and to fan hatred between these two groups. The point of the penetration thesis is that some wholly 'other' kinds of practices – practices of domination – are at work in connection with and even within juridical institutions.[3]

The polyvalence thesis claims that the law can be made use of by numerous other practices of power, so that the law on the whole appears entirely differently in its different connections with other practices. In the materials studied in this work, the law has been practised in connection with the practices of immigration administration that forms part of the state security services. Similarly, the law has been practised in connection with the European integration, at the time when it was still considered to be an economic mission.

Throughout the book, however, the problem of polyvalence is present in a more general way in that each positioning of the law by Foucault depends on the anti-juridical knowledge that forms its complete opposite. The law on the whole is constructed differently in each context: discussions of economic, psychological and historical knowledges, as well as knowledge of the state, society and the individual – all present the law in different ways, because these presentations are never of the law in itself, but always of the constitutive 'other' of something else. Foucault's characterisations of law depend on the primary presentation of some other practice.[4] The point of the polyvalence thesis is that the law has no essence of its own, but is always relationally constructed.

The expulsion thesis claims that, because of the historical gradient, juridical reason no longer grasps the reality of power.[5] The crucial reality of power is not only practices of domination, but also normalisation: the capillary power that society's immanent norms exert on individuals. From the scattered discussions by Foucault on normalisation, his depiction of the market as a site of normalisation best represents the idea. Yet Foucault's work on the whole, if looked at from the vantage point of knowledge-power, is based on an idea that exercise of power may connect with the anonymous power of normalisation.[6] (Needless to say, the primitive fear of strangers – xenophobia – that underlies immigration law – thus, too, the problem of the European individual – is one motor of normalisation.) Looked at from the perspective of normalisation, the point of the expulsion thesis is that the force by which society regulates itself from the inside, notably through market mechanisms, has pushed the juridical representation of power into a marginal position.

All these three theses inform ways of theorising about law that are in one way true to Foucault, but in another way not. Their fidelity lies in that they take certain of Foucault's claims very seriously and adopt Foucault in their cognitive schemata. Their infidelity lies in the fact that Foucault was, in spite of all, depicting the law, its practice and reason, as something else. In his mind, law was not disciplinary power or biopower, and it was not normalisation. Juridical stands for the complete opposite of all that.[7] The present work has proceeded from this basis, which is why it has departed from all the above three theses. Despite the fact that other practices may be at work in juridical institutions, what mainly works there is legal practice. Despite the fact that law is relationally constructed, it could not be so at all if it had no identity of its own. Finally, despite the fact that normalisation is at work – perhaps even inside the law – what also works is law which is by nature destructive to normalisation. Microscopic analyses of legal cases purported to make this visible.

The law exists in its relations with the two other forces in the general field of power. These relations constitute the framework for the practice of law in its own field. On the one hand, the framework sets up the marginal boundary conditions to the practice of law. On the other hand, the boundary conditions come into existence in the concrete operations of legal practice. However, boundary conditions are not directly manifest in concrete operations. Directly manifest are the tactical manoeuvres of purposively and strategically oriented actors.

The boundary conditions emerge in the performance of legal practice in another way: in its ateleological dimension. Regardless of the aims of the actors, they emerge in each performance that enacts the fundamental categories of law, the ultimate principles of justification and the basic concepts of justice. The law's organisational relations to other forces in the general field of power dwell in the practical operations of law, but they are nonetheless different things. In Michael Polanyi's language, the relations of law in the general field of power are *the tacit dimension* of the practice of law (Polanyi 1967). These relations are threefold: the law's self-relation, the breaking down of domination and the breaking down of normalisation.

In order to be a member in the general field of power, the law needs to have its own principle to establish a self-relation, a relation that constitutes its own power (as domination has a self-relation in reason of state, and normalisation in the gravitational pull of normality). Law's self-relation emerges in the interplay between the field of law and *homo juridicus* through which juridical power functions. When juridical power is exercised, its effect is an emergence of the specific equivalence between social structure and individual agency: properties of the legal field are mirrored in the legal form of individuality.[8] Both the legal field and the legal subject are split by the two fundamental categories of legal practice: individual rights and authoritative decisions. Behind authoritative decisions exists the counterpart of *homo juridicus*: the sovereign legislator as a form and subject of power.

So there is a form and subject of power, on the one hand, and a form and subject of individuality, on the other hand. Both are fully contained by the field of law, where the emergence of juridical force is generated by practising their relationship. In its tacit dimension (that is, in its dimension of boundary conditions in the general field of power), this force is meant not only for the subjection of individuals, but also as a counterforce against domination and normalisation. What matters is that an element of possible resistance is woven into the functioning of the legal principle of power from the very beginning. Against any exercise of power, the possibility of taking counter-measures by asserting rights is always available. However, by asserting rights, one at once recognises the power and authority of the law.

The second relation, the breaking down of domination, emerges from the specific form of struggle that the legal field imposes on actors: provision of justifications.[9] As long as legal practice exists, it imposes this form not only on the players who enter the field of law. In its tacit dimension, it also imposes the requirement of justification on the general field of power. On this plane, practice of law is a counterforce to forces of domination, that is, to all practices that attempt to impose a solid order on people. Between order and docility, law exists as a layer of recalcitrance into which one's own interpretations and discourses may be inserted. Ultimate principles of justification – the rule of law and general good – lie under all legal disputing, excusing and cavilling. As long as this is open to individuals, they have already shaken off the yoke, as Bacon lamented.[10]

The field of law forces the 'essential power' of reason of state into another kind of discourse, where power can no longer be exercised for the sake of power.

The requirement of justifications is imperative in the legal field; an individual who has accessed it has at once escaped pure domination. As the possibility of resistance is necessary for the existence of relations of power, the field of law is constitutive of the general field of power by preventing it from turning into a consolidated order of domination. Each time a practice of domination tries positing legal force as an element of its own game, it at once enters the game of justification that must be played between a sovereign legislator and *homo juridicus*.

Finally, in the third relation, the law breaks down normalisation that is a force immanent to society. This relation emerges from the interplay between the basic principles of justice, legality and equity. The Aristotelian system (of justice *kata nomos* and justice as *epieikeia*) is more precise: it is the interplay between positive law, on the one hand, and factual circumstances that generate extra-positive law, on the other hand. This constitutes a system for making representations and reflections on social reality, which create the law as a force against normalisation. The automatic result of application of this system is that social norms are deprived of their immanence. Immanently working social norms are replaced by legal representations, an artificial organisation comprising norms that will have to be learned, remembered and applied.

The system also has the capacity to reveal, and thereby destroy, the silent jurisdictional operation that is at work in the guise of veridiction. The Aristotelian system inserts a space of divergence, distance and delay between the rule and regulation, whereas normalisation has its prescriptive effects, effects of jurisdiction, hidden in its descriptive and codifying effects. Normalisation loses its proper functioning if the jurisdictional nature of its operation – determination and exclusion of abnormality – is brought to light.

The practice of law constantly reveals the nature of knowledge of society as culturally arbitrary. Arbitrary power will no longer be concealed by misrecognition of society's immanent norms as the truth.[11] Before the law, society's immanent norms mean nothing as such, but are always filtered through legal norms that are openly jurisdictional – given by the sovereign, in other words. The practice of law may or may not give relevance to social normality, in some cases it may even assimilate 'customary' social norms in the artificial organisation that it tries to remember and apply. However, legal norms cannot reproduce the silence in the operation of social norms, because legal norms and their applications are acts of awareness.[12]

The field of power, of which the law is one member, has three major instances. The state, which is better conceived of as consisting of all the practices that work by reason of state, is the agent of order as domination. Society, which again is better conceived of as consisting of society's immanent and self-executing norms, is the agent of order as normalisation. The juridical sovereign, which is better conceived of as a structural element or property of the field of law, is the agent of power constituted by the communion between *homo juridicus* and *corpus juris*. Three major forces in the general field of power pass through individuals in practices of power: domination, normalisation and the law.

The omni-historical elements of legal practice

'Let's suppose that universals do not exist', said Foucault at the beginning of *The Birth of Biopolitics*, and started as always with concrete practices (Foucault 2008: 3). This brings us to the difficult problem of history. In order fully to grasp the reality of history – that is, the reality of change – one must suppose that universals do not exist. What makes things change? For Machiavelli, the source of change – variation of our *fortuna* – is human desire that is elementarily insatiable.[13] Desire is given as the universal property in every man and woman, and this is the reality of history, the reason why things change. However, history does not seem to let even desire walk out of history. Desire too is a historically changing category that appears differently in different practices of power.

Throughout the book, the field of legal practice seems also to be one of pervasive change. The legal game is a game of changing the rules, principles and interpretations; even the most fundamental legal concepts are exposed to this game. Accordingly, I have tried not to forget to make perceptible what legal materials manifest beyond everything else: the richness of the protean transmutations that will never fully comply with one's analytical devices, however rigorous. Yet this is not the final moral of the story, there is one that is more interesting. At this point, the omni-historical nature of the elements of legal practice needs to be addressed.

There seems to be a reason why all the 'knowledges' presented in this book have historically made connections with the juridical institutions and the rationality of law. That connection is a way for a knowledge to make itself effective in reality, to enter history and become material. Economic knowledge could be materialised only if institutionalised legally. Psychological knowledge was made real by connecting it to the criminal justice system. The target of historical knowledge is the legally conceived political system, through which knowledge of history is inserted into history as a means of struggle. Knowledge of the state materialises in laws that it holds as instruments, but finds these instruments capable of turning against their users. Knowledge of society should try to work in silence in the factual presuppositions of legislators. Finally, knowledge of the individual is extracted by procedures subtly modelled by juridical forms.

All of these historical connections are instances of the logic of strategy. Once again, what is the logic of strategy? For Foucault, it seems to have substituted for the principle of causality, which allows him to see history as a pervasively contingent affair. It was a way for him to 'welcome the cunning assembly that simulates and clamours at the door. And what will enter, submerging appearance and breaking its engagement to essence, will be the event' (Foucault 1998c: 345). So history is a matter of events. What Foucault calls 'eventalisation' of history is critical use of history: first, eventalisation is 'a breach of self-evidence' that 'means making visible a *singularity* at places where there is a temptation to invoke a historical constant' (Foucault 2000f: 226).

> Second, eventalisation means rediscovering the connections, encounters, support, blockages, plays of forces, strategies and so on, that at a given

moment establish what subsequently counts as being self-evident, universal and necessary. In this sense, one is indeed effecting a sort of multiplication or pluralisation of causes. (Foucault 2000f: 227)

For Foucault, there certainly is no ending to this transmutation of things in the course of history. The whole point of eventalisation is to deny the possibility of making an 'extrahistorical mechanism or structure available' (Foucault 2000f: 227) that would in the end explain all historical change and make everything intelligible. Clearly, an introduction of the idea of omni-historical element departs from Foucault at this point. For Althusser, omni-historical meant something that is 'not transcendent to all (temporal) history, but omnipresent, trans-historical and therefore immutable in form throughout the extent of history' (Althusser 2008: 35). What matters is the fine distinction between omni-historical and extra-historical. Omni-historical elements belong to history itself: they constitute the reality of change.

Accounting for elements of legal practice as omni-historical is not possible without a view of the general field of power. Without this view, and only in terms of the operations and tactical manoeuvres of the practice of law, nothing of the kind can be seen: the only thing that practice manifests is constant change itself. However, the backdrop of law's tacit dimension – that is, the power-relations between law, domination and normalisation – allows one to see more. In the general field of power, the function of law is precisely to maintain the constant possibility of change. Whereas domination and normalisation would stabilise society, the law makes it move.

Traditionally, the legal system has been considered either as a stabilising element of society or as an element that reacts to changes that occur somewhere else.[14] In this view, legislation is the main modern instrument providing a possibility of responding to any new need and balance of interests that emerges externally to law. However, the microanalysis of legal practice carried out in this work shows that the instrument of legislation, as a receiver of social and political momentum that legislation should change into a heavier material reality, is not the major contribution of the law to historical change. Rather, it is the practice of law that constitutes the field of law as a layer of possible change in the general field of power. The field of law as a field of practice is a site of emergence; the becoming of things occurs there.

Here is the second appearance of the logic of strategy. In the general field of power, the logic of strategy meant the conjoining of different practices of power and knowledge. But in the field of law it means the strategic and tactical conjoining of the omni-historical elements of legal practice: rights and decisions, the rule of law and general good, legality and equity. These fundamentals, ultimates and basics are indeed the deep structure of the practice of law, but this deep structure is a moving structure for constant movements. Their enactment is action that makes time travel and things change, not by terrible shifts that make breaks between huge epochs, but from moment to moment in the micro level of legal practice. In other words, the elements of constant change are not to be found in anthropological universals, such as human desire. These elements are to be found in the practices that pass power through the individual. And this work has been an attempt to grasp the moment they passed through the European individual.

The European individual

It is often said that total exclusion of dangerous individuals is no longer possible because modern society no longer has a geographical outside. The wilderness beyond the walls of the city can no longer serve as a depository of abnormal and dangerous individuals. What matters more, however, is that imaginative space in modern society no longer exists for subjects whose thinking and conduct does not stand to reason. This is because society and politics were at the beginning of modernity founded on the image of the universal subject. Political ideas were justified in that they stand to reason for everyone. In turn, the techniques and mechanisms of power implemented in the practices of domination and normalisation worked on the underside of law to guarantee the reality of the modern universal subject. Producing this subject is vital, because it forms the ideological foundation of the polity.

Existence of fundamentally irrational 'otherness' poses formidable threats to the norms at the foundations of the polity, because these foundations hold together only on the presumption that everyone in principle has the capacity to understand and accept them. In the words of Habermas, everyone must be capable of agreeing to norms 'as participants in rational discourses' (Habermas 1996: 107). This is really an old paradox, already present in the so-called Great Speech of Protagoras. Zeus had ordered Hermes to distribute political senses (justice and shame) to everyone equally, because only this can warrant the existence of sustainable political societies. But Zeus added: 'And establish this law as coming from me: Death to him who cannot partake of shame and justice for he is a pestilence to society' (Plato *Protagoras*: 322d). Hence, a polity is based on the idea that 'all can', but right next to this foundation it implies that 'all cannot'.

The law of liquidation by Zeus expresses the principle by which the intersections between veridiction and jurisdiction work. Zeus presents something in the indicative mood which is at once a norm: every human being will from now on be capable of shame and justice. This is not an element of syllogism, but a command. However, some people do not abide by or fit this norm. The universal subject, who can participate in rational discourses, has a concealed constitution in the universal law of liquidation. However, liquidation has no other purpose but to produce and uphold the universal subject. The latter belongs to the former's constitution as well.

The European individual born in this work is not the universal form of humanity, but its failure. The European individual is three things in this work: a textual figure, a problem and a hologram.

The European individual has a reality in the texts of the cases. It is not flesh and bone, as are the concrete individuals whose stories were presented in those cases. Drawing on Marc Bloch, one can say that the existence of the European individual in these legal cases is one of 'interrelations, confusions, and infections of human consciousness' (Bloch 2008: 125). In other words, it is a mental creature born in the mind of someone who has read these texts. Yet the reality of the texts is not flat and uncomplicated, but has its own deep structure and archaeology. For those of us who read texts as reality, 'that which the text tells us expressly has ceased to be the primary object of our attention'; 'we prick up our ears far more eagerly when we are permitted to overhear what was never intended to be said' (Bloch 2008: 52).

Analysis of texts can 'no longer confine itself to weighting the explicit assertions of the documents. It has been necessary to wring from them further confessions which they had never intended to give' (Bloch 2008: 74). A reality exists that the text does not present, but rather hides, and 'from the moment we decide to force [texts] to speak, even against their will, cross-examination becomes more necessary than ever' (Bloch 2008: 53) However, because all one has is texts, the analyses cannot but try 'making use of the internal characteristics of the [. . .] texts' (Bloch 2008: 96). Other texts exist in texts.

The European individual has another reality as a problem. What is a problem? A problem is something that allows entry into the field of thought, said Foucault. To be a problem, 'it is necessary for a certain number of factors to have made it uncertain, to have made it lose familiarity, or to have provoked a certain number of difficulties around it' (Foucault 1997c: 117). Behind every problem exists a process of problematisation, and these processes are what cross-examination of texts tries to wring from them.

The European individual was already a problem for the participants in the proceedings: it was uncertain and provoked difficulties. Beyond that level of explicit assertion, the European individual exists as a problem owing to certain rather more important problematisations: the problematisation of human forms, the problematisation of power and the problematisation of knowledge. To enter the field of thought through the problem of the European individual, one has had to 'reject a priori theories of the subject in order to analyse the relationships that may exist between the constitution of the subject or different forms of subject and games of truth and practices of power' (Foucault 1997b: 290). The European individual has provided a view on exactly these three problematisations: forms of subject, practices of power and games of truth.

Finally, the European individual as a hologram connects the two ends of the work: the genealogy of the modern subject and the event of the birth of the European individual. Whereas the genealogy provided a view on the general field of power, the European individual provided a view on the omni-historical elements of legal practice. In this way, this work has attempted to make perceptible the connecting texture of forces and practices between the two forms of individuality. What, then, could be the more direct relationship between the European individual and the modern subject?

'This brings us to the more general problem of preservation in the sphere of mind', as it brought Freud when he asked himself: 'But have we a right to assume the survival of something that was originally there, alongside of what was later derived from it' (Freud 1962: 16, 15). Freud's intuition was that 'in mental life nothing which has once been formed can perish – that everything is somehow preserved and that in suitable circumstances (when, for instance, regression goes back far enough) it can once more be brought to light' (Freud 1962: 16). His famous parable of the Eternal City was meant as a metaphor for the psychic system, where former layers will continue to exist despite their being buried by newer layers:

> Now let us, by flight of imagination, suppose that Rome is not a human habitation but a psychical entity with a similarly long and copious past – an entity, that is to say, in which nothing that has once come into existence will have passed away and all the earlier phases of development continue to exist alongside the latest one. [. . .] And the observer would perhaps only have to change the direction of his glance or his position in order to call up the one view or the other. (Freud 1962: 17)

The European individual is finally just such a hologram. Entering the field of thought through problematisations of the European individual – human forms, power and knowledge – one is able to glimpse the historical backgrounds of our present being. These were produced, and then again buried, in intersections between practices of power and games of truth. In the problem of the European individual one has suitable circumstances that bring to light forces that have passed through the individual for centuries. Moreover, the European individual has the capacity to prove that these forces have survived, because in the European Individual regression goes back far enough.

Notes

1 Plato: 'people use the word "learn" not only in the situation in which a person who has no knowledge of a thing in the beginning acquires it later, but also when he who has this knowledge already uses it to inspect the same thing, whether this is something spoken or something done (as a matter of fact, people call the latter "understand" rather than "learn", but they do sometimes call it "learn" as well)' (Plato *Euthydemus*: 277e–78a).
2 In a psychoanalytic reading, the law stands for prohibition that in fact gives birth to human desire. One such reading is provided by Panu Minkkinen: 'Man cannot reign autonomously in his world because law engages him into the conflictive universe of contradicting desires. But neither can he plunge into the rage of his instinctive life because law imposes orderly meaning into the world. Like the prohibition of incest, law both constitutes the originary object of desire and maintains the indispensable distance in relation to it' (Minkkinen 1999: 118).
3 Foucault 1991 (the last two chapters) and Foucault 1986a. Despite their heavy criticism of these and other views of Foucault, Alan Hunt and Gary Wickham adopt the perspective of interpenetration of the law and the practices of governing, where they rely on Foucault's disposition on 'governmentality'. See Foucault (2007a: 87–123) and *The Foucault Effect* (Burchell, Gordon and Miller (eds) 1991). In their programme for

sociology of law as governance, Hunt and Wickham consider the law as one of the practices of governing: 'all operations of law are distinctive instances of governance' (Hunt and Wickham 1998: 99).

4 This is a sort of Hegelian 'characterisation in which things are in essential or polar opposition to each other. In polar opposition, each term is such that its interaction with another opposed entity is constitutive of its own entity' (Taylor 1983: 261). Ben Golder and Peter Fitzpatrick build their work *Foucault's Law* by and large on the idea of polyvalence, where the tension between law's responsiveness and recalcitrance is depicted neatly as law's 'insistent capacity to be otherwise than it is' (Golder and Fitzpatrick 2009: 86).

5 See Hunt and Wickham (1998: ch 3) and Hunt (1992).

6 François Ewald has reconstructed a new concept of law based on Foucault's idea of normalisation. He claims that the different mechanisms of normalisation that have appeared in different compartments of today's legal systems – for example the mechanism of quantitative calculation of risks in insurance law – have put the reality of law as a whole on a new foundation, which has replaced law's former foundation in juridical reason that makes qualitative distinctions between rights and wrongs. See Ewald (1990; 1988; 1986). For discussion, see Tuori (2002: ch 3; 2003), Minkkinen (1999: 107–108) and Golder and Fitzpatrick (2009: 35–39, 103–107).

7 Ultimately, of course it does not matter how loyal one is to Foucault if these viewpoints facilitate research that can be good in its own right.

8 As Bourdieu says, the individual internalises into its *habitus* the social structure in which it moves, and it maintains the field by externalising these structures again in its action. This is a matter of the 'dialectic of social structures and structured, structuring dispositions through which schemes of thought are formed and transformed' (Bourdieu 2007: 40).

9 Drawing again on Bourdieusian theory of practice: 'Entry into a field requires the tacit acceptance of the rules of the game, meaning that specific forms of struggle are legitimated whereas others are excluded' (Swartz 1997: 125).

10 Bacon (1858: 98), discussed in Chapter 8 of this book.

11 This is the place to refer to Bourdieu's basic axiom concerning symbolic violence (*la violence symbolique*): 'Every power to exert symbolic violence, i.e., every power which manages to impose meanings and to impose them as legitimate by concealing the power relations which are the basis of its force, adds its own specifically symbolic force to those power relations' (Bourdieu and Passeron 2000: 4). For Bourdieu, law is one form of symbolic violence: 'Law does no more than symbolically consecrate – by reducing it in a form that renders it both eternal and universal – the structure of power relations among the groups and classes that is produced and guaranteed practically by the functioning of these mechanisms', ie the social mechanisms of domination. See Bourdieu (2007: 132). In my view, the law rather reveals symbolic violence and destroys the functioning of misrecognition, *méconnaissance*, that presents arbitrariness as truth.

12 Minkkinen depicts Foucault's law as a '"juridico-epistemological" matrix [. . .] through which the social world penetrates language'. Speaking of the law as an original form for production of truth, Minkkinen's discussion comes close to mine: 'law first relays the human world into language and then opens the seemingly closed system to speech' (Minkkinen 1999: 118).

13 'Da questo nasce il variare della fortuna loro' (Machiavelli 1994: 189).

14 A classic example of this view is Maine's *Ancient Law* (1920); a modern example would be Philippe Nonet and Philip Selznick's *Toward Responsive Law* (2005).

Bibliography

Agamben, G. (1999) *Potentialities: Collected Essays in Philosophy*, trans. D. Heller-Roazen, Stanford: Stanford University Press.

Althusser, L. (2000) *Machiavelli and Us*, trans. G. Elliot, London & New York: Verso.

Althusser, L. (2008) *On Ideology*, trans. B. Brewster, London & New York: Verso.

Althusser, L. and Balibar, E. (2006) *Reading Capital*, trans. B. Brewster, London & New York: Verso.

Arendt, H. (1989) *The Human Condition*, Chicago and London: The University of Chicago Press.

Aristotle (1934) *Nicomachean Ethics*, trans. H. Rackman, Aristotle in 23 Volumes, Vol. 19. Cambridge, MA: Harvard University Press.

Aristotle (1944) *Politics*, trans. H. Rackman, Aristotle in 23 Volumes, Vol. 21, Cambridge, MA: Harvard University Press.

Aristotle (1926) *Rhetoric*, trans. J. H. Freese, Aristotle in 23 Volumes, Vol. 22, Cambridge, MA: Harvard University Press.

Arnull, A. (1999) *The European Union and its Court of Justice*, Oxford: Oxford University Press.

St Augustine (1984) *Concerning City of God Against the Pagans*, trans. H. Bettenson, Harmondsworth: Penguin Books.

Bacon, F. (1858) *The Essays: or Counsels, Civil and Moral and the Wisdom of the Ancients*, Boston: Little, Brown and Company.

Bataille, G. (1986) *Eroticism: Death and Sensuality*, trans. M. Dalwood, San Francisco: City Lights Books.

Bengoetxea, J. (1994) 'Legal system as a regulative ideal', *Archiv für Rechts- und Sozialphilosophie*, 53: 65–80.

Bentham, J. (1970) *Of Laws in General*, London: University of London and The Athlone Press.

Bloch, M. (2008) *The Historian's Craft*, trans. P. Putman, Manchester: Manchester University Press.

Böckenförde, E.-W. (1998) 'The concept of the political: a key to understanding Carl Schmitt's constitutional theory', in D. Dyzenhaus (ed.) *Law as Politics: Carl Schmitt's Critique of Liberalism*, Durham and London: Duke University Press.

Bogdandy, A. von and Bast, J. (2002) 'The European Union's vertical order of competences: the current law and proposals for its reform', *Common Market Law Review*, 39: 227–68.

Botero, G. (1956) *The Reason of State & The Greatness of Cities*, trans. P. J. Waley, London: Routledge & Kegan Paul.

Bourdieu, P. (1977) *Outline of a Theory of Practice*, trans. R. Nice, Cambridge, UK: Cambridge University Press.

Bourdieu, P. (1987) 'The Force of Law: toward a sociology of the juridical field', trans. R. Terdiman, *The Hastings Law Journal*, 38: 814–53.

Bourdieu, P. (1989) 'Social Space and Symbolic Power', trans. L. J. D. Wacquant, *Theory and Practice*, 7(1): 14–25.

Bourdieu, P. (1990) *In Other Words. Essays Towards a Reflexive Sociology*. Cambridge: Polity Press.

Bourdieu, P. (2007) *The Logic of Practice*, trans. R. Nice, Cambridge (UK): Polity Press.

Bourdieu, P. and Passeron, J.-C. (2000) *Reproduction in Education, Society and Culture*, trans. R. Nice, London, Thousand Oaks and New Delhi: Sage Publications.

Bourdieu, P. and Wacquant, L. J. D. (1992) *An Invitation to Reflexive Sociology*, Cambridge, UK: Polity Press.

Bourdieu, P., Chamboredon, J.-C. and Passeron, J.-C. (1991) *The Craft of Sociology: Epistemological Preliminaries*, trans. R. Nice, Berlin and New York: Walter de Gruyter.

Butler, J. (1997) *The Psychic Life of Power: Theories in Subjection*, Stanford: Stanford University Press.

Burchell, G., Gordon, C. and Miller, P. (eds) (1991) *The Foucault Effect: Studies in Governmentality with two lectures and an interview with Michel Foucault*, Chicago: The University of Chicago Press.

Canguilhem, G. (1991) *The Normal and the Pathological*, trans. C. R. Fawcett, New York: Zone Books.

Clapham, A. (1991) *Human Rights and the European Community: a Critical Overview*, Baden-Baden: Nomos Verlagegesellschaft.

Craig, P. and Búrca, G. de (1998) *EU Law: Text, Cases, and Materials*, 2nd edn, Oxford: Oxford University Press.

Dinan, D. (1994) *Ever Closer Union: an Introduction to the European Community*, Basingstoke and London: MacMillan.

Durkheim, É. (1997) *The Division of Labor in Society*, trans. W.D. Halls, New York: The Free Press.

Ewald, F. (1986) 'A concept of social law', trans I. Fraser, in Teubner G., (ed.): *Dilemmas of Law in the Welfare State*, Berlin and New York: Walter de Gruyter.

Ewald, F. (1988) 'The law of law', trans. I. Fraser, in Teubner, G. (ed.) *Autopoietic Law: a New Approach to Law and Society*. Berlin and New York: Walter de Gruyter.

Ewald, F. (1990) 'Norms, discipline and the law', *Representations*, 30: 138–61.

Foucault, M. (1986a) 'On popular justice: a discussion with Maoists', trans. J. Mepham, in M. Foucault, *Power/Knowledge: Selected Interviews and Other Writings 1972–1977*, Brighton: The Harvester Press.

Foucault, M. (1986b) 'The confession of the flesh', trans. C. Gordon, in M. Foucault, *Power/Knowledge: Selected Interviews and Other Writings 1972–1977*, Brighton: The Harvester Press.

Foucault, M. (1989) *The Birth of the Clinic: an Archaeology of Medical Perception*, trans. A. M. Sheridan, London and New York: Routledge.

Foucault, M. (1990) *The Care of the Self: the History of Sexuality: 3*, trans. R. Hurley, London: Penguin Books.

Foucault, M. (1991) *Discipline and Punish: the Birth of the Prison*, trans. A. Sheridan, London: Penguin Books.

Foucault, M. (1992) *The Use of Pleasure: the History of Sexuality: 2*, trans. R. Hurley, London: Penguin Books.

Foucault, M. (1993) 'About the beginning of the hermeneutic of the self: two lectures at Dartmouth', *Political Theory*, 21(2): 198–227.

Foucault, M. (1994a) *The Order of Things: an Archaeology of the Human Sciences*, New York: Vintage Books.

Foucault, M. (1994b) *The Archaeology of Knowledge*, trans. A. M. Sheridan Smith, London: Routledge.

Foucault, M. (1997a) 'What is revolution?', trans. L. Hochroth, in M. Foucault *The Politics of Truth*, Los Angeles: Semiotext(e).

Foucault, M. (1997b) 'The ethics of the concern for self as a practice of freedom', trans. P. Aranov and D. McGrawth, in M. Foucault *Ethics, Subjectivity and Truth: Essential Works of Foucault 1954–1984, vol. 3*, ed. P. Rabinov, New York: The New Press.

Foucault, M. (1997c) 'Polemics, politics, and problematizations: an interview with Michel Foucault', trans. L. Davis, in M. Foucault *Ethics, Subjectivity and Truth: Essential Works of Foucault 1954–1984, vol. 3*, ed. P. Rabinov, New York: The New Press.

Foucault, M. (1998a) 'Nietzsche, genealogy, history', trans. D. F. Brouchard and S. Simon, in M. Foucault *Aesthetics, Method, and Epistemology: Essential Works of Foucault 1954–1984, vol. 1*, ed. J. D. Faubion, New York: The New Press.

Foucault, M. (1998b) *The Will to Knowledge: the History of Sexuality: 1*, trans. R. Hurley, London: Penguin, London.

Foucault, M. (1998c) 'Theatrum philosophicum', trans. D. F. Brouchard and S. Simon, in M. Foucault *Aesthetics, Method, and Epistemology: Essential Works of Foucault 1954–1984, vol. 1*, ed. J. D. Faubion, New York: The New Press.

Foucault, M. (2000a) 'Truth and juridical forms', trans. R. Hurley and others, in M. Foucault *Power: Essential Works of Foucault 1954–1984, vol. 3*, ed. J. D. Faubion, New York: The New Press.

Foucault, M. (2000b) 'Truth and power', in M. Foucault *Power: Essential Works of Foucault 1954–1984, vol. 3*, trans. R. Hurley and others, ed. J. D. Faubion, New York: The New Press.

Foucault, M (2000c) 'The political technology of individuals', in M. Foucault *Power: Essential Works of Foucault 1954–1984, vol. 3*, trans. R. Hurley and others, ed. J. D. Faubion, New York: The New Press.

Foucault, M. (2000d) '"Omnes et singulatim": toward a critique of political reason', in M. Foucault *Power: Essential Works of Foucault 1954–1984, vol. 3*, trans. R. Hurley and others, ed. J. D. Faubion, New York: The New Press.

Foucault, M. (2000e) 'Lemon and milk', in M. Foucault *Power: Essential Works of Foucault 1954–1984, vol. 3*, trans. R. Hurley and others, ed. J. D. Faubion, New York: The New Press.

Foucault, M. (2000e) 'The subject and power', in M. Foucault *Power: Essential Works of Foucault 1954–1984, vol. 3*, trans. R. Hurley and others, ed. J. D. Faubion, New York: The New Press.

Foucault, M. (2000f) 'Questions of method', in M. Foucault *Power: Essential Works of Foucault 1954–1984, vol. 3*, trans. R. Hurley and others, ed. J. D. Faubion, New York: The New Press.

Foucault, M. (2000g) 'Space, knowledge and power', in M. Foucault *Power: Essential Works of Foucault 1954–1984, vol. 3*, trans. R. Hurley and others, ed. J. D. Faubion, New York: The New Press.

Foucault, M. (2000h) 'Questions of method', in M. Foucault *Power: Essential Works of Foucault 1954–1984, vol. 3*, trans. R. Hurley and others, ed. J. D. Faubion, New York: The New Press.

Foucault, M. (2000i) 'The risks of security', in M. Foucault *Power: Essential Works of Foucault 1954–1984, vol. 3*, trans. R. Hurley and others, ed. J. D. Faubion, New York: The New Press.

Foucault, M. (2003a) *Abnormal: Lectures at the Collège de France, 1974–1975*, trans. Graham Burchell, ed. V. Marchetti and A. Salomoni, London and New York: Verso.

Foucault, M. (2003b) *'Society Must be Defended': Lectures at the Collège de France, 1975–1976*, trans. D. Macey, eds M. Bertain and A. Fontana, New York: Picador.

Foucault, M. (2006) *Psychiatric Power: Lectures at the Collège de France, 1973–1974*, trans. G. Burchell, ed. J. Lagrange, Basingstoke and New York: Palgrave Macmillan.

Foucault, M. (2007a) *Security, Territory, Population: Lectures at the Collège de France 1977–1978*, trans. G. Burchell, ed. M. Senellart, Basingstoke and New York: Palgrave Macmillan.

Foucault, M. (2007b) 'What our present is', in M. Foucault: *The Politics of Truth*, trans. L. Hochroth, Los Angeles: Semiotext(e).

Foucault, M. (2008) *The Birth of Biopolitics: Lectures at the Collège de France, 1978–1979*, trans. G. Burchell, ed. M. Senellart, Basingstoke and New York: Palgrave Macmillan.

Freud, S. (1962) *Civilization and its Discontents*, trans. J. Strachey, New York: W.W. Norton & Company Inc.

Golder, B. and Fitzpatrick, P. (2009) *Foucault's Law*, Abingdon: Routledge.

Guicciardini, F. (1994) *Dialogue on the Government of Florence*, ed. and trans. A. Brown, Cambridge: Cambridge University Press.

Habermas, J. (1996) *Between Facts and Norms: Contributions to a Discourse Theory of Law and Democracy*, trans. W. Rehg, Cambridge: Polity Press.

Hart, H. L. A. (1997) *The Concept of Law*, 2nd edn, Oxford: Oxford University Press.

Hart, H. L. A. (2001) 'Bentham's *Of Laws in General*', in Hart *Essays on Bentham: studies in jurisprudence and political theory*, Oxford: Clarendon Press.

Homer (1991) *The Iliad*, trans. R. Fagles, New York: Penguin Books.

Hegel, G. W. F. (1964) 'The German constitution', trans. T. M. Knox, in *Hegel's Political Writings*, Oxford: Clarendon Press, Oxford.

Hunt, A. (1992) 'Foucault's expulsion of law: toward a retrieval', *Law and Social Inquiry* 17(1): 1–38.

Hunt, A. and Wickham, G. (1998) *Foucault and Law: Towards a Sociology of Law as Governance*, London: Pluto Press.

Hurri, S. (2005) 'The twelve tables', *No Foundations* 1: 15–23.

Hurri, S. (2011) 'Liberal battle form: *eidos* of competition', *No Foundations* 8: 123–33.

Hurri, S. (2013) 'Justice *kata nomos* and justice as *epieikeia* (legality and equity)', in Huppes-Cluysenaer, L. and Coelho, N. (eds) *Aristotle and the Philosophy of Law: theory, practice and justice*, Dordrecht: Springer.

Jhering, R. von (1879) *The Struggle for Law*, trans. J. J. Lalor, Chicago: Callaghan and Company.

Jhering, R. von (2003/1972) *Der Kampf ums Recht*, Frankfurt am Main: Vittorio Klosterman.

Kant, I. (1917) *Perpetual Peace: a Philosophical Essay*, trans. M. Campbell Smith, London: George Allen & Unwin Ltd.

Kant, I (1997) *Critique of Pure Reason*, trans. J. M. D. Meicklejohn and V. Politis, ed. V. Politis, J.M. Dent: London.

Koskenniemi, M. (2007): *Fragmentation of International Law: Difficulties Arising from the Diversification and Expansion of International Law*, report of the study group of the International Law Commission, Helsinki: The Eric Castrén Institute.

Kumm, M. (2010) '*Internationale Handelsgesellschaf, Nold* and the new human rights paradigm', in Maduro, M. and Azoulai, L. (eds) *The Past and Future of EU Law: the Classics of EU Law Revisited on the 50th Anniversary of the Rome Treaty*, Oxford and Portland: Hart Publishing.

Lea, H. C. (1896) *A History of Auricular Confession and Indulgences in the Latin Church, vol 1, Confession and Absolution*, London: Swan Sonnenschein & Co.

Luhmann, N. (1988) 'Closure and openness: on reality in the world of law', trans. I Fraser, in G. Teubner (ed.) *Autopoietic Law: a New Approach to Law and Society*, Berlin and New York: Walter de Gruyter.

Machiavelli, N. (1989a) 'The prince', trans. A. Gilbert, in Machiavelli *The Chief Works and Others*, vol. 1, Durham and London: Duke University Press.

Machiavelli, N. (1989b) 'Discourses on the first decade of Titus Livius', trans. A. Gilbert, in Machiavelli *The Chief Works and Others*, vol 1, Durham and London: Duke University Press.

Machiavelli, N. (1994) *Il Principe e altre opere politiche*, Milano: Garzanti Editore.

Maine, H. S. (1920) *Ancient Law: its connection with the early history and of society and its relation to modern ideas*, London: John Murray.

Meinecke, F. (1988) *Machiavellism: the doctrine of raison d'État and its place in modern history*, trans. D. Scott, New Brunswick (U.S.A.) and London: Transaction Publishers.

Mill, J. S. (1962) *Considerations on Representative Government*, South Bend, Indiana: Gateway Editions, Ltd.

Minkkinen, P. (1999) *Thinking without Desire: a First Philosophy of Law*, Oxford & Portland: Hart Publishing.

Mouffe, C. (1998) 'Carl Schmitt and the paradox of liberal democracy' in D. Dyzenhaus (ed.) *Law as Politics: Carl Schmitt's Critique of Liberalism*, Durham & London: Duke University Press.

Nietzsche, F. (2003) *The Genealogy of Morals*, trans. H. B. Samuel, Mineola, N. Y: Dover Publications, Inc.

Nietzsche, F. (2007) *Twilight of the Idols with the Antichrist and Ecce Homo*, trans. A. M. Ludovicki, Ware: Wordsworth Editions Limited.

Nonet, P. and Selznick, P. (2005) *Toward Responsive Law: Law and Society in Transition*, New Brunswick and London: Transaction Publishers.

Plato (1997) *Complete Works*, ed. J. M. Cooper, Indianapolis and Cambridge: Hackett.

Polanyi, M. (1967) *The Tacit Dimension*, Garden City: Doubleday & Company.

Radbruch, G. (1950) 'Legal philosophy', trans. K. Wilk in *The Legal Philosophies of Lask, Radbruch, and Dabin*, Cambridge Mass: Harvard University Press.

Radbruch, G. (2006) 'Statutory lawlessness and supra-statutory law (1946)' trans. B. Litschewski Paulson and S. L. Paulson, *Oxford Journal of Legal Studies* 26(1): 1–11.

Rousseau, J.-J. (1955) *The Social Contract*, trans. G. D. H. Cole, London: J. M. Dent & Sons Ltd.

Schmitt, C. (1988) *The Crisis of Parliamentary Democracy*, trans. E. Kennedy, Cambridge Mass. and London: MIT Press.

Schmitt, C. (1993) *Über die drei Arten des rechtswissenschaftlichen Denkens*, 2nd edn, Berlin: Dunker & Humblot.

Schmitt, C. (2003) *The Nomos of the Earth in the International Law of the Jus Publicum Europaeum*, trans. G. L. Ulmen, New York: Telos Press Publishing.

Schmitt, C. (2004a) *On the Three Types of Juristic Thought*, trans. J. W. Bendersky, Westport Connecticut and London: Praeger Publishers.

Schmitt, C. (2004b) *Legality and Legitimacy*, trans. J. Seitzer, Durham & London: Duke University Press.

Schmitt, C. (2008) *Leviathan in the State Theory of Thomas Hobbes*, Chicago and London: The University of Chicago Press.

Swartz, D. (1997) *Culture & Power: the Sociology of Pierre Bourdieu*, Chicago & London: The University of Chicago Press.

Taylor, C. (1983) *Hegel*, Cambridge: Cambridge University Press.

Tuori, K. (2002) *Critical Legal Positivism*, Aldershot: Ashgate.

Tuori, K. (2003) 'Sosiaalisen oikeuden arkeologia' [Archaeology of Social Law] in F. Ewald *Normi yhteisen käytännön mittapuuna*, Helsinki: Suomalainen Lakimiesyhdistys.

Tuori, K. (2007) *Oikeuden ratio ja voluntas* [Law's Ratio and Voluntas], Helsinki: WSOYpro.

Tuori, K. (2011) *Ratio and Voluntas: the Tension Between Reason and Will in Law*, Aldershot: Ashgate.

Viroli, M. (1992) *From Politics to Reason of State: the Acquisition and Transformation of the Language of Politics 1250–1600*, Cambridge: Cambridge University Press.

Waldron, J. (2005) 'Torture and positive law: jurisprudence for the White House', *Columbia Law Review* 105(6): 1681–750.

Weber, M. (1949) 'The Meaning of "ethical neutrality" in sociology and economics', trans E. A. Shils and H. A. Finch in M. Weber *The Methodology of Social Sciences*, New York: The Free Press.

Weber, M. (1978) *The Economy and Society: an Outline of Interpretive Sociology*, vol. 2, trans. E. Fischoff and others, Berkeley: University of California Press.

Weiler, J. H. H. (1999) *The Constitution of Europe: "Do the new clothes have an emperor?" and other essays on European integration*, Cambridge: Cambridge University Press.

List of cases

Primary case material

van Duyn. Case 41/74, *Yvonne van Duyn v Home Office* Judgment of the Court of 4 December 1974 [1974] ECR 1337.

Bonsignore. Case 67/74, *Carmelo Angelo Bonsignore v Oberstadtdirektor der Stadt Köln* Judgment of the Court of 26 February 1975 [1975] ECR 297.

Rutili. Case 36/75, *Roland Rutili v Ministre de l'intérieur* Judgment of the Court of 28 October 1975 [1975] ECR 1291.

Royer. Case 48/75, *Jean Noël Royer* Judgment of the Court of 8 April 1976 [1976] ECR 497.

Bouchereau. Case 30/77, *Régina v Pierre Bouchereau* Judgment of the Court of 27 October 1977 [1977] ECR 1999.

Adoui and Cornuaille. Joined Cases 115/81 & 116/81, *Rezguia Adoui v Belgian State and City of Liège; Dominique Cornuaille v Belgian State* Judgment of the Court of 18 May 1982 [1982] ECR 1665.

Secondary case material

Stork. Case 1/58, *Friedrich Stork & Cie v High Authority of the European Coal and Steel Community* Judgment of the Court of 4 February 1959 [1959] ECR (English special edition) 17.

Van Gend en Loos. Case 26/62 Judgment of the Court of 5 February 1963 *NV Algemene Transport – en Expeditie Onderneming van Gend & Loos v Netherlands Inland Revenue Administration* Judgment of the Court of 5 February 1963 [1963] ECR (English special edition) 1.

Costa v. ENEL Case 6/64, *Flaminio Costa v ENEL* Judgment of the Court of 15 July 1964 [1964] ECR (English special edition) 585.

Stauder. Case 29/69, *Erich Stauder v City of Ulm* Judgment of the Court of 12 November 1969 [1969] ECR 419.

Internationale Handelsgesellschaft. Case 11/70, *Internationale Handelsgesellschaft mbH v Einfuhr- und Vorratsstelle für Getreide und Futtermittel* Judgment of the Court of 17 December 1970 [1970] ECR 1125.

Nold. Case 4/73, *J Nold, Kohlen- und Baustoffgroßhandlung v Commission of the European Communities* Judgment of the Court of 14 May 1974 [1974] ECR 491.

Commission v France. Case 167/73, *Commission of the European Communities v French Republic* Judgment of the Court of 4 April 1974 [1974] ECR 359.

Pecastaing. Case 98/79, *Josette Pecastaing v Belgian State* Judgment of the Court of 5 March 1980 [1975] ECR 691.

Luisi and Carbone. Joined Cases 286/82 & 26/83, *Graziana Luisi and Giuseppe Carbone v Ministero del Tesoro* Judgment of the Court of 31 January 1984 [1984] ECR 377.

Cinéthèque. Joined Cases 60/84 & 61/84. *Cinéthèque SA and others v Fédération nationale des cinémas français* Judgment of the Court of 11 July 1985 [1985] ECR 2605.

ERT. Case C–260/89, *Elliniki Radiophonia Tiléorassi AE and Panellinia Omospondia Syllogon Prossopikou v Dimotiki Etairia Pliroforissis and Sotirios Kouvelas and Nicolaos Avdellas and others* Judgment of the Court of 18 June 1991 [1991] ECR I–2925.

Grogan. Case C–159/90, *The Society for the Protection of Unborn Children Ireland Ltd v Stephen Grogan and others* Judgment of the Court of 4 October 1991 [1991] ECR I–4685.

Opinion 2/94, *Opinion on Accession by the Community to the European Convention for the Protection of Human Rights* Opinion of the Court of 28 March 1996 [1996] ECR I–1.

Olazablal. Case C–100/01, *Ministre de l'Intérieur v Aitor Oteiza Olazabal* Judgment of the Court of 26 November 2002 [2002] ECR I–10981.

Index

For Product Safety Concerns and Information please contact our EU
representative GPSR@taylorandfrancis.com
Taylor & Francis Verlag GmbH, Kaufingerstraße 24, 80331 München, Germany